Developing Women Leaders in Corporate America

Recent Titles in
Women and Careers in Management

How Women Can Make It Work: The Science of Success
Eden King and Jennifer Knight

Women as Leaders in Education: Succeeding Despite Inequity, Discrimination, and Other Challenges
Jennifer L. Martin, Editor

Women as Transformational Leaders: From Grassroots to Global Interests
Michele A. Paludi and Breena E. Coates, Editors

Developing Women Leaders in Corporate America

BALANCING COMPETING DEMANDS, TRANSCENDING TRADITIONAL BOUNDARIES

Alan T. Belasen

Women and Careers in Management
Michele A. Paludi, Series Editor

 PRAEGER

AN IMPRINT OF ABC-CLIO, LLC
Santa Barbara, California • Denver, Colorado • Oxford, England

Library of Congress Cataloging-in-Publication Data

Belasen, Alan T., 1951–
   Developing women leaders in corporate America : balancing competing demands, transcending traditional boundaries / Alan T. Belasen.
      p. cm. — (Women and careers in management)
   Includes bibliographical references and index.
      ISBN 978–0–313–39573–4 (cloth : alk. paper) — ISBN 978–0–313–39574–1 (ebook)
   1. Women executives—United States. I. Title.
HD6054.4.U6B445   2012
658.4′07124082—dc23   2011045329

ISBN: 978–0–313–39573–4
EISBN: 978–0–313–39574–1

16 15 14 13   3 4 5

This book is also available on the World Wide Web as an eBook.
Visit www.abc-clio.com for details.

Praeger
An Imprint of ABC-CLIO, LLC

ABC-CLIO, LLC
130 Cremona Drive, P.O. Box 1911
Santa Barbara, California 93116-1911

This book is printed on acid-free paper ∞

Manufactured in the United States of America

This book is dedicated in memory of my sister, Dalia S. Belasen, whose commitment to the values of fairness, righteousness, helping others ("Ezra Lazulat"), moral courage, and personal integrity brought hundreds—from top company executives to public officials, employees, and customers—to her Shiva. I was touched by each and every personal story about my sister. She was a true company's hero whose performance put her office on the map in the banking industry. Mourners recalled Dalia's values of teamwork, work ethic, and empowerment; she was a friend to everyone who knew or needed her for personal, social, or financial reasons. Dalia had the unique ability to listen with an open heart and embrace causes with love and courage. Mother, daughter, and sister. Dalia epitomizes what I am advancing in this book: the innate power to balance transactional and transformational leadership; the ability to think and act holistically: to see the dynamic interplay between two opposing goals and navigate between competing tensions with love and passion, empathy and compassion, assertiveness and openness. I admired my sister. I will miss her forever.

Contents

Series Foreword

Ma muaka kite a muri
Ma muri ka ora a mua
(Those who lead give sight to those who follow,
Those who follow give life to those who lead)

—Pauline Tangiora

Welcome to the "Women and Careers in Management" Series at Praeger. This series examines the status of women in management and leadership and offers discussions of issues that women managers and leaders face, including:

Differences in leadership styles.

Traditional gender roles reinforcing women's subordinate status in the workplace.

Obstacles to advancement and pay.

Benefit and resource inequity.

Discrimination and harassment.

Work/life imbalance.

This series acknowledges that gender is one of the fundamental factors influencing the ethics, values, and policies of workplaces and that the discrimination against women managers and leaders explains the pervasiveness of institutionalized inequality. This series also discusses interconnections among equality issues: sex, race, class, age, sexual orientation, religion, and disability. Thus, this series brings together a multidisciplinary and multicultural discussion of women, management, and leadership.

"Women and Careers in Management" encourages all of us to think critically about women managers and leaders, to place value on cultural experiences, and integrate empirical research and theoretical formulations with experiences of our family, friends, colleagues, and ourselves. It is my hope that the books in "Women and Careers in Management" serve as a "life raft" (Klonis, Endo, Crosby & Worrell, 1997), especially for the Millennial and subsequent generations.

I am honored to have Dr. Alan Belasen's book, *Developing Women Leaders in Corporate America*, published in the "Women and Careers in Management" Series. Dr. Belasen offers empirical research and best practices for employers and employees for managing this aspect of diversity in organizations. Dr. Belasen has provided communication audit consulting and leadership development curricular design and training to government, not-for-profit, and business organizations in the United States and abroad. His clients range from entrepreneurial organizations, healthcare systems, academic institutions, and business enterprises. Examples include a petroleum company in Brazil, an online leadership program in Missouri, and a healthcare provider group in New Jersey.

We benefit from Dr. Belasen's expertise when reading *Developing Women Leaders in Corporate America*. Readers will, in all likelihood, find new understandings and insights about the role of women in leadership positions. Dr. Belasen offers an impressive compendium of research that clarifies women's leadership styles and how employers must embrace women's leadership styles as they are transforming of organizations and respectful of employees. Dr. Belasen replaces myths with facts about women and leadership.

Dr. Belasen's book shares Pauline Tangiora's sentiment for women leaders:

> Those who lead give sight to those who follow,
> Those who follow give life to those who lead.

—Michele A. Paludi
Series Editor

Reference

Klonis, S., Endo, J., Crosby, F., & Worrell, J. (1997). Feminism as life raft. *Psychology of Women Quarterly, 21*, 333–45.

Acknowledgments

First and foremost I would like to thank my wife, Susan, for her steadfast support and unparalleled encouragement to accomplish the task of writing this book. I am also indebted to my five "A's": Ari, Amy, Anat, Amanda, and Abby whose creative ideas and constructive criticisms helped shape some of my thinking about this book and its purpose.

Special thanks to Michele Paludi, Series Editor, renowned human resource management professor, author of many books, and expert on diversity in leadership for her confidence, guidance, and feedback. Brian Romer, Senior Acquisitions Editor, was enormously helpful in bringing the manuscript to closure. Robin Tutt, Submissions Coordinator, was helpful in the pre-production phase of this book.

Many thanks to Dr. Nancy Frank, my colleague and research partner, for the years of working together on numerous research projects leading to conference papers, book chapters, and journal articles. Nancy's influence on my thinking is well reflected in this book. My colleague, Elliot Luber, was instrumental in providing insights and ideas for this book. Much appreciation goes to Dr. Nancy Kymn Rutigliano whose expertise in the area of crisis leadership and whistle-blowing has helped shape important sections of this book. I would also like to acknowledge the insights and ideas that Dr. Rosalyn Rufer, my colleague, provided while I was working on the different drafts of this book. I am very grateful to Dr. Laura Schweitzer, President, Union Graduate College, for her insights, encouragement, and support.

I am especially thankful to the many graduate students at the University at Albany who attended my leadership communication course and helped refine my thinking about many of the issues and topics raised in this book.

Special mention goes to: Naomi Krakower, Jaclyn Holmes, Kelly Tu, Jessica Dillard, Shuang Zhao, Jessie Festa, Liwen Tang, Amanda Thompson, Theresa Gasper, Pornchanok Tuancharoensri, Sandra Lynn Pabis, Georgianna Rowe, and Rana Fayez. Many professionals contributed to the sections on self assessment and self improvement: Hermeata Porcher, Megan Campbell, AnnMarie Hutchison, Wendy Coonrod, Amanda Mitchum, April Coulson, Melissa Leander, Kimberly Stackhouse, Ana Maria Chanaba, and David Kamen. Thanks goes to the Office of Academic Affairs, SUNY-Empire State College, for providing the research funds to support the research for this book.

Special thanks to my mother, Daisy Belasen, for her constant support and confidence in my ability to bring this book to fruition. Thanks for your inspirational motivation, Ema.

—Alan

Introduction

According to Paludi (in press), women are eminently qualified for leadership and management positions in business and in academia. Research has indicated that women's strength in interpersonal and social skills (e.g., nurturing, compassion, sharing information with all) contributes to their expertise as leaders and managers. However, several scholars on organizational behavior (e.g., Rosabeth Moss Kanter, 1997; Su Maddock, 2002) have argued that organizational cultures are "gendered." Although women and men have reached numerical parity in management overall, evidence suggests that fewer women than men lead organizations. In addition, access to middle management and executive positions remains elusive for most women (Paludi, 2008). To date, 16 Fortune 500 companies are run by women; a total of 35 Fortune 1000 companies have a woman CEO. Furthermore, stereotypes depict men, but not women, as having the requisite skills and characteristics for managerial and leadership positions. Business professionals indicate a strong preference for male applicants for a stereotypically masculine job, even when similar information on the resumes of women and men applicants had led to perceptions of similar personality traits. These stereotypes persist even though gender differences are not found in leadership ability or job performance.

Research on gender stereotypes also suggests that gender bias is an invisible barrier—the glass ceiling—preventing women from breaking into the highest levels of management in organizations. Women, especially women of color, experience the glass ceiling, most commonly in male-populated organizations (Paludi & Neidermeyer, 2007). Their advancement within the hierarchy of organizations is blocked at a lower level as a consequence of sex and/or race discrimination. Because of the glass ceiling with respect to leadership positions, women shift into a state of "hypereffectivity" or "overachievement" to advance their careers. Women shift their energy from personal, non-value maximizing behaviors to performance-enhancing activities in areas that have been traditionally dominated by men (Irby et al., 2002). Hence, women attempt to demonstrate their leadership skills over male colleagues by taking on more assignments to show how much more effective they are at their job. The old style of management based on trade relationships and authority lines, which focuses on short-term goals and competition among subordinates, stands in stark contrast to the transformational style of women with its focus on shared responsibility, communication lines, and distributed leadership. This style fits well with rapid organizational change and the shift toward horizontal structures of management allowing women to perform their leadership roles naturally through inclusive decision-making processes that encourage participation and ownership. Serious health consequences that result from hypereffectivity, including job stress and job burnout, are self-evident (Belasen, 2000).

This book will assist women leaders and managers as well as employers to recognize hypereffectivity and develop strategic approaches to helping reduce stereotyping associated with women in male-populated careers.

This book differs from other books on women and leadership because it focuses on the empirically research-based Competing Values Framework (CVF). The Competing Values Framework (CVF) serves as an organizing schema, roadmap, and memory jogger that enables leaders to assess personal strengths and weaknesses, analyze and manage organizational situations. A critical element of the CVF is the concept of constrained optimization. That is, goals and activities across the CVF quadrants compete for the limited attention of the leader creating an inevitable tension between diametrically opposing demands [diagonal quadrants]. This book emphasizes the importance of identifying the tradeoffs among the competing demands and the challenge of balancing them using appropriate communication tools and message orientations. Effective leaders have a strong belief in themselves. They have a sense of self-efficacy and self-assurance in their ability to deal with competing and often contradictory pressures. The framework used in this book highlights the dynamic interplay across the quadrants and the set of skills and communication responses used by leaders to address diverse stakeholders.

If effective managers are more successful in handling novel or exceptional situations and generally exhibit greater behavioral and cognitive complexity (Denison et al., 1995; Hart & Quinn, 1993) than less effective managers, do men and women alike manifest these behaviors in playing organizational leadership roles across hierarchical levels? Extending the CVF to women in leadership given the expanded presence of women in managerial positions, it becomes increasingly important to understand whether men and women share similar behavioral characteristics when it comes to playing the CVF leadership roles. Are there any significant differences between men and women across managerial levels? Do they emphasize the same roles across different situations or task environments?

Also relevant, however, is the question of whether women actually manage in accordance with the predictions of feminist approaches. Given present-day attention to feminist approaches of leadership, it is appropriate to ask whether women align with traditional feminist role strengths within the CVF when compared to men, and, in particular, whether men and women demonstrate different or similar role strengths with the CVF.

Chapter 1—The Catch 22 of Women's Leadership

Chapter 1 sets the context for the paradox of why more women have not yet shattered the metaphorical glass ceiling. Although women, more so than men, go to great lengths to educate themselves and gain important leadership skills, they continue to be represented only marginally in high-level positions in the corporate world. They are also grossly underrepresented in boardrooms and executive suites, with only 3.2% of Fortune 500 CEOs being women. In fact, women hold only about 14% of company board seats. As of October 2011, there were only 35 women CEOs listed in the Fortune 1000, leading many to believe that this problem is associated with a "pipeline condition," the untested explanation that women leaders with the appropriate skills sets and abilities are very scarce. Corporate and cultural barriers, including the double-bind situation, in which women are trapped in a "catch-22" vicious cycle, are also discussed.

Chapter 2—Corporate and Cultural Barriers: The Paradox of the Glass Ceiling

This chapter traces corporate and cultural causes and trends that lead to prejudice and discrimination. Organizations, particularly those that are male-dominated, are not gender-neutral reflecting settings, performance criteria, and leadership styles in which women's behaviors and accomplishments are judged against male norms. Men in leadership roles, however, are seen as acting in congruence with expected masculine roles. The gender stereotypes that inhibit women from reaching the top still exist, especially when standards of success are measured in male terms, where hierarchy and power are preferred over social equality and persuasion. Organizations must not only recognize the barriers that prevent women from fully committing to work, but they must also offer support to help women balance their contradictory roles.

Chapter 3—Corporate Greed and the Anguish of Executive Failure; or Why More Women Should Lead

Chapter 3 describes bad habits that often lead to executive failure and unanticipated consequences. What happens when the vision goes wild? Why would an otherwise successful executive take the organization through an out-of-control spin into uncertain environments in an attempt to accomplish an untested vision? Why do most executives refrain from pursuing a practical vision? How do CEOs get to the point where deception appears acceptable? What kinds of leadership skills are now necessary for CEOs to prove their worthiness to lead companies? The chapter explores qualities for successful leadership, including the abilities to focus, take initiative, communicate, and stand behind decisions. The ability to see outside the box and the readiness to take responsibility for one's actions are also examined. Several profiles of effective women CEOs who manifest these abilities in their behaviors and decision-making styles with strong emphasis on values, morality, and leadership integrity are highlighted to distinguish their approach and orientation from the self-destructive behaviors of male CEOs who have overemphasized power and greed.

Chapter 4—Competing Values and Women's Leadership

Given the expanded presence of women in managerial positions, it becomes increasingly important to understand whether men and women share similar behavioral characteristics when performing vital leadership roles. The theoretical basis for this book is the Competing Values Framework (CVF), which serves as an organizing schema, roadmap, and memory jogger that enables leaders to assess, analyze, and manage interpersonal relations and organizational situations. A critical element of the CVF is the concept of constrained optimization. That is, goals and activities across the CVF quadrants compete for the limited attention of the leader, creating an inevitable tension between diametrically opposing demands [diagonal quadrants]. This book emphasizes the importance of identifying tradeoffs among competing demands and the challenge of balancing them using appropriate communication tools and message orientations. Confident leaders have a strong belief in themselves. They have an innate sense of self-assurance in their ability to deal with competing and often contradictory pressures. The framework used in this book highlights the dynamic interplay across the quadrants and the set of skills and communication responses used by confident leaders to address diverse stakeholders.

Chapter 5—Aligning Personality Traits with Leadership Roles

Chapter 5 draws on CVF studies to highlight the relationship between personality traits and leadership behaviors of women and men, including interpersonal skills, communication strategies, and transformational leadership. The relationship between traits and behaviors is an important factor in dealing with stress and organizational crises. Implications for leadership development, especially for women, set the stage for examining leadership skills and behaviors across the CVF quadrants.

Chapter 6—Women's Traits and Leadership Roles: The Danger of Becoming Hypereffective

In spite of the apparent connection between transformational leadership and feminist theories of leadership, are we correct in assuming that women in particular are more likely to demonstrate CVF-based transformational behaviors? This question does not hypothesize that transformational leadership is the exclusive domain of women. Rather, it suggests that women can become effective leaders in relational, inclusive, and empowered social settings by balancing transformational and transactional leadership roles. It is not uncommon to conclude that women, wanting to demonstrate superior skills over their male counterparts, tend to resort to overemphasizing important transactional roles such as the monitor and producer roles, in addition to transformational roles thus becoming hypereffective. The causes and consequences for hypereffectivity are discussed and possible remedies are offered.

Chapter 7—Women's Self-Development

The importance of self-development first begins with the understanding of one's strengths and weaknesses. The chapter includes examples of women managers working in various organizations, who have participated in leadership development programs aimed at helping to facilitate their professional goals among other things. The Competing Values Framework was used to map out their leadership roles and competencies, identify strengths and weaknesses, and develop a path for self-improvement.

Chapter 8—Qualities Unique to Women

It has been shown that the presence of female directors in a company leads to increased profitability. In fact, of the 50 most profitable U.S. companies in the Fortune 500 listing, 82% had at least one female director, and all top 10 companies had female directors on their boards. Porter & Daniel's (2007) definition of transformational women's leadership roles includes the following dimensions: values, vision, action, learning, understanding, ethical practices, and social constructivism. These seven dimensions, when combined, form a robust definition of great leadership that is also consistent with Goleman's (2009, p. 44) description of emotional intelligence as the "sine qua non of leadership." Examples of successful women executives are highlighted for each of these dimensions. One of the crucial survival skills that successful female leaders have in common is adaptability. Women are also more likely than men to engage in conversations, elicit opinions and seek to better understand how their superiors, peers, and subordinates would feel about their attempts at influence. The chapter also includes a discussion about ethical leadership, moral courage, and organizational integrity as important factors characterizing women's leadership.

Chapter 9—Women's Secret Power

The most difficult barrier for women to overcome with regard to being good at both management and leadership are women themselves. Even though women were found to be stronger in a producer role, scored higher in conscientiousness, are detailed oriented, and have strong analytical skills, they can still learn to develop their visionary skills further and aim for the top. Women can excel at both transactional management and transformational leadership if they so desire. Not reaching the top is not because of lack of talents. Women's career ladder is blocked by systemic barriers, self-limiting social and organizational processes, and cultural stereotypes that prevent them from being successful in their careers. The chapter discusses these barriers as well as how female managers can sustain their skills and styles, build confidence, and lead effectively.

Chapter 10—When It Comes to Leadership, Women Rule

This chapter includes examples of successful women leaders in the media and technology industries who have demonstrated extraordinary talents and visionary skills in initiating and leading change and transformation in their organizations.

Chapter 11—Women as Global Leaders

Chapter 11 examines important concepts and tools essential for managing global operations effectively. For much of the last 25 years women were largely prevented from reaching global business ventures because it was assumed that locals would not respect or accept them undermining or weakening the business relationship. Another reason that women were not considered was that it was believed (erroneously) that they weren't interested in these assignments. The same vicious cycle described throughout this book appeared to face women aspiring to fit into offshore positions. Male managers seemed to be less of a "risk" in international assignments than women and therefore would be afforded opportunities even without all of the "required" qualifications. However, change does occur although the patterns of misrepresentation in top executive positions so pervasive domestically also pervades international assignments. Although women have recently increased their international presence, this is really only due to the fact that men no longer want the positions. And while more women are being placed on international assignments than ever before, only 22% of senior positions are occupied by women.

In this chapter we contextualize the discussion around the ideas and arguments that global management requires cosmopolitan leadership with skills and behaviors displayed by women. It is also argued that companies who promote women to senior positions tend to do very well financially. As globalization infiltrates the world's businesses, executives, men and women, will choose transformational leadership as their means for successfully leading their organization. Transformational leadership, characteristically women's leadership, will become the dominant form of leading in the next wave of conducting business in the global market.

Chapter 12—Fundamental Change

Two levels of intervention must be considered for lowering or neutralizing the negative effects of evaluative biases: (1) informal or personal initiatives by women and men in organizations; and (2) change in formal institutional mechanisms such as policies, evaluation criteria, and codes of behavior. On the personal side, women need to find the right balance between agentic and communal behaviors through feedback, mentoring, and developmental plans. Balanced behaviors between transformational and transactional roles will allow women to communicate competence and self-confidence. Second, women are encouraged to self-promote and make lateral and vertical connections. Institutionally, organizations need to reassess their mission statements and remove corporate barriers that limit or inhibit women's access to upper-level positions.

1

The Catch 22 of Women's Leadership

During the 1960s and 1970s women's participation in the workforce has reached 40% with women primarily occupying professions such as teaching, nursing, and social work. The majority of women were still in nonmanagement positions due to the prevailing assumption that managerial responsibilities require managers to be assertive, with an analytic mindset and with commitment that transcends regular work time. Hence, women filled support staff positions such as assistants and secretaries. With the passage of the 1964 Civil Rights Act that made discrimination in employment unlawful on the basis of gender, race, and social status, women began to chisel away at the concrete wall that buffered them from reaching managerial positions that traditionally have been the exclusive territory of men. The concrete wall began to crack in the 1970s and 1980s when women were advancing to lower middle management positions. Nevertheless they were still excluded from top executive jobs.

In the 1990s, as organizations have begun shifting away from vertical structures rooted in male conceptions of power that emphasize command and control approaches toward horizontal structures of management based on commitment and empowerment, new values such as diversity, participation, integrity, trust, honesty, and inclusion have also signaled a shift to a new management paradigm. This new paradigm involved a shift from transactional management to transformational leadership; and from command structures designed exclusively around reporting and compliance to commitment structures emphasizing relational power and open communication lines. Upper management was expected to shift from "taking charge" to "taking care" and was evaluated on abilities to "transform" people and organizations, not only "transact" around core business competencies.

Today's flatter, team-based organizations are no longer looking for top-down authority figures but for more collaborative and inclusive approaches to leadership based on facilitative power and consultation. Leadership is becoming more interactive, and women's style of leadership seems to be more appropriate than that of men's in diversified and globalized work environments (Daft, 2011). Moreover, the past 40 years marked a significant transformation in women's participation in the labor force. The U.S. Bureau of Labor Statistics (2009, p. 8) reported that women's proportion in the civilian labor force increased steadily from 43.3% in 1970 to 59.5% in 2008. Women have also increasingly attained college degrees. Among women aged 25 to 64 who are in the labor force, the proportion with a college degree roughly tripled from 1970 to 2008. Women's earnings as a proportion of men's earnings also have grown over time. In 1979, women working full time earned 62% of what men did; in 2008, women's earnings were 80% of men's (U.S. Bureau of Labor Statistics, 2009).

At the same time, the question remains of why more women, whose feminine gender role suggests teamwork, empowerment, sharing information, and caring for employees, have not yet shattered the metaphorical glass ceiling. Why are women grossly underrepresented in boardrooms and executive suites?

In 2007, McKinsey & Company, an international management consulting firm, conducted a study to offer valuable insight regarding the importance of female representation within top management positions. The report, *Women Matter: Gender diversity, a corporate performance driver*, documented the reasons that hinder diversity in senior management positions. The study predominantly focused on European companies, providing evidence that gender gaps are palpable globally. Interestingly, the study also pointed out that "companies where women are most strongly represented at board or top-management levels are also the companies that perform best" (McKinsey & Company, 2007, p. 3). If companies truly do perform best when women hold top positions, one might wonder why gender gaps persist.

Higher Education, Greater Skills

Women's self-reports of assertiveness, dominance, and masculinity (Twenge, 1997, 2001), and the value that women place on job attributes such as freedom, challenges, leadership, prestige, and influence have all become more similar to those of men (Konrad, Ritchie, Lieb & Corrigall, 2000). They also work harder and wiser to choose the leadership style that they feel comfortable with and that does not contradict with their feminine image. They can be go-getters in management and, at the same time, inspire others as transformational leaders. Moreover, women are not submissively waiting for opportunities, but rather seeking them out, proactively and diligently. They reach for those opportunities by themselves. Nevertheless, to prove they are able to achieve the same level of managerial leadership as men, women need to "prove" they have strong upper management skills in many areas. Paradoxically, women now outnumber men at almost every level of higher education, with three women attending college and graduate school for every two men. They get more master's degrees and more PhDs. Most law school students are women, as are almost half of the medical students. In Canada, women earned 35.3% of all MBAs in 2007, up from 33.4% in 2006. Women earned 32.1% in 2005, 34.3% in 2004, and 34.1% in 2002 (Catalyst, 2009).

At lower managerial levels, women are slated to earn more money than men. The number of women with $100,000+ income is rising at a much faster pace than it is for men. Nationwide, about 1 in 18 women working full time earned $100,000 or more in 2009, a jump of 14% over two years; in contrast, 1 in 7 men made that much, up just 4% (Carol Morello, *Washington Post*, Oct. 7, 2010). Furthermore, the February 2010 *U.S. Bureau of Labor Statistics Report* provided evidence confirming that "Women outnumbered men on the nation's payroll" for the first time in history (Calvert Group, October 2010). Interestingly, surveys indicate that women, and especially highly educated women, are more likely to be motivated by a job's intrinsic values than by extrinsic rewards.

Corporate Mental Blinders

These results bear the question of why, with women advancing in both education and leadership, the number of women in top corporate positions is so small. While women pursue more education and earn more money, they are still hitting the glass ceiling when it comes to corporate upper echelons. Although women are going to great lengths to educate themselves, they continue to be marginally represented in higher level positions in the corporate world (Perry, 2009).

If women have the ability to influence followers to emulate their actions as well as the ability to motivate them to embrace and enact their vision, then they certainly possess qualities of successful managerial leaders. Notably, very few women have upper management line experience in the areas of marketing, finance, or operations, which are typically needed to become a company CEO. And so goes the saga of the glass ceiling: About 70% of women and 57% of men "believe an invisible barrier—a glass ceiling—prevents women from getting ahead in business, according to a study of 1,200 executives in eight countries, including the U.S., Australia, Austria and the Philippines" (Clark, 2009). Moreover, it was found that only 4% of the companies interviewed in a study attempted to get women the line experience they needed to become a CEO (Oakley, 2000). Another corporate practice that hinders women's chances of success includes compensation practices. In general, women receive a lower salary as well as less perks and time off. In fact, according to a 2008 survey of CEO pay, women on average made only 85% of what men made (Jones, 2009). Furthermore, a study conducted by Kulich, Ryan, and Haslam (2007) suggested that decisions about performance-based pay related directly to male CEOs, while they were mediated by evaluations of leadership characteristics and abilities in the case of female CEOs.

Kulich, Ryan, and Haslam (2007, p. 595) explain: "While men were both rewarded and punished in line with their company's performance, the amount of bonus received by the female CEO did not significantly differ in contexts of increasing versus declining company performance. Apparently, relative to male executives for whom the standard romance of leadership pattern was found, company performance did not matter so much when allocating a bonus to female executives. Hence, for women the romance of leadership was observed on perceptual dimensions (i.e., assessments of charisma and leadership ability) but not on behavioral and tangible dimensions such as bonus allocation . . . [thus] men's success seemed to be acknowledged without needing to scrutinize their leadership abilities, whereas women's abilities were subject to greater interrogation before conclusions about their leadership were inferred from company performance."

Aside from the barriers in company policies and procedures for women, behavioral and cultural prohibitions also exist. For one thing, there is the double-bind situation—a woman cannot succeed no matter what she does. In these cases, women are told to act authoritatively to be taken seriously but are then perceived as "bitches" for acting tough (Oakley, 2000); but when women act in ways that are consistent with the feminine stereotype, they can be seen as too nice (Valerio, 2009). Ultimately, the double-bind view depicts women in a paradoxical lose-lose situation.

If Women Are Better, then Promote Them!

The majority of women experience multiple goals in life and don't just set out to snag the biggest monetary prize when they plan their career (Pinker, 2009). Women seem to prefer intrinsic rewards such as self-development and quality of work life whereas men value more extrinsic rewards and opportunities to advance up the corporate ladder (Sturges, 1999).

In 2008, the Pew Research Center conducted and published the survey *Men or Women: Who's the better leader?* The survey was based on telephone interviews with a nationally representative sample of 2,250 adults living in the continental United States. The survey respondents were asked to report if they believed eight traits—honesty, intelligence, hardworking, decisive, ambitious, compassionate, outgoing, and creative—were true for men or women. The findings from this particular survey question were quite revealing: On seven of eight leadership traits measured in this survey, women were rated either better than or equal to men. Of those eight traits men prevailed over women only on decisiveness. Although women were viewed as more likely to possess most leadership traits, the survey findings unveiled a puzzling paradox: when respondents were asked whether men or women make better political leaders, only 6% stated they believe women make better political leaders than men and 21% stated they felt men make better leaders than women (Pew Research, 2008).

Would You Prefer to Have a Woman Boss?

In a report posted titled: Americans prefer male boss to a female boss (http://www.gallup.com/poll/24346/americans-prefer-male-boss-female-boss.aspx), Carroll (2006) writes:

> Gallup first asked this question in 1953, and at that time, two in three Americans said they would prefer a male boss, while just 5% said they would prefer a female boss, with 25% volunteering it would make no difference. Beginning in 1982, sentiments shifted and greater numbers of Americans said they would prefer a female boss or said their boss's gender didn't matter to them. In more recent years, a plurality of Americans have volunteered that gender makes no difference to them, but the preference for a male boss among those who have a preference has been observed in every poll in which this question has been asked over the years (see Table 1.1).

Other results from the poll:

- By a margin of 37% to 19%, Americans would prefer to have a male boss than a female boss.
- 43% say that it makes no difference.
- In the history of the question, no more than 22% have said they would prefer a female boss.
- Women are more likely to have a preference; men are more likely to say gender does not matter.

TABLE 1.1
Percentage of Americans Preferring a Male or Female Boss

Gender of respondent	No preference	Prefer a male boss	Prefer a female boss
Male	56%	34%	10%
Female	32%	40%	26%

Poll taken August 7–10, 2006. (Carroll, J., http://www.gallup.com/poll/24346/americans-prefer-male-boss-femaleboss.aspx)

Are Women Well Represented in Management? Not Enough!

On September 28, 2010, the U.S. Government Accountability Office (GAO) released the findings of its 2000–2007 study, using the U.S. Census Bureau's American Community Survey (ACS), covering three questions:

1. What is the representation of women in management positions compared to their representation in nonmanagement positions by industry?
2. What are the key characteristics of women and men in management positions by industry?
3. What is the difference in pay between women and men in full-time management positions by industry?

Overall, the GAO results showed that female managers' representation and differences between female and male managers' characteristics remained largely similar. However, differences narrowed substantially in level of education and slightly in pay (GAO-10-1064T). In 2007, women comprised an estimated 40% of managers and 49% of non-managers across 13 industry sectors, virtually unchanged from 2000. On average for the 13 industry sectors, an estimated 14% of managers in 2007 were mothers to children under age 18 in the household, compared to 17% of non-managers. The largest proportion of women managers were healthcare and social assistance (70%), educational services (57%), financial activities (50%), and leisure and hospitality (45%). While both male and female managers experienced increases in obtaining undergraduate degrees or higher (up 6%), women's gains surpassed men's, up 3%. Across the industry sectors, on average, female managers earned 81 cents for every dollar earned by male managers in 2007 as compared to 79 cents in 2000. The narrowing of the gap between 2000 and 2007 for all managers without children in the household was statistically significant at the 95% confidence level.

The Anomaly of Women Executives

Women are sparsely represented at the upper echelons of business and only 3.2% of Fortune 500 CEOs are women. In fact, women hold only about 14% of company board seats (Arfken, Bellar & Helms, 2004). As of October 2011, there were only 35 women CEOs listed in the Fortune 1000 leading many to believe that the problem is associated with a "pipeline condition," that is, the explanation that women leaders with the appropriate set of skills and abilities are simply scarce, the catch 22 paradox in action.

One of the most serious issues regarding the scarcity of women in executive suites and corporate boards is the vicious cycle where negative stereotyping, discrimination, and prejudice traverse from traits (women are friendly, cooperative, relational, inclusive) to consequences (women are dominated and opportunities for upward mobility are blocked) leading many successful women to believe there are little or no incentives for women to fight through systemic barriers (Mceldowney, Bobrowski & Gramberg, 2009). The paradox that exists reveals the prevailing gap: "In an era when women have made sweeping strides in educational attainment and workforce participation, relatively few have made the journey all the way to the highest levels of political or corporate leadership" (Pew Research Center, 2008, p. 3).

Women are more likely to be siloed into staff positions such as corporate communication, human resources, and diversity although they often play key roles in marketing and customer relations primarily because of their superior people and communication skills in these areas (Bilimoria & Piderit, 1994). Contrast the siloing of women into staff positions with line positions with profit and loss responsibilities that are often reserved for men, supporting their upward mobility aspirations. PepsiCo Corporation is a case in point.

While PepsiCo is led by the very talented Indra Nooyi, a quick look at the PepsiCo leadership team's pictures reveals an interesting fabric—with men populating important line positions and women responsible for an array of communication and HR functions (http://www.pepsico.com/Company/Leadership.html). One study found that this is not just an issue in the United States, but worldwide, as indicated in the low number of women appointed to company boards (Burgess & Tharenou, 2002). Why is this? How can we explain the discrepancy between mounting evidence of women leadership effectiveness on one hand and the shortfall of women in boardrooms and executive suites on the other? If women outperform men in most leadership traits and if men excel primarily on traits associated with less formidable transactional, command, and control attributes—how can we explain the contradiction between desired leadership qualities and the shunning of women? If coaching and mentoring work better to inspire people than authority and control as sources of motivation, why aren't women more prevalent in upper executive positions? Is it possible that women's relational communication and communal leadership style put them at a disadvantage when it comes to managing bottom line operations in a cutthroat marketplace?

The simple answer is the "glass ceiling"—the invisible wall that prevents groups such as women and minorities from advancing in their careers. The glass ceiling was introduced in a *Wall Street Journal* article in 1987 that used the term to describe what was occurring in American businesses and other parts of the world. The metaphor references the unseen "artificial barriers" that inhibit women from attracting top executive jobs. Twenty-five years later, the majority of women in corporate America are still struggling with this invisible wall. Furthermore, the glass ceiling is no longer a single barrier, but a combination of multiple factors that push against women in management, leading Anna Marie Valerio (2009) to conclude that even with the progress that has been made so far in corporate America, women seeking upper executive positions face persistent barriers to their success.

2

Corporate and Cultural Barriers: The Paradox of the Glass Ceiling

Judith Oakley describes the "glass ceiling" as not just one wall that women strive to shatter, but "many varied pervasive forms of gender bias that occur frequently in both overt and covert ways" (2000, p. 321). In fact, her study found that in male-led companies the voices of women are often stifled and the current approaches that exist to help women move up in the hierarchy usually are geared toward getting women to blend in rather than speak their minds.

Ultimately, women who seek top management positions must weed through culturally formed stereotypes and at the same time avoid crossing culturally generated barriers. Alice Eagly and Linda Carli (2007) describe this barrier as "labyrinth leadership." I see the labyrinth as a centripetal force, invariably unicursal, that sends women to the center followed by a centrifugal force that then keeps them from reaching their goals. This centrifugal force is associated with inertia that moves in a circular path—a catch 22.

Eagly and Johnson (1990) categorized leadership styles of men and women, arguing that women are more interpersonally oriented and democratic than men, and men are more task-oriented and autocratic than women. Janice Yoder (2001) extended this categorization suggesting that both men and women perform leadership roles on a continuum ranging from a male-dominated, hierarchical, power-oriented context to a female-oriented, relational, influence-based context. She therefore argued that leadership is *gendered*, supporting earlier observations that gender provides an implicit, background identity in the workplace, and that most people have internalized gender roles to some extent.

Paradoxically women are judged against male norms, often eliciting negative evaluations about their behaviors and performance. When gendered organizations value the disembodied employee, the expectations are for women to fit this male-normed mold regardless of the perceived incongruity between the predominantly agentic qualities and the predominantly communal qualities characterizing women. The perceived incongruity could lead to two forms of prejudice: a less favorable evaluation of women's fitness for leadership roles; and a less favorable evaluation of the actual leadership behavior displayed by women because agentic behavior is perceived as less desirable in women than men (Eagly & Karau, 2002). When women perform leadership roles they are often perceived as having violated their stereotypically prescribed feminine roles.

Gendered Leadership

Eddy and Cox (2008, p. 72) pointed out in their research of women presidents in community colleges that: "although some of the women described their leadership as open and participatory, the hierarchical structure was most apparent," leading them to the same conclusion: Women should not be judged against male norms. Furthermore, women should not be penalized for acting in ways that are outside of what is expected of them. One of the women presidents told the story of being forceful on her side of an argument and being called a "bitch." She reflected, "I walked out of his office and said, 'I can't work for this man, and what's more, I probably can't work for anyone. I've got to be my own boss.' Indeed, she was penalized for acting tough outside her gender. Another president, petite in stature, noted that a female board member advised her to wear glasses 'to appear more serious.' The women needed to act tougher to meet the expected work roles but could not appear too tough" (p. 74).

Men in leadership roles, however, are seen as acting in congruence with their prescribed masculine roles. Therefore, successful female leaders generally work hard and seek leadership styles that do not elicit resistance to their authority by challenging norms dictating that women be egalitarian and supportive of others (Eagly et al., 2003, p. 825). Hence, gender role congruence theory, consistent with social identity theory and similarity-attraction models of interactions, typecasts males as high in masculine traits that are more task-focused or agentic, whereas females are high in feminine traits in tune with interpersonal and communal orientations.

Existing structures of pay and reward systems tend to reinforce this incongruity—women are judged less favorably than men in spite of exhibiting identical behaviors and accomplishments. Male contributions are measured in terms of bottom line results and numeric values such as ROI and ROE. Dominance, aggression, and competitiveness are overvalued and overemphasized. Traditional women's strengths such as maintaining relationships, resolving conflicts, sharing power, caring for employees, and reaching a consensus tend to be undervalued. Good communication skills, collaboration, mentoring, and developing others are important but less significant than quantitative measures of success—bottom line factors used to reward male managers. Women are particularly vulnerable to these evaluative biases when they work in male-dominated settings, paradoxically suffering harsh consequences for displaying excellent leadership, communication, and sensitivity skills (Heilman, Wallen, Fuchs & Tamkins, 2004).

Female managers reportedly "were forceful about getting their way" and needed to work hard to persuade senior managers to see their side, while male managers were able to negotiate, bargain, and achieve compromises (Lauterbach & Weiner, 1996). Feminine traits such as concern for others (relatedness), consensual approach to decision making, and consideration of feelings of others prior to initiating action may limit the extent of upward influence because women may act on different kinds of opportunities.

Organizations, particularly those that are male-dominated, are not gender-neutral—they reflect settings in which women's behavior and accomplishments are scrutinized, measured, and evaluated differently from men's (Hopkins, O'Neil & Bilimoria, 2008). Success becomes increasingly challenging in organizations with bosses that see loyalty and "fit" with their norms and values. Managers whose styles match those of their executives and senior managers may benefit from "fit effects" in performance evaluation and promotion decisions.

The perceived incongruity and subsequent prejudice reinforces a vicious cycle from two directions: Because leaders are expected to have more agentic than communal qualities, women conforming to their gender role are "failing" to meet the requirements of their leadership role; while conforming to their leader role can produce a failure to meet the requirements of their gender role (Eagly & Johannesen-Schmidt, 2001). Men, on the other hand, produce expectations that are consistent with current views of agentic leadership roles and behaviors (e.g., confidence and assertion), their natural tendencies. However, because agentic behaviors are perceived incompatible with communal behaviors, women are particularly vulnerable to becoming targets of prejudice, placing them at a disadvantage (e.g., rewarded differently).

Corporate Long-Term Success

Sometimes people view women as lacking the stereotypical directive and assertive qualities of good leaders—that is, as not being tough enough or not taking charge. "Sometimes people dislike female leaders who display these very directive and assertive qualities because such women seem unfeminine—that is, just like a man or like an iron lady. Carly Fiorina, former CEO of Hewlett-Packard, complained, "In the chat rooms around Silicon Valley . . . I was routinely referred to as either a 'bimbo' or a 'bitch'—too soft or too hard . . ." (Fiorina, 2006, p. 173). The anomaly of a woman executive in a male-populated executive suite may itself affect the ratings of her leadership skills and abilities.

A second major reason for female disadvantage is due to prevailing assumptions that male bosses are preferred by the masses. The Gallup Poll described earlier in the book confirmed this attitude in a study that showed a preference for male bosses over female bosses although the numbers started to tilt toward the middle (no preference). In 2006, men bosses were preferred by 37% of the respondents compared with 19% preferring a female boss. Forty-three percent showed indifference breaking away from any male-female categorization. What's more interesting was the fact that 40% of women prefer to have a male boss (Carroll, 2006).

Another barrier involves company boards. Company boards serve numerous roles, some of which include providing continuity for the organization and often selecting and appointing a CEO who is charged with the administration of the organization. The board governs by broad objectives and policies and publicly accounts for all organizational expenditures and funds (Arfken, Bellar & Helms, 2004). Because CEOs are usually men and board members are usually chosen from the pool of CEOs, many CEOs will select mirror-like board members who possess the qualities they have, surrounding themselves with figureheads that match their own attributes. They will likely select individuals with whom they feel more comfortable, leaving the opposite gender (women) behind, excusing their decisions with the "pipeline condition" described earlier.

Without women on company boards, innovation and creativity might be stifled or suppressed in favor of dominating males' views. Having women on company boards can give the company unique and fresh ideas and make connections between consumers and employees (Arfken, Bellar & Helms, 2004). Studies have shown that having women in positions of executive leadership can be linked to long-term success for the company as well as competitive advantage. Because women have a strong influence on what people buy, companies would be able to access the full range of resources available to a company. Notably, the Fortune 500 companies with the highest percentage of women corporate officers achieved, on average, a whopping 35% higher return on equity and 34% higher stakeholder satisfaction than did competitors with less diversity in the corporate suites (Catalyst, 2004).

Women help boost a company's public image and reputation through support of social responsibility and philanthropic programs. They add value to the company with unique adaptability skills and are masters in creating positive work climates based on inclusion and diversity. They typically have a stronger moral orientation and possess more social sensitivity than men, a necessary attribute to have on a socially accountable company's board. It is not that women and men compete in a zero sum game—it is that they bring something new and different to the table for an organization (Jones, 2009). As Eagly (2007) pointed out: Business journalists often echoed some of these themes by highlighting the important role that women have in dealing with employees and stakeholders while delivering consistent results—CEO qualities that are pursued by many boards of directors.

Stereotyping—What Else?

While male CEOs and senior VPs are praised for forceful and assertive behavior and given low marks for being cooperative and empathic, the exact opposite is "reserved" for women. Notably, the gender stereotypes that are hurting women to reach the top still exist especially when standards of success are measured in male terms where hierarchy and power are preferred over egalitarianism and persuasion. One is prejudice, which is when someone holds a negative view of another based on their cultural identity. The other is discrimination, which is when prejudice becomes observable. Research shows that both of these components exist in the workplace where agentic or instrumental behaviors are valued rather than empowerment, influence, and care for employees. Assessments of leadership inherently reflect gender stereotypes and prejudices.

Stereotyping can be particularly risky due to the fact that the descriptions of certain groups are often mutually exclusive. Moreover, the fact that women in upper management positions are almost always "tokens" instead of "dominants" hurts their chances of making it to the top (Oakley, 2000). Because "dominants" have a tendency to act in ways that affirm the group's solidarity, the "tokens" are often made to feel excluded as well as face more pressure at work. Kanter's (1977) theory of tokenism suggests that underrepresented individuals at the senior ranks require unique strategies and talents because they must respond to different expectations and are evaluated with different lenses than mainstream peers. In fact, the likelihood of women who work with groups of 85% or more of men to experience negative consequences associated with tokenism is relatively high (Yoder, 1991). There is also a widely held stereotypical belief that women will allow their emotions to get in the way of their work and managing others, especially men (Huffman & Cohen, 2004). A woman who loses composure may be seen as weak and will lose credibility. A man who loses composure may be seen as sensitive (Ruderman & Ohlott, 2005).

Gmür (2006) reported on the results of a study on male and female attributes in which 376 professionals were asked to provide descriptions of masculine, feminine, and neutral attributes. The results indicated that "the ideal manager is predominately described using male attributes, whereas stereotypical female attributes, to the extent they enter at all, are selected only in

TABLE 2.1
Typical Stereotypes

Female Stereotypes	Male Stereotypes
Communal (connecting with others, cooperative, sensitive, empathetic, and nurturing)	Agentic (assertive, autonomous, self-promoting, dominant, and tough)
Emotional and often cry; unable to control emotion; less credible	Hard-headed and able to control emotion; knows when to display emotion (if at all)
Back-stabbing, manipulative	Assertive

combination with male characteristics" (p. 107). Table 2.1 lists typical stereotypes of males and females in management positions.

Paradox in Action

Women in the media industry have markedly higher turnover rates than in most other industries. Many women choose to leave the media profession at an earlier age compared to many other professions, on the ground that they suffer from a higher level of stress and a higher percentage of failure in balancing the double burden of family and career due to the demanding, intense, and unpredictable nature of their working conditions (e.g., when breaking news takes place, journalists need to arrive at the scene upfront right away). This becomes a vicious cycle: As more women leave the industry, the few women who remain with years of experience are expected to stay overtime, and few of the already low percentage of women that persist compete for top-ranking positions. The very nature of media work, coupled with the traditional responsibility imposed on women of having to take good care of their families before focusing primarily on their careers has led to the diminishing representation of women with years of experience. The difficulties of balancing family obligations with career goals has proved to be a significant rationale accounting for the scarcity of females in executive positions in general and the media industry in particular. The McKinsey & Company (2007, p. 9) study describes the "double burden" as a syndrome with global implications. European women, for example, devote on average twice as much time as men to domestic tasks. Quite often women feel it is too heavy of a burden to try to manage work with their life at home and domestic activities. Many women choose to work part-time or not at all so they can tend to their families and have a strong presence within the home.

Within the media industry, a dividing line exists between men and women when it comes to task assignments. Men have access to high-visibility projects while the door is closed to women for these same projects a large majority of the time. Men are the favorite representatives for international, high-visibility assignments while most women are passed over for the opportunity to expand their careers to the international arena. Surveys show that while female and male MBA graduates expressed equal interest in international assignments, only 3% of women managers are sent abroad. In fact, 75% of companies indicated that the prejudice against women in international assignments is so great that sending them abroad would be a setup for failure (Adler, 1994).

Many women in the field reported that this common practice prevented them from potential advancement. Women have less access to challenging projects (e.g., international assignments) and high-risk assignments that also lead to high-visibility, which is so important for advancement to senior executive positions (Lyness & Thompson, 2000). Successful completion of high-risk assignments typically comes with public recognition that is often translated into top positions. While men tend to place a high priority on visibility and recognition, women with a track record of success depend on peer support to advance their career. Contrast the barrier of exposure to high-risk assignments and responsibilities with the paradox of the "glass cliff" on which women are likely to be appointed to positions associated with crisis situations, and the likelihood for failure and criticism increases (Haslam & Ryan, 2008).

Many women report that to be successful, they need to demonstrate super-human levels of commitment, technical proficiency, meeting bottom line results, exhibiting strategic thinking, demonstrating effective decision-making skills, applying creativity, having effective conflict-resolution skills, and coping with change and uncertainty—all coupled with long hours at work. What's more, women have to deal with the inconsistency of their own sense of success and the way organizations measure it (Ruderman, Ohlott, Panzer & King, 1999). Women also experience cross-pressures for their time and the constant need to balance competing priorities across life and career goals that are different for men

(Mainiero & Sullivan, 2006; O'Neil & Bilimoria, 2005). Consequently, many women choose to work part-time or not at all so they can attend to their families at home. Others telecommute by working from home, most commonly on a part-time basis. Indeed, Ruderman and Ohlott (2004) reported a higher turnover rate for women than for their male counterparts in executive positions with at least ten years of experience.

Some organizations offer on-site daycare as well as flex time where an employee can choose to work four days a week for ten hours rather than five days a week for eight hours. The Johnson & Johnson Finance Vice President Kendall O'Brien stated, "If J&J hadn't had on-site day care, if I hadn't had a supervisor supportive of my working flexible hours, if I weren't part of an organization that's cognizant of the talent pipeline and that recognized I didn't want to leave, I wouldn't be here today" (*Women Leaders of NAFE's Top Companies*, 2010). Organizations must not only recognize the barriers that exist that prevent women from fully committing to work, but also must offer support to help women balance their contradictory roles.

Christine Todd Whitman: First Female Governor of New Jersey

Former New Jersey Governor and EPA Secretary Christine Todd Whitman was interviewed on 1/2/2011 by CNN's Fareed Zakaria in a segment, "How does a woman lead in what is still a male-dominated world?"

---

http://archives.cnn.com/TRANSCRIPTS/1101/02/fzgps.01.html

> **Zakaria:** In the 112th Congress, only 17 percent of the seats will be filled by women, and just 12 percent of America's states are governed by females. Women don't do much better in the corporate world. Christie Todd Whitman was the first female governor of New Jersey and a member of President George W. Bush's cabinet. She now sits on several major corporate boards.
>
> **Zakaria:** Governor Whitman, thank you for joining me.
>
> **Whitman:** My pleasure.

(continued)

Zakaria: The thing that one often wonders about when dealing with a very accomplished woman like you, who has succeed in many different realms is, is it different being a woman?

Whitman: I wouldn't know. I've never been a man. I—I don't mean to say that facetiously, but I used to get the question a lot, what's it like being a woman governor? And I can say I can tell you what it's like to be a governor. I don't know what it's like to be a woman versus a male.

Zakaria: But do you think there are different styles of leadership? Because you —

Whitman: Yes.

Zakaria: —you must have dealt with a lot of men—

Whitman: No. No, no, no. I—

Zakaria: —and you've seen the—the differences.

Whitman: Yes. No, that's very true. I think there really are differences, which is why I argue that we need a better mix at the decision making table, not just men and women, but minorities as well, because we do bring a different approach, different life experiences, different frames of reference.

I mean, I've—I've often found and the minute you generalize you get into trouble. But it was often the case when I'd be in a meeting and I'd be the only female there, and I would say something, and the conversation would continue on, and then a man down the table would say exactly the same thing, and oh, what a brilliant idea. And I go, OK, right. It's OK. As long they got the idea, it's all right by me.

Zakaria: And what about the idea that there is a kind of a—a softer style and a more consensus-building style? Do you think that's true?

Whitman: Yes, I do. I mean, there used to be—Millicent Fenwick was a congresswoman from New Jersey who the Lacey Davenport on the "Doonesbury" series, a cartoon series, used to say that if you give— when women have been in power as long as men, they'll act just the same way. I don't think that's true. I think we will always see a difference.

And I used to remember, I'd send a bill as governor to the legislature, and they would deal with it as they're supposed to and then make changes. And then it would come back to me with changes, and I'd sign it. And—and I can remember seeing headlines saying, well, it wasn't what she wanted. Well, that's not true. If we finally were moving an issue forward, it didn't have to be exactly the way I'd sent it in. That's what the legislature's supposed to do.

That was not a loss, as far as I was concerned. That was a victory. That was getting things done, moving into a place we hadn't been before. But, very often, the pundits, usually male, would be saying, well, that didn't get the way you wanted it, and so that wasn't a victory. And I'd say, you don't get it.

Zakaria: You know the famous story of Harry Truman, he—

Whitman: The buck stops here?

Zakaria: Well, no. He's—Harry Truman, when he's about to hand over the office to Eisenhower, tells one of his aides, he says, poor Ike. He's—all he's done is be a general. He's going to pick up the phone and say do this, do that—

Whitman: Oh, right.

Zakaria: —and he's going to—not going to realize none of it is ever going to happen.

Do you feel like that's another difference, that in—in politics you can't just command?

Whitman: No, you can't just command. You have to get people—it—it goes back to a definition of leadership that I always liked, which is leadership is getting other people to do what you want them to do because they want to do it. And that's what it takes.

You have to convince people. You have to work with people. You have to get people to support you on these things. You have to get them to understand. Communication becomes enormously important.

And while it's important for a CEO of a—of a major company, it's even more so for a person in—in political office, because it's a daily thing, and it—it does require getting that support—

Zakaria: Is you're constantly persuading, you're—

Whitman: You're constantly persuading. You're constantly explaining. You're constantly trying to prioritize.

(continued)

And the other thing that I think is quite different, you know, as CEO you do decide what's in the best interests of the company and what's in the best interests of the shareholders. But it's not the same thing as when you're—when you're coming up with a policy in government.

Getting to understand the fact that there are always going to be people you're going to hurt, no matter how good a policy is, it's not going to benefit everybody. And you will have people coming to you saying, this is going to kill me. I mean, this is going to put me out of business, this is going to hurt my children, whatever it is. And it's that ability to stand back and say, what's going to be in the greatest good for the greatest number?

Zakaria: Do you—do you think that there are still glass ceilings for women in America?

Whitman: Yes. I mean, there's still—you can certainly see it on the—on the business side. And for women in politics, it's fortunately breaking down a bit, but it's still there more in presumptions.

It's interesting. My daughter ran for Congress, and she's —was a mother. She was 30. She had twin boys, who were young at the time, very young. And—but she worked on Capitol Hill, she'd been communications director for a pretty prominent congressman. She'd worked at the Department of Labor, running programs for them. She'd had her own business, management consulting business, events planning. And she was a licensed realtor in the state of New Jersey.

And yet, when she ran, people would look at her and say, well, you're—you don't have enough experience. And who's going to take care of the kids? And yet, the fellow whose seat she was seeking had been 30 when he'd run. He had young children, and he'd been a substitute teacher. And nobody said you don't have enough experience or who's going to take care of the children?

So there is still that bias there which does, in fact, create a ceiling on expectations, and it makes it tougher on—on women. But it's breaking down, fortunately.

Business world not so much. We still don't have pay equity. But it's getting better. It's just taking a long time.

Zakaria: Governor Whitman, thank you very much.

Whitman: Pleasure.

Systemic Barriers that Inhibit Women's Abilities to Lead Effectively

The effects of prejudices against female managers and professionals are widespread and transcend country lines. After comparing almost 11,500 female professionals with 16,700 male workers in 34 countries for their latest book, Dudley and Goodson (2008) concluded that women are still far more timid than men in the office and that, generally, women are less likely to promote their personal successes. When women promote themselves verbally it could be construed as bragging or boasting. Indeed, only 6% of women feel that they have been successful due to continuously promoting their accomplishments in the workplace.

The list assembled below includes typical barriers and obstacles that prevent women from reaching the top.

1. Lack of access to positions of power; discrimination: men are favored for upper echelon positions

2. Domination and lack of respect

3. Bias, prejudice, negative stereotyping based on traits and behavioral characteristics attributed to women

4. Perceived incompetency and therefore viewing women as less credible as influence agents

5. Cross-pressures and competing priorities between leadership and gender roles

6. Lack of adequate mentoring and lack of female role models in the workplace

7. Organizational culture with a bias toward hiring men: Competent women are perceived as violating prescriptive gender role norms that expect women to be communal

8. Agentic women are considered less socially competent or accepted

9. Succession planning that ignores women's careers

10. The "vision thing" that is perceived to be lacking from women's transformational leadership style

11. Female managers are isolated from social networks

12. Women are more internally motivated by self-improvement and goals related to team success, not only quantitative benchmarks

13. Reward systems organized around extrinsic values and hard skills; intrinsic values and soft skills are less emphasized

14. Greater preference for male bosses

15. Outright discrimination based on sex as well as on race

The rest of the book explores these and other corporate and cultural barriers and presents ideas to reduce the effects of these barriers, to deal with them at the personal or organizational level, and, when possible, to make them irrelevant or eliminate them.

3

Corporate Greed and the Anguish of Executive Failure; or Why More Women Should Lead

In the past decade, corporate America's faith in the larger-than-life CEO has been shaken by numerous scandals. Those entrusted to lead major companies to greatness have instead led them to their demise. Jeffrey Skilling was regarded as taking Enron to a new level of success by Wall Street's standards, while making himself, his senior management, and even Enron's employees—multi-millionaires. This Cinderella story ended in a twenty-four-year jail sentence for Skilling, who was found guilty for inside trading, securities fraud, and conspiracy, among others (Burns, 2006). His counterpart, Kenneth Lay, was also facing charges but suffered a fatal heart attack prior to being convicted. Yet another fallen CEO, Bernard Ebbers of WorldCom, was also convicted of fraud and conspiracy and is serving a 25-year prison term in Louisiana, according to an article published in the *New York Times* on September 27, 2006.

How do CEOs get to the point where deception appears acceptable? What kind of leadership skills is now necessary for CEOs to prove their worthiness to lead companies? It is simply no longer enough to graduate from an Ivy League business school.

The next few sections describe bad habits that often lead to failures and unanticipated consequences and ways to deal with these habits to divert failure. The book will also explore a list of qualities for successful leadership, including the ability to focus, to take initiative, to communicate and stand behind decisions, to see outside the box, and the readiness to take responsibility for one's actions. Several profiles of successful women CEOs will be used to highlight traits and competencies that distinguish their careers focusing on leadership integrity and moral courage.

The Ability to Focus

There is one skill set that seems to override all others as a common element of success, and that is the ability to *focus*. As Marcus Buckingham (2005) has pointed out, to focus can refer either to your ability to systematically identify the most critical of factors among various others—in this case to focus well is synonymous with the ability to filter well. In another sense, to focus may mean the ability to bring sustained pressure to bear after identifying those critical factors—what Buckingham refers to as the "laser-like quality of focus." Both of these variations have been found to be crucial to success in top-management positions, and both will come up again in the discussion of other important characteristics.

Taking the Initiative

One of the most crucial of all qualities common among winning companies is a focus on growth (Joyce, Nohria & Robertson, 2003). Target Corporation has used growth strategies to find success in a highly competitive sales sector where others have failed in comparison. Target's founder, John Geisse, was a well-known trend-spotter from the start. In some sense, the success of Target can be attributed to a good deal of opportunistic situations; however, none of the chain's status would have been possible had the company's early leaders been unable to recognize and take advantage of some of the larger trends of the time. The company has maintained this competitive edge over the years by using proactive strategies to sustain its competitive advantage in a market dominated by its chief archrival Wal-Mart (Belasen, 2008).

Top-to-Bottom Communication

The ability to communicate consistent messages both internally and externally is an important leadership skill. The success of the company resides in the ability of the company to act as a whole and to share new and innovative strategy from the top down. At Merck, Ray Gilmartin realized this critical role of leadership: "My job is really to set the overall strategic direction of the company, to ensure that we are organized to carry out that strategy, and that we have the right management processes in place. I need to create an environment where everyone in the organization can achieve their full potential so that our company . . . [Succeeds in the highly competitive market]" (Neff, Citrin & Brown, 1999).

Adaptability and Risk Taking

There are many setbacks to purely responsive reactions on the part of the CEO. If a founder does not grow and adapt rapidly enough there is a fundamental risk of not evolving past the point where one person can manage it. In fact, there are many interesting examples of this, including heads of such companies as Dell, FedEx, Intel, Microsoft, Schwab, and Starbucks—each CEO founded (and in some cases co-founded) the companies they are still leading. The key is to learn to adapt constantly and, in the words of Steve Case of America Online, to "hire great people, people you can have confidence in and trust." Consider the following quote along these same lines from Mike Armstrong, former CEO of AT&T:

> I don't expect anyone to be perfect. It's not human nature. What I do expect is that you will take risks, correct mistakes, and learn from both. And if you don't—judging by market results—then we'll make a change. It's nothing personal. And I'll do it, even if you're my best friend. We must have this company execute to its full potential.

This "anything-it-takes" attitude exhibited by Armstrong is not unique among CEOs known for their success stories. Larry Bossidy, former CEO of AlliedSignal states,

> I think the CEO today has to be . . . more communicative . . . and I think he has to be far more nimble. Companies used to have five-year strategic plans. Now most people have cut it down to three years, and probably that's too long. With the pace of the world changing as it does, you've got to look at where you are ever more frequently or the bus goes by.

It is not merely enough to have a strong strategy; the business environment is highly dynamic and unstable. What works today may not work tomorrow, hence the need for individuals who can pinpoint the "next big thing," and inherent in that ability is the acceptance of risk. In the words of Armstrong, "You've got to have the guts to make a decision." The known winners in today's business world are individuals who do not shrink from the challenge of tracking potential competitors and trends in the market alike. Lou Gerstner of IBM understood this need for change, "we are constantly changing what we do—building a culture of restless self-renewal." Successful leaders acknowledge this dynamic aspect and install systems and programs to anticipate change, recognizing the fact that early anticipation of new developments is what will bring success.

Leadership Integrity, not Management Control

According to Kell and Carrott (2005), corporate cultures—weak and strong alike—have been found to influence employees leadership styles more than any other aspect of their jobs. Fundamental to leadership are trust, integrity, transparency, personal relationships, and innovation. Because leadership is focused on construction of a common agreement over organizational goals, leadership must be participatory and shared. In leadership, executives *delegate* authority to team members or other individuals; they *depend* on followers' *respect* and *commitment* for the completion of goals. While managers do things right, leaders do the right thing. A manager's job is to make sure that things get done right, on time, under budget, and with maximum profits. Managers generally focus on very short-term outcomes, schedules, and specific goals. Leaders, on the other hand, focus on creating vision for the future, foresighted strategies, as well as uplifting moralities and the values of their followers. Managers will tell employees exactly what to do, while a leader meaningfully motivates them to do their jobs.

A Downward Spiral

The vast number of scandals involving CEOs in the late '90 s and early 2000s rocked not only the stock market, but also commercial America's view of these all-powerful individuals. There have been many investigations as to why these people succumbed to the pressures of committing crimes such as fraud, insider trading, and conspiracy. One popular opinion is greed, the same kind Gordon Gekko (Michael Douglas) spoke of in the classic 1987 film *Wall Street*. However, Tom Walker (2007) of the *Houston Chronicle* clarifies, "there's another explanation, one that suggests corporate executives are akin to celebrities who believe the rules don't apply to them, or that they have the wealth to get themselves out of trouble, or that they're simply invincible" (p. 6). Invincibility is a tricky concept, yet in this case, it makes sense. We live in a world where celebrities are far from normal, everyday people. We put them on pedestals because of their riches and good looks, and we make excuses for their downfalls—they are, in fact, invincible. There is no doubt that this type of outlook is appealing, especially to CEOs. CEOs like Tyco's former chief Ted Kozolowski, who was certainly swept up in the feelings of invincibility that came along with his status. He even threw a Mediterranean-themed birthday party for his wife, a social gathering whose total cost was in excess of $2 million. While this would be perfectly acceptable for celebrities spending their own money, Kozolowski's event was paid for in part by company funds.

These examples show that CEOs become blindsided by the prospect of luxury and fame that they lose sight of what is important. They do not realize that when celebrities spend and make other important decisions recklessly, they are usually doing the greatest damage to themselves. When CEOs take full advantage of celebrity-style benefits, they do colossal damage to their employees and shareholders, as well as to themselves (Walker, 2007, p. 6). Those employed by Enron, WorldCom, and Tyco lost everything when their CEOs went down due to many pensions tied to stock options that became obsolete when Wall Street caught wind of scandal. Charles Prestwood, a 33-year veteran of Enron, says all he has to show for his time with the firm are gifts in honor of his tenure. He explains, "I had $1.3 million and now all I've got to show for it is two clocks" (Burns, 2006, p. 1). Employees at Enron were even told to keep their money right where it was when talk of problems within the company began, even though Skilling had begun exercising his options. Employees trusted Skilling, as many trust CEOs to do the right thing and to make decisions in the best interest of the corporation. Unfortunately, in the past this has proved to be the exception to the rule in several instances.

Yet another aspect of this invincibility is the fact that business leaders are strapped with few required qualifications to rise to their status. While doctors, lawyers, and architects are responsible for completing rigorous testing and securing licenses, business leaders are not subject to the same rigmarole. Harvard University's Howard Gardner, a psychologist, explains "you don't need a license to practice . . . the only requirements are to make money and not run afoul of the law" (Walker, 2007, p. 6). Being in the public eye can be a hindrance to even those who are qualified to be CEOs. In his "beautiful mind" theory, Professor Todd Kendall of Clemson University argues that the same "genetic factor that leads to brilliance also causes behavior outside of societal norms" (Walker, 2007, p. 6). Another theory, called "substitutability," claims that those who are especially talented or knowledgeable in one particular subject area are more likely to get away with their bad behavior because that person is either difficult or temporarily impossible to replace. Those CEOs who are well versed in their particular business and industry are similar to actors who are chosen to play a certain part that is difficult for another to emulate in that both are difficult to substitute, at least in a short amount of time. CEOs and actors who misbehave are likely to get away with their irresponsibility because their expertise is a necessity. These theories are likely to explain why CEOs who were eventually brought to justice were not only allowed to get away with their deceitful behavior for so long, but also why they felt they were entitled to conduct themselves in this way.

Though invincibility is an explanation for why CEOs find themselves engaging in questionable decision-making practices, there is also the possibility of the presence of an overpowering ego. Gordon Quick (2007), of the *St. Louis Post*, argues in his article aptly titled "They're Not All Bad, Just Big-Headed" that CEOs do not necessarily begin their tenure as bad people (p. 5). Quick explains that corrupt CEOs are often those people, without regard to humility, who believe that they are what keeps their firm successful to the point that they lose sight of those below them who could provide valuable suggestions and feedback. This leads to their inability to acknowledge limitations, the belief that the rules no longer apply to the CEOs, and the belief in the entitlement to far more compensation than they are currently receiving, despite previously agreeing to a lucrative contract. CEOs with excessive egos frequently have an "it's all about me attitude," to the point where their names become completely synonymous with the company's brand—which Quick (2007) terms the "cult" CEO. Unlike some companies like GE, which are synonymous with former CEO Jack Welch in a positive way, Quick (2007) argues that a cult CEO creates many vulnerabilities to their organizations. Nevertheless, Quick's

(2007) position on this issue does not attempt to claim that an ego is necessarily a bad thing. CEOs need to be aggressive, self-sufficient, and driven to get results. The key is the ability to harness the ego's power and balance it with humility.

Executive Failures

In his book, *Why Smart Executives Fail* (2003), Sydney Finkelstein identifies four destructive syndromes that often occur simultaneously or lead to each other if the symptoms are not quickly recognized and corrected.

Brilliantly Fulfilling the Wrong Vision—A flawed executive mindset that relies on magic answers, "the holy grail," or "the wrong scoreboard" and that throws off a company's perception of reality. The founder of Wang Labs, An Wang, was fixated on the idea of crushing IBM as a competitor. In this case, we can say that Wang was using IBM as the "scoreboard" for his factor of success. This led him down a decision-making path to try and compete directly with IBM, which was much bigger in size. This ultimately led to the loss of revenues and profits.

Delusions of a Dream Company—A delusional attitude that keeps a constant picture of inaccurate reality in place. This syndrome relates to overconfidence and illusion of control leading executives to worship their own ideas and disregard many warning signs around them. Border, the founder of Webvan, ignored the research that would have given him more insight into the profitability estimates of his strategic move to create a new venture, Webvan. Border believed that acting quickly and capitalizing on opportunities would prevent the loss of market leadership. As a result of poor oversight, billions of dollars were spent on assets and infrastructure resulting in poor ROI.

Tracking Down Lost Signals—Breakdowns occur in communications systems developed to handle potentially urgent information. Saatchi & Saatchi, NASA, Oracle, Nissan, and Xerox have all fallen into this trap. NASA is perhaps the most serious of these examples: the rigid hierarchical culture did not facilitate the flow of information across hierarchical levels. Employees could not go over their immediate managers' heads, and managers did not interact with anyone not directly beneath them. This created a culture where subordinates did not feel comfortable going above their managers when the managers did not act on the information, thus stopping the flow of critical information that could have prevented the Challenger explosion. Ease of availability of information could prevent a great deal of executive corporate failures had the information been communicated properly across the appropriate channels to the necessary people and oversight ensured that the proper action was being taken. Another example is J&J's decision to disregard the comments and concerns that were presented to them by the cardiologists who used their product. J&J's rationalization for this was that their patents protected them enough to get by without addressing customer concerns or investing any further money into a more advanced product.

However, that decision remained untrue. Other European competitors developed a superior product and marketed it to the same cardiologists who complained to J&J. This was a major reason for the severe decline in J&J's market share. J&J continued to ignore the situation. Because it was the mindset that the patents were the end all and be all of J&J's stent business, no importance was put on the outside threats that indeed did exist. Instead, the communication channels within J&J needed to be open and fluid. For instance, the marketing department of J&J should have seen the competitors out there and relayed this as a threat, prompting further action to be taken.

Seven Bad Habits—The leadership mindsets that keep top executives from correcting their course of actions include: dominant personality; having no boundaries between personal and corporate interests; having all the answers; disregarding colleagues who do not support their views; obsession with visibility and public image; rationalizing major obstacles in their strategy; and, worshipping the status quo.

Today's CEOs and those of the future must be well aware of the importance of possessing an unassuming nature, and of the need for letting go of the reigns from time to time to empower employees and promote bottom-up learning. CEOs must also continue to concern themselves with the increasing significance and sustainability of corporate social responsibility. Each of these three points is essential for leading an organization in a path that is both ethical and profitable.

Regaining Trust

It is evident that CEOs face an array of pressures when taking on this important role. They are required to be aggressive, yet approachable; proud, yet humble; and powerful, yet open. Their ideal leadership profile resembles that of a circle: perfectly balanced across many organizational facets. In reality, however, only a few great leaders display behavioral complexity and paradoxical skills that capture this balance.

What qualities do CEOs need to possess to win the approval of stake-holders and corporate America? Quick (2007) explains that they need CEOs who understand their strengths and weaknesses, who recognize their own needs and motivations, and who can align them with the interests of the company. CEOs must believe that openness, candor, and respect are the fundamental elements of a high-performance company. In the end, we need CEOs with true humility—CEOs who can capitalize on the strength of their ego, without letting themselves sabotage their success and that of their company. We need enlightened CEOs.

Along with humility, a truly great chief has the ability to cultivate a leadership attitude all through the organization, not just at the top. James Kelly and Scott Nadler (2007) speak to the importance of this tactic in their *Wall Street Journal* article "Leading from Below: CEOs can't change companies on their own." The secret is to foster a leadership mentality throughout the ranks. Managers outside of the "C-suite" should exercise upward leadership to influence executives' minds and direction. Kelly and Nadler's suggestions for successful leadership include the following:

- Make the decision to be a leader
- Focus on influence, not control
- Make your mental organizational chart horizontal rather than vertical
- Work on your "trusted advisor" skills
- Don't wait for the perfect time, just find a good time
- Integrate a broader range of risks and potential impacts into your business decisions

- Expose yourself to a broader range of perspectives
- Create vacuums rather than imposing solutions
- Encourage questions without answers
- Ask "what if" questions
- Openly discuss values as well as value
- Refresh your radar screen periodically

Female CEOs: Successful Stories

Currently there are 16 women who hold the title of Chief Executive Officer in Fortune 500 companies. The following analysis examines the educational backgrounds, employment history, and leadership styles of three such female CEOs. By examining the noteworthy careers of these three extraordinary women, a unique pattern is identified: female CEOs combine the powerful ability to impact the bottom line with a passion for motivating employees and a considerate ear for consumer needs, giving them a dynamic edge in business today.

Virginia Rometty: First Female President and CEO at IBM

IBM announced on October 26, 2011 that its board had elected the first female president and chief executive officer in the company's 100-year history who will take office on January 2, 2012. Virginia "Ginny" Rometty, 54, joined IBM straight from Northwestern University with a computer science degree in 1981 as a systems engineer and rose through the ranks, bringing the business-to-business company closer to its clients in industries such banking, insurance, telecommunications, manufacturing, and health care.

Ms. Rometty will report to the current CEO Samuel J. Palmisano, staying on in his role as Chairman, who has led the company on a day-to-day basis since Louis V. Gerstner, Jr., stepped down from the CEO role in 2002. Ms. Rometty's work was noted for leading IBM—ranked number 18 in the Fortune 500 with more than $99 billion in 2010 revenue—in its efforts to move from narrowly addressing a company's technical needs to addressing its broad industry agenda though her decade-long leadership of IBM's services organization.

The most dramatic move in that campaign was her advocacy and stewardship of IBM's $3.5 acquisition of Price Waterhouse Coopers

Consulting (PWCC) in the fall of 2002, giving the company more authority in its discussions with c-suite executives. She has also led IBM's move to higher-value integrated product and services solutions, a major strategy begun by former Chairman Gerstner, through her tenure leading various functional IBM groups.

After Ms. Rometty convinced PWCC's technology-agnostic partners to stay with IBM through the acquisition, CEO Palmisano put her in charge of IBM's global sales force, where she led a new client-centric integrated approach to sales, research, marketing, service, and support. In her current position as Senior Vice President and IBM's global sales leader, she is today accountable for revenue, profit, and client satisfaction in the 170 global markets in which IBM does business, with responsibility for both the company's worldwide business results and its global strategy, marketing, and communications functions.

Sources

- IBM press release
  http://www.businesswire.com/news/home/20111025007083/en/
  Virginia-M.-Rometty-Elected-Ibm-President-CEO

- IBM G. Rometty biography
  http://www-03.ibm.com/press/us/en/biography/10069.wss

- New York Times article, Oct. 26, 2011, by Steve Lohr: "IBM names Virginia Rometty as New Chief Executive."
  http://www.nytimes.com/2011/10/26/technology/ibm-names-a-new-chief.html?pagewanted=all

Anne Mulcahy, CEO, Xerox: A Turnaround Strategist

Ranked closely behind Nooyi in the #2 slot on *Fortune Magazine*'s 2006 Top 50 Most Powerful Women in Business is Anne Mulcahy, Chairman of the Board and Chief Executive Officer of Xerox. A 24-year veteran of the $16 billion document management company, Mulcahy is the first woman CEO in the company's history. Although not the obvious choice for the job (Xerox's stock tanked 15% on the day of the announcement), Anne has fulfilled her strategic leadership role restructuring the company, which was debt-riddled at the time of her appointment, for an extraordinary turnaround (Tsiantar, 2006). In the summer of 2009 Anne was replaced by Ursula Burns, the first Fortune 500 headed by a black woman.

Anne Mulcahy completed a Bachelor of Arts degree in English and Journalism from Marymount College in Tarrytown, NY before beginning her career at Xerox in 1976 as a field sales representative. She remained at Xerox for the next 16 years working in a sales capacity, taking on increasingly responsible sales and senior management positions. In 1992 Mulcahy was named Vice President for Human Resources where she was responsible for compensation, benefits, human resource strategy, labor relations, management development, and employee training. Four years later she spent a short period serving the company as Vice President and Staff Officer for Customer Operations, covering South America, Central America, Europe, Asia, and Africa before becoming Chief Staff Officer in 1997 and Corporate Senior Vice President in 1998. She finally moved into her position of President and Chief Operating Officer where she remained until being named CEO of Xerox on August 1, 2001, and Chairman on January 1, 2002. In addition to her seat on the Xerox Board of Directors, Anne is a board director of Catalyst, Citigroup Inc., Fuji Xerox Company, Ltd., Target Corporation, and is Chairman of the corporate governance task force of the Business Roundtable.

Despite having many years of company experience under her belt, Mulcahy was not exactly groomed to take on the top role of CEO. With a degree in English/Journalism and little executive experience, many were surprised at the promotion, although none more than Mulcahy herself. The Xerox veteran candidly admitted that she had never planned to become the CEO, saying, "I took on this position feeling equal parts excitement and dread" (Vollmer, 2004). Nonetheless, the now-respected executive is widely credited for leading the company away from the grasps of bankruptcy of Chapter 11. When Anne took over in 2001 Xerox was awash in $17 billion in debt. Realizing the impending battle, with much candor, Anne warned employees of tough times ahead and enlisted the help of a colleague to give her a crash course in finance to supplement her lacking background in the subject matter. "There wasn't a lot of time for false pride," she said. Through aggressively restructuring Xerox's debt, closing divisions, and cutting expenses, within one year Anne successfully directed Xerox out of the red zone (Tsiantar, 2006).

The success of the company reorganization relied heavily on Mulcahy's open communication strategy. "I feel like my title should be Chief Communication Officer," the Xerox executive has said, emphasizing the importance of honesty, confidence, and listening for effective communication with customers and employees. She believes strongly that her success as a leader is driven by a "commitment to understanding and meeting customers' requirements, as well as developing and nurturing a motivated and proud workforce . . . When your organization is struggling, you have to give people the sense that you know what's happening and that you have a strategy to fix it. Beyond that, you have to tell people what they can do to help." And let them help, she did; the CEO has been known to accept nothing less than total support from not only her executive team, but from all Xerox employees. She is known for her no-nonsense, without fear or favor approach, which has born a dedicated workforce (Vollmer, 2004).

Mulcahy has been characterized by colleagues as "extremely focused and decisive," qualities she has credited to her upbringing. As the only daughter in a family with four boys, Mulcahy was encouraged by her parents to compete equally with her brothers, which taught her not only to handle criticism but to listen to it as well—an ability that has helped her to make difficult decisions. Today, working at Xerox is still all in the family for Anne; her husband is a retired Xerox executive and her older brother runs the global services group. Anne also has two sons (Kharif, 2003). Regardless of her non-traditional background, Mulcahy has proven her ability to make strategic decisions that affect the bottom line. In addition, her experience within the HR function has left her with a powerful ability to motivate and sustain a productive workforce, even in the face of massive organizational change.

Ursula Burns, Xerox's Visionary CEO

Here is an excerpt from Geoff Colvin's interview of Ursula Burns that appeared in the May 3, 2010, issue of *Fortune Magazine*. Burns has been CEO of Xerox since July 2009 and succeeded Anne Mulcahy as Chairman in May 2010. She is the first African-American woman to run a Fortune 500 company.

Fortune: In a nonstop infotech revolution, Xerox's long-term strategy is a really interesting issue. So let me ask you Peter Drucker's famous question: What business are you in?

UB: We're in the business of enabling our clients to focus on their real business while we take care of their document-intensive business processes behind the scenes. I'll use *Fortune* as an example. You're not in the business of printing a magazine. What we see about *Fortune* is the printed magazine.0:00 /3:10Xerox making itself 'obsolete.'

Fortune: That's right—we don't own any printing presses.

UB: But without someone who could supply you with that solution, Fortune would be less than it could be. What we do is manage document-intensive business processes for our clients around the world so that they can focus on what they really do. We do that by applying technology. We do it in a global way, so that if you have locations around the world and you want to communicate with your people in a fairly consistent way, I can do that for you. It will look the same, feel the same, be delivered in the same time and the same format. All the information you want present will be there; anything you want redacted will be gone. You shouldn't have to worry about that.

Fortune: That leads to the deal you recently closed: your acquisition of Affiliated Computer Services. Wall Street initially didn't like it. What did you find so compelling?

UB: It was all about extending our capabilities, expanding our reach. Xerox is a technology company that's global and has an amazing brand. ACS is a business-process outsourcing company that knows business processes and how to manage them to be significantly more efficient. Business processes are all around documents, containers of information.

Fortune: So a document doesn't have to be a piece of paper.

UB: ery often it's not. At the end phase, many documents end up on paper. But in the beginning they are digital files, photographic images, phone calls, voice data. All of that is key to having a business process work. Xerox is really good at managing documents, and we're definitely good at managing through a process. So what's close to our core that we're really great at, that we can extend by utilizing the things we have that are differentiators—technology, brand, global reach? Business process was what we settled on. In ACS we saw a great company that was already diversified. It needed a brand. It needed technology to make this work more efficient, more auto-mated. And it needed global reach. And we have all three.

Fortune: Your stock dropped on the announcement of this deal. Why were investors worried, and what did you say to make them understand?

UB: We announced that we were spending quite a bit of money, a lot of it in the form of stock, so investors were not too thrilled about the dilution, obviously. But they were also just confused. Who is ACS? What is business-process outsourcing? And why are you engaged in it? The stock took a big drop, and we had to start speaking to our shareholders and go back to basics: explain what Xerox was about, the capabilities of our company, and why this acquisition was a natural extension of the company. We also had to explain that it was a finan-cially good deal. Will it be accretive in all aspects for the shareholders? Is it a reasonable price? We got over that fairly quickly. People under-stood the dilution. We also had to explain the longer-term story about how this will grow cash generation, and remind them that we are pretty good operators.

Fortune: When the infotech revolution was getting started in the 1960s, reputable experts said paper would soon disappear. Of course, exactly the opposite happened—we use more every year. How come?

UB: I don't think paper will go away. I do believe that the value of paper will change, and Xerox is working on changing that value. Con-sider a color page. Actual life is in color, but you keep reproducing it in black and white. You remove value. It's a bad thing to do. You retain more information, you act quicker, you can learn faster if things are in color. The reason they're not in color is that it's too expensive. So we're working to make color less expensive. I bring that up because as color becomes more available, black-and white becomes less necessary. We are making things obsolete as we invent and

(continued)

create. We cannot be afraid of driving ourselves out of certain businesses. We're the creator of digital publishing with the Docutech machine years ago. We could say, "We're going to protect that at all costs," but if we did that, we would close a whole bunch of doors that have opportunity behind them, and we'd go out of business because somebody else would open those doors. The copying machine literally obsolete a whole bunch of secretaries' work, right? But we opened up a whole new set of opportunities. Every move we make is focused on doing that same thing.

Fortune: Xerox has a famously strong culture, but you've said it could use a little adjusting. What did you mean?

UB: Let me note the strong points. We are nice. And I mean that in a very good way. If you get sick, we'll take care of you. We're not one of these mechanical cultures. We are real people working with real people. It's phenomenal. We are a team-based company. Diversity is important. Everybody thinks racial and gender diversity is important for sure, but differences in how you work, what your points of view are, are things that we love. Some of those things can become a hindrance, especially when you need to move quickly, which is just about every day. This niceness sometimes leads to lack of motion, lack of decision. We have great operators in our company all around the globe, and we haven't quite given them comfort in operating independently. They can do it. So I want them to actually start doing it. Walk in here and use your brain, take chances. Not being reckless. But they know what to do. They don't have to call me to do it.

Fortune: You're passionate about math, science, and engineering. What's the state of education in those things in the U.S. today?

UB: Very, very, very poor.

Fortune: How big a problem is that?

UB: It's one of the most important structural problems we have in this nation. The world is full of opportunities—every day there's something new that you can do. For example, you could make dirty water potable. Why does anyone not have potable water? Because it's a problem that hasn't been solved yet, but it can be. Working on telephone lines—you don't need a Ph.D. to do it, but you need to be able to read, discern, analyze problems. We are structurally creating an underclass that will be hard to fix. If we don't have people who can create value, they will be servers forever. This is not an insurmountable problem. If you get kids when they're young from just about any background, you can create people who are capable of utilizing science, technology, math, and engineering to solve problems. If you look at the list of the top nations and try to find out where we are in reading, math, and any science, it is stunning. I don't look at the list anymore because it's an embarrassment. We are the best nation in the world. We created the Internet and little iPods and copying and printing machines and MRI devices and artificial hearts. That's all science and engineering. Who's going to create those things?

Fortune: You've been president or CEO through this entire historic recession. What did you learn?

UB: What I learned is that it could be, and it was for us, a good time to change. When things are okay, there's not that much of an impetus to turn things around. I learned that sitting still is probably not the best thing to do when things are changing a lot. The best thing to do is move. We lost almost $2 billion of revenue. We changed the inside operations to ensure that we were liquid and profitable. We hunkered down, but we wanted to make sure we kept investing to differentiate ourselves.

Fortune: That's an exercise that many companies go through in tough times—deciding "What's our essence—what won't we cut even if we have to cut everything else?"

UB: This is not the first time that we've done this. The last time was in 2000, a little bit more self-inflicted. This time it was not self-inflicted. But every time we get into a really big shake, we have to step back and say, "Really, what are you about?"

Fortune: What are some of the technologies you're developing now that you believe will be most important?

UB: One is fairly simple but very important. Hundreds of billions of pages are printed in the world, not all of them on digital devices. I'm trying to get them all to digital devices. Eighty-plus percent of those

(continued)

are printed in black and white. So one of the big investments we have is in trying to make color more affordable. We launched a product last year called ColorQube that lowers the price of color printing for an average business document by 62%. It's solid-ink technology, sustainable, 90% less solid waste, significantly less energy utilization.

Fortune: Solid ink?

UB: It's basically a crayon, but don't try to put a crayon in this machine, please. It's obviously a higher formulation. It's a crayon that you melt, and you can print with less of everything. The second big investment we have is in smart document technologies. Most containers of information—paper, whatever—have tons of information, and it's generally manipulated by human beings. For example, during discovery in litigation, lawyers and their clerks look at stacks and stacks of paper, and they might say, "Okay, everything that has Geoffrey in it, I want it in pile A." Then if it has your Social Security number, your last name, any private information, I want it redacted—you get a marker and you black it out. Smart document technologies allow us to scan, store, categorize, and retrieve documents intelligently.

Fortune: You've spent your whole career in one organization. I think you were on the speed-dial lists of all the headhunters, but you didn't leave. What's your advice to a young person starting out today who wants to be a CEO?

UB: First, don't start out wanting to be a CEO. You're going to be really disappointed if you do that because you may end up doing things you don't love. Find something that you love to do, and find a place that you really like to do it in. I found something I loved to do. I'm a mechanical engineer by training, and I loved it. I still do. My son is a nuclear engineer at MIT, a junior, and I get the same vibe from him. Your work has to be compelling. You spend a lot of time doing it. And the reason I never left—even though I had, as you say, opportunities to leave—is that this company was my family. I don't mean that in a mooshy way. I had friends here. I saw the world with this place. I learned to lead in this company. I got to work on these great problems. And whenever I felt like leaving, it was generally because something bad was happening to this company. A good friend of mine who's a board member said to me, "You can't stay when times are good only. You've got to stay when times are bad. If you have a relationship that's a good one, you have to help in the tough times." And every single time I could have left, the day or the month after I didn't leave, I was so happy I didn't.

Source: http://money.cnn.com/2010/04/22/news/companies/ xerox_ursula_burns.fortune/index.htm Reprinted with permission, PARS International Corp, Inc. FORTUNE is a registered trademark of Time Inc. and is used under license.

4

Competing Values and Women's Leadership

Given the expanding presence of women in management, it becomes increasingly important to understand whether men and women share similar behavioral characteristics when performing the Competing Values Framework (CVF) transformational and transactional leadership roles. The CVF is highlighted in the literature as one of the 40 most important frameworks in the history of business and the framework has been studied and tested in organizations for more than 25 years (Cameron, Quinn, DeGraff & Thakor, 2006). The purpose of this chapter, therefore, is to extend the CVF to investigations of women in leadership.

Can the CVF, a tool made of integrated, inevitably bonded paradoxes, help us understand the origin and implications of this apparent Glass Ceiling paradox?

If effective managers, particularly upper-level managers, are more successful in handling novel or exceptional situations and generally exhibit greater behavioral and cognitive complexity (Denison et al., 1995; Hart & Quinn, 1993) than less effective (and presumably lower-level) managers, do men and women alike manifest these behaviors in performing organizational leadership roles across hierarchical levels? Are there any significant differences between men and women in using the CVF roles across managerial levels? Do they emphasize the same roles across different situations or task environments?

Because women are often seen as more emotional and people oriented, it would seem that their behaviors would align more closely with their fundamental predispositions and personality traits, consistent with beliefs that women are biologically and temperamentally different from men.

Belasen and Frank (2008) found direct influences of personality traits on managerial styles, thus indicating that gender differences in traits or response predispositions do correspond to gender differences in managerial styles. Controversial as it is, biological determinism views men and women as hardwired to behave in certain sex-based ways. Others view the human genome as a matrix of information constantly evolving through subtle changes induced by the environment and technology. Gender roles and attitudes are a complex socio-psychological construct that reflects how individuals determine which managerial leadership roles are appropriate for women and men. As Yoder (2001, p. 815) clearly stated: "doing leadership may differ for women and men, and . . . leadership does not take place in a genderless vacuum." Given contextual differences, what is effective for men is not necessarily effective for women. This distinction has important implications for leadership development programs that need to be tailored to meet the unique developmental needs of women managers (Hopkins, O'Neil, Passarelli & Bilimoria, 2008). Several examples of self-analysis and developmental plans for 30, 60, and 180 days of women managers are highlighted in later chapters.

The current studies, as well as more recent findings (Frank & Belasen, 2008a; 2008b) are also consistent with this body of research. The next section is based on my work published in various sources including my book, *Leading the Learning Organization* (SUNY Press, 2000). While I examine the competing tensions that exist between two sociological paradigms, I also note the efforts by researchers and practitioners to bridge the gap between competing organizational and managerial commitments (e.g., stability versus change) and subsequent integrated view presented by the CVF approach.

Balancing Polar Opposites: From either/or to and/both

The best managers and leaders create and sustain a tension-filled balance between two extremes. They combine core values with elastic strategies. They get things done without being done. They know what they stand for and what they want and they communicate their vision with clarity and power. But they also know that they must understand and respond to the complex array of forces that push and pull organizations in so many different directions (Bolman & Deal).

Control has become a limitation, it slows you down. You've got to balance freedom with some control, but you've got to have more freedom than you ever dreamed of (Jack Welch).

For much of the past half-century, management philosophy has coalesced around two broad schools of thought: A rationalistic school based on the principles of scientific management and the theory of bureaucratic control, and a humanistic school based on the view of organizations as interactive systems evolving around the need to respond to the psycho-social needs of the individuals within them.

The Rationalistic and Humanistic Approaches to Management

The rationalistic approach is positioned as an efficiency-driven, control-oriented ideology with a strong emphasis on the centralization of decision making, development of clear policies and procedural specifications, unambiguous roles and responsibilities, a high degree of formalization, divisible tasks, high specialization, standardization, and functional departmentation to reduce duplication. Running like a machine, this organization is viewed as highly efficient, yet inflexible and anti-innovative. Its strict hierarchy and unchallenged authority is aimed at achieving obedience, facilitating administrative innovations, and exchanging good performance and compliance with rewards, while sanctioning poor performance and undesirable behavior.

The humanistic approach has distanced itself from the rationalistic view by centering on individual well-being, employees' work conditions, job satisfaction, training, and communication. Evolving into what has been called a human resource perspective, this approach calls for giving employees greater opportunities for involvement in decision making over work processes. The philosophy is that free from the burden of being overcontrolled, with more autonomy and greater discretion, and with more influence over the outcomes of work, employees will synergize their efforts and perform with excellence. The prognosis is simple, yet powerful—a humanistic approach can lead to high commitment and morale—employees would regain trust and confidence in their managers and ultimately become accountable for the results of their work. Proponents of the humanistic approach (e.g., Argyris, Herzberg, Likert, Maslow, McGregor) enthusiastically have called for integration of the needs of individuals with those of the organization. Particular attention was focused on the idea of making employees feel more useful and important by giving them meaningful jobs and as much autonomy, responsibility, and recognition as possible as a means of getting them involved in their work. Job enrichment, combined with a more participative, democratic, and employee-centered style of leadership, arose as an alternative to the excessively narrow, authoritarian, and dehumanizing work orientation generated by scientific management and classic management theory (Morgan, 1986, p. 42).

This humanistic approach, then, advocates the need for flexibility, development of employees through delegation and cross-training, open communication, tolerance for ambiguity, the nurturing of creativity, and risk taking. For these reasons, the humanistic approach became quite popular during the 1960s and 1970s. Many mid-level managers and corporate executives began to participate in T-groups and management development programs designed to enhance self-awareness and interpersonal skills.

Polar Relationships

If you are part of the scientific management tradition, you may view competencies as the specifications for the human machinery desired to provide maximum organizational efficiency and effectiveness. If you are part of the humanistic management tradition, you may view competencies as the key that unlocks the door to individuals in realizing their maximum potential, developing ethical organizational systems, and providing maximum growth opportunities for personnel. (Richard Boyatzis, 1982)

The differences between the rationalistic and humanistic approaches have been captured by such popular distinctions as theory "X" and theory "Y," and have been referred to as mechanistic versus organic systems of management (Morgan, 1986). This distinction has also been reinforced in contemporary approaches to management and organization as the contingency and congruence theories, which claim that organizations must develop isomorphic relationships with their external environments to increase their chances to survive. Commonly known as "survival of the fittest," these theories propose that organizations with forms congruent with their environments can be naturally selected in and thrive. Placid, stable environments with little competition and with lower customer expectations enable an organization to predict marginal shifts and respond to them with incremental changes. Changes that are manageable and do not disrupt the routine flow of work call for a bureaucratic form of organization.

In dynamic, changing environments with customers demanding higher product and service quality and with stiff domestic and global competition, organizations are propelled to maintain high flexibility and quick responses of the kind found in organic or interactive systems. Organic systems are nimbler and quicker to respond to market demands. They are decentralized, problem-oriented, informal, fluid, and have on-line information that flows laterally and can reach different parts of the organization at the same time. Organic systems of management provide the flexibility, quickness, and smart response needed to deal with the fluctuations of the environment Ivan Seidenberg, Chairman and Chief Executive Officer of NYNEX Corporation, then Bell Atlantic Corporation, both predecessors of Verizon, captured the essence of the differences between the two approaches by suggesting that the technological and market changes in the telecommunication industry forced his company to drift toward an organic configuration. Shaking off 100 years of traditional, bureaucratic culture to become a market-driven, customer-focused system was necessary to make NYNEX agile and able to respond quickly to external pressures, while competing effectively against the leanest and meanest industry start-ups. Accordingly, under the pretense of social and economic change, managers found themselves confronting problems for which a bureaucratic system seemed ill-suited to handle. Bluestone and Bluestone (1993) elaborate: "by the 1980s, bureaucratic firms were too bloated with mid-level managers to be efficient and much too burdened by rules and regulations to keep up with foreign competition. More and more organizations began to realize that top-down bureaucratic control was antithetical to productivity, quality, and innovation" (p. 131).

It was in this context that discourse on organizational culture and employee commitment began to attract attention of both practitioners and management gurus. Management consultants as well as organizational researchers shared the view that an altered approach was needed to help managers create adaptive, more effective systems that were based on the principles of shared knowledge, accessibility, innovation, empowerment and high involvement (Bradford & Cohen, 1984; Kanter, 1983; Peters & Waterman 1982; Piore & Sabel, 1984). Quality pioneers such as Juran, Deming, Feigenbaum, Crosby, and Peters have claimed that Japan's industrial success is attributed to the Japanese ideology, which centers on the value of human resources, employee loyalty, free communication, and joint decision making. They suggested that American firms would do well to emulate the Japanese success story by emphasizing and developing strong cultures that foster concern for quality, flexibility, and customer satisfaction (Ouchi, 1981).

Deming's appearance on a National Broadcasting Company (NBC) TV program on June 24, 1980, highlighted this necessity: "If Japan can, why can't we?" By the end of the 1980s, the notions of culture and commitment began to gain a stronghold in many organizations. Managers initiated change programs aimed at rethinking the way organizations are structured, work is conducted, and people are managed and rewarded. Organizations began to take on a whole new outlook, as one writer described:

> Ideas provoked action, and business people began experimenting . . . More than anything else, companies began monkeying with their methods of managing people. New cross-functional teams were designed to break down barriers between departments. New pay-for-performance systems were supposed to get everyone pulling in the same direction. Managers learned new techniques of motivation. Directives were out, coaching was in. Sitting in an office was out, walking around was in. The very word 'employee' began disappearing in favor of associate (Case, 1993, p. 83).

More and more companies experiencing severe competition found resolution in the revival of the quality circle movement. Companies wanted to reexamine their operating assumptions about management approaches and experiment with various ways of involving employees in improvement of work processes. Quality circles were the most common vehicles for eliciting suggestions on how to improve operations. However, problems began to arise when little attention was given to how the quality circles fit into the new core values, vision, and mission of organizations utilizing the quality circle concept. Quality circles were quickly subdued by the rigid, autocratic approach to management in which the old style still governed and dominated the infant and not yet proven a successful quality circle.

TQM Philosophy

Other organizational researchers have claimed that Total Quality Management (TQM) brings the two paradigms, rationalistic and humanistic, into agreement by establishing an optimal balance in calling for a socio-technical approach, where technical and human needs are interdependent with one another (Trist & Murray, 1993) to achieve the goal of adaptation without the need to give up on the premises of either one of the paradigms. These researchers argued that the TQM scientific approach is consistent with the theories of the rationalist school and its emphasis on streamlining and standardizing work processes, while the structural elements of TQM are consistent with the humanistic approach, which centers on individuals and groups (Drucker, 1993; Schmidt & Finnigan, 1992, 1994). Schmidt and Finnigan (1992) succinctly explain how the two major streams of management practices come together in the management ideology of TQM: Technology-oriented theories have focused on how to do things with greater precision and efficiency and socially oriented theories have focused on how to get people in an organization to work together in ways that are more productive and satisfying. Some managers have been guided more by the first stream, believing that a rigorously controlled approach to running an organization is more realistic than any approach that depends too heavily on the interest, commitment, and judgment of people (especially lower-level workers). Other managers have followed the preachments of the "humanistic" approach—trusting, developing, and involving people as their strategy for producing organizational health. In Total Quality Management, these two approaches come together in ways that reinforce each other (p. 12).

Total Quality Management provided frustrated managers with a feasible set of principles to integrate the technical and social systems of the organization into a well-coordinated system unified by external objectives. The message that came from the TQM gurus was astonishingly simple—take on an outside-in perspective to managing organizations. Effectiveness is not an internal measure but rather an external measure defined by the ultimate consumer of organizational goods and services. Articulating this view into the mission and strategy of the organization has led many organizations to adopt the inverted pyramid structure with customers on top and managers on the bottom. Employees were seen as a resource and were expected to meet customer needs proficiently. Accountability was outward to customers, with managers being responsive to the needs of employees. As organizations increasingly spent millions of dollars on training and development programs in support of the quality vision, a puzzling pattern emerged: there were as many ways to implement TQM as there were companies adopting it. Nevertheless, four principles seem to be common to all manifestations of TQM: synergy and empowerment, continuous improvement, process orientation, and customer-focus. These principles were supported by the values of:

- Creating a climate of openness and trust
- Harnessing the power of teamwork
- Solving problems systematically by thinking in the long term
- Motivating employees by rewarding both intangible and measurable contributions
- Developing commitment to the goals of continuous improvement and learning in the organization

These principles and values also required ownership that is supported by a shared vision, process champion, and exemplary leadership (i.e., precious commodities in turbulent times in which attention is given primarily to responding to short-term pressures, as well as turf and status issues). The implementation of TQM, quite naturally, has turned much attention to the role of the middle manager, the mediator or information transmitter, who is centrally located within the chain of command, between the strategic apex and the operating core of an organization. TQM appeared to be a major threat to the power balance within the organization and a destabilizing, menacing force that should be counteracted, fended off, or extinguished. Paradoxically, those managers who in the past were in favor of change were now opposing it. Change became a self-limiting process. In light of the important position that middle managers occupy, quality practitioners and researchers have offered advice and techniques on how senior managers should handle the middle managers' subversion of the change process (Brigham, 1993; McDermott, 1993). They warned that supervisors and middle managers may not understand or welcome the new roles they must play. McDermott (1993) went on to describe what the senior manager is up against when trying to convince middle managers to embrace and lead a total quality effort. Unless middle managers are convinced that the new world is a better place, they may react negatively. They may engage in battles for turf.

Although other problems with TQM have involved lack of vision and the inability to communicate clearly the goals of achieving greater quality through an organization-wide effort, it seems that the quality movement has never been able to solidify its underlying assumption as a gestalt or an integrative approach to management. Positioning itself on the shaky ground between the humanistic and the rationalist paradigms, TQM quickly became the target for criticism from both sides, with the rationalists leading the way. It was not surprising then to find that seven out of ten TQM efforts were nothing more than enhanced problem-solving efforts aimed primarily at improving processes, with a little lip service given to "changing culture" (Crouch, 1992). Others (Schmidt & Finnigan, 1992) criticized the lack of vision on the part of the TQM sponsors, who neglected to embrace the systemic, integrative notion of TQM, and instead focused primarily on design specifications, manufacturing processes, and statistical tools. Still others attributed the failure of TQM to the narrow focus of senior managers, who viewed the quality program as a way of stamping out quality problems, rather than as a transformation in philosophy, values, and ultimately a state of well-being and purpose (Bass & Avolio, 1994). Rationalizing the new reality, Galbraith (1993) excused the quality pioneers by claiming that "they are nothing more than engineers, statisticians, and consultants who are naive to the importance of the human behavior dimension" (p. 144).

Change and Accountability

This shift away from the underlying assumptions of the quality movement must be restored on two levels—cognitive and behavioral. Cognitively, senior and mid-level managers must turn their attention to shifting their thinking and energy toward sustaining the subtle balance between the rationalistic and the humanistic approaches. Behaviorally, they must take the necessary steps to become the architects of change and become accountable for the process and outcomes of the quality effort. Managers must abandon their control stronghold and learn to lead, to unleash the creativity of their staff, and to coach them for continuous improvement (Galbraith & Lawler, 1993). Middle managers are being asked to shift their paradigms by eliminating their entrenched bureaucratic attributes and establishing new ones that are more suitable for an entrepreneurial culture. In other words, instead of being turf conscious and using defensive communication, managers are expected to maintain openness and to see the socio-technical movement from a broader, more systemic point of view. They see the shift in paradigms from the prism of a cultural transformation that can help the organization transcend to higher levels of performance. Schmidt and Finnigan (1994, p. 11) list the key elements of the newly integrative approach:

- Organizational structure becomes flatter, more flexible, and less hierarchical.
- The focus shifts to continuous improvement in systems and processes (continue to improve it even if it is not broken).
- Workers perceive supervisors as coaches and facilitators.
- Supervisor-subordinate relationships shift to interdependency, trust, and mutual commitment.
- The focus of employee effort shifts to team effort; workers see themselves as teammates.
- Management perceives labor as an asset and training as an investment.
- The organization asks customers to define quality and develops measures to determine if customers' requirements are being met.

Other contemporary views of organization and management appeared to avoid the control-flexibility dichotomy in favor of an integrative, or holistic, approach. This approach, often referred to as "gestalt," was aimed at evaluating managerial effectiveness based on universal principles that embrace contextual, informational, and judgmental variables. One example of such an integrative approach came from developers of behavioral models of decision making (Vroom, 1973; Vroom & Jago, 1988): "We were tired of debates over the relative merits of theory X and theory Y and of the truism that leadership depends on the situation. We felt that it was time for the behavioral sciences to move beyond such generalities . . . Our aim was to develop a set of ground rules for matching a manager's leadership behavior to the demands of the situation. It was critical that these ground rules be operational, so that any manager could determine how he should act in any decision-making situation" (Vroom, 1973, p. 66).

This integration, however, requires a different prism to understand and explain how organizations work and how managers should function. One example of this view is the Competing Values Framework of organizational effectiveness developed by Quinn and Rohrbaugh (1983) and expanded by Quinn (1988).

The Dimensions of the Competing Values Framework

Originated by Quinn and Rohrbaugh (1983) and Quinn (1988), the Competing Values Framework (CVF) highlights the contradictory nature inherent in organizational environments and the complexity of choices faced by managers when responding to competing tensions using different roles. For example, the innovator and broker roles rely on creativity and communication skills to bring about change and acquire resources necessary for change management. The monitor and coordinator roles are more relevant for maintaining internal consistency and integrating work units. The director and producer roles are geared toward goal setting and meeting performance targets. The facilitator and mentor roles focus on relations and synergy among organizational members as well as motivating employees and encouraging participation. The framework is also useful in distinguishing the roles that are transformational from roles that are transactional (Figure 4.1).

The CVF points to the need to guard against personal and organizational biases in treating certain roles: When managers focus on certain roles extensively without considering the tradeoffs among other roles the organization may become dysfunctional. Giving priority to certain organizational environments (e.g., internal processes) might impede the accomplishment of goals in other areas (e.g., human relations). Paying special

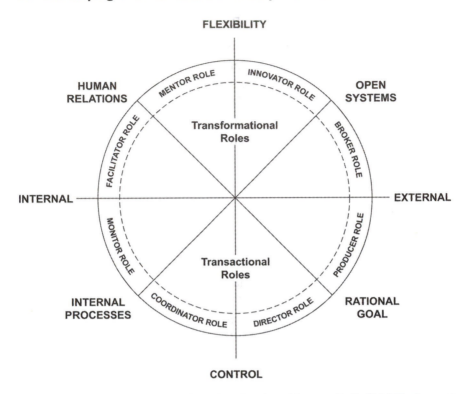

Figure 4.1 Competing Values Leadership (Quinn, R. E. [1988]. *Beyond Rational Management*, Jossey-Bass: San Francisco. Used by permission).

attention to particular roles directs managerial activities and resources away from other value maximizing activities and roles. In the long term, the imbalance in using the roles may create unnecessary conditions of instability.

As discussed later, communication audit and gap analysis can help managers avoid blind spots that are often ignored or engrained in daily behaviors and practices. Managers who are able to master the paradoxical behaviors and skills associated with all the roles also have the capacity to use a set of adaptive responses to deal with complexity in a variety of situations. The concept of paradox underscores the importance of developing behavioral flexibility and considering the dynamic interplay across the various roles.

Traits Affecting the Choice of Roles

While the task environment often determines the type of roles managers choose to perform, a related question is how managers actually choose appropriate roles and how cognitive styles, reflected in personality traits, affect these choices. The interplay of traits and leadership roles, for example, is a well-known tool for selecting individuals and matching them with organizational positions (Dastmalchian, Lee & Ng, 2000). The recent work by Belasen and Frank (2008) also reports causal paths that illustrate the influence of traits on corresponding CVF role strengths. The trait, conscientiousness, for instance, was causally related to the strengths in the Internal Processes quadrant of the CVF (see Table 4.1)

Roles and Skills across Hierarchical Levels

An interesting question is how managers at different hierarchical levels classify their behaviors across the CVF roles. To answer this question, the results of a study involving managers in a large financial institution are reported below (Belasen, 1998; 2000). One central finding of these surveys is that there are many striking similarities in the importance of the roles played by managers at different levels. Overall, the evidence

TABLE 4.1
Traits Associated with CVF Roles

Personality Traits	CVF Leadership Roles
Agreeableness	**Human Relations:**
	Mentor
	Facilitator
Openness to New Ideas	**Open Systems:**
	Innovator
	Broker
Assertiveness	**Rational Goal:**
	Director
	Producer
Conscientiousness	**Internal Process:**
	Coordinator
	Monitor

TABLE 4.2
Similarities and Differences in Motivating Employees and Goal Setting

Level	Producer	Director
All managerial levels	• Maintains a high level of energy, motivation, and effort • Motivates others	• Makes important work decisions • Sets goals • Sets objectives for accomplishing goals • Defines roles and expectations for employees
First level	• Focuses on results and accomplishments • Gets others to excel in their work • Uses time- and stress-management strategies to handle delays and interruptions	• Assigns priorities among multiple goals
Middle level	• Creates high-performance expectations • Focuses on results and accomplishments • In motivating employees, considers their individual differences	• Garners support for goals from managers at lower levels
Top level	• Creates high-performance expectations • In motivating employees, considers their individual differences •Gets others to excel in their work	• Establishes a context for decision making at lower levels

suggests that managers at each level were able to identify with all eight CVF roles (Tables 4.2 through 4.5).

The results suggest that first-level managers can be classified as "committed intensive." These managers place greater emphasis on the importance of the innovator, broker, and producer roles than on all other roles. These managers serve as the primary point of contact for providing financial products and services to business clients within the assigned market area. Committed intensives are characterized by the high intensity they bring to their work. They are almost obsessive about personal productivity for themselves and others, to the point that they may have difficulty understanding, and perhaps tolerating, individuals who are not willing to work as hard as they do (Quinn, 1988).

The middle-level managers in the sample can be described as "conceptual producers," who work well with developing and selling new ideas. This is consistent with the fact that these managers have a higher level of formal

TABLE 4.3
Similarities and Differences in Controlling Work and Tracking Details

Level	Coordinator	Monitor
All managerial levels	• Ensures that work is going according to schedule • Reallocates resources to accommodate the needs of work units • Coordinates tasks and people	• Disseminates information regarding policies and procedures • Relies on reports from others • Ensures flow of information among necessary personnel and units • Sets up and maintains necessary communication channels
First level	• Anticipates workflow problems	• Oversees compliance with procedures • Plans workload adjustments as needed
Middle level	• Anticipates workflow problems • Schedules workflow of tasks and projects	• Interprets financial and statistical • reports
Top level	• Determines subordinates' assignments based on individual skills and abilities • Coordinates units as well as individual employees	• Carefully reviews the work of others

TABLE 4.4
Similarities and Differences in Mentoring and Facilitating Interactions

Level	Mentor	Facilitator
All managerial levels	• Gives credit to subordinates for their work and ideas • Maintains an open, approachable, and understanding attitude toward subordinates • Takes a personal interest in employees	• Works to enhance employee participation • Creates a cohesive work climate in the organization • Creates a sense of belonging to the organization
First level	• Helps employees work toward a clear set of objectives and prepares them for promotion	• Fosters a sense of teamwork among employees

(continued)

TABLE 4.4 (*continued*)

Level	Mentor	Facilitator
	• Does on-the-job training	• Facilitates and leads meetings
Middle level	• Does on-the-job training • Creates opportunities for first-line supervisors to challenge themselves	• Fosters a sense of teamwork among employees • Involves subordinates in discussions about work matters
Top level	• Advises lower level managers on how to handle difficult employee situations • Challenges lower levels	• Involves subordinates in discussions about work matters • Facilitates and leads meetings

TABLE 4.5

Similarities and Differences in Managing Change and Persuasion

Level	Innovator	Broker
All managerial levels	• Supports changes imposed on the organization • Nurtures contacts with external people even when disagreeing with the changes	• Builds coalitions and networks among peers • Represents the unit to clients and customers
First level	• Helps employees deal with ambiguity and delay • Assesses the potential impact of proposed changes • Comes up with ideas for improving the organization • Assesses the potential impact of proposed changes	• Interacts with people outside the organization • Presents ideas to managers at higher levels
Middle level	• Turns problems into opportunities • Encourages creativity among employees • Helps employees deal with ambiguity and delay • Helps subordinates see the positive aspects of changes	• Represents the unit to others in the organization

TABLE 4.5 (*continued*)

Level	Innovator	Broker
Top level	• Turns problems into opportunities • Encourages creativity among employees • Develop vision • Personally helps individual employees adjust to changes in the organization • Helps subordinates see the positive aspects of change	• Represents the unit to others in the organization • Mobilizes support for the vision • Exerts lateral and upward influence in the organization

Source: Belasen, A. T. (2000). *Leading the Learning Organization: Communication and Competencies for Managing Change*. Albany, NY: SUNY Press.

education than do first-level managers. These individuals perceive themselves as being conceptually skilled, production focused, effective managers even though they pay little attention to details. This is supported by evidence that the managers in our sample emphasized the high importance of the innovator, broker, producer, facilitator, and director roles at their level. The coordinator, mentor, and monitor roles were assessed to be of less importance as indicated by lower mean scores relative to the overall profile mean for middle-level management.

Upper-level management appears to be characterized as "open adaptive." These managers scored highly on the importance of the innovator, broker, producer, director, facilitator, and mentor roles relative to their management level's overall profile mean. It was evident that upper-level managers placed less emphasis on the coordinator and monitor roles. This is consistent with empirical research suggesting that upper-level managers spend more time dealing with the institutional environment and the well-being of the organization as a whole and are less concerned with internal processes and operations management.

Leadership Roles and Message Orientations

An important question is how managers select the right role to communicate different tasks and goals and use the most effective message orientation, or right approach, for each task or goal they encounter? DiPadova and Faerman (1993), for example, observed that often the levels are experienced as so discrete and stratified that members see themselves as separate constituencies in the same organization, rather than as members of the same team.

The common language offered by the CVF ameliorates the separateness because it is essentially an organizational language that identifies performance criteria that are common across the hierarchy. Clarifying managerial roles and expectations can help minimize role ambiguity as well as reduce the potential for role conflict. Likewise, interpersonal conflicts associated with turf issues, status, and power can be avoided in favor of developing a constructive dialogue and encouraging positive communication.

Rogers and Hildebrandt (1993) suggested that each quadrant in the CVF represents a different message orientation with significant parallels and polar opposites: relational, hierarchical, promotional, and transformational (see Figure 4.2). When managers use the mentor and facilitator roles, for example, they use a relational approach to communication which places emphasis on receivers' insights and feedback. A promotional orientation fits the behaviors displayed by the director and producer roles that rely on persuasion strategies to meet functional objectives. A transformational orientation matches the styles and behaviors of the innovator and broker roles that are geared toward selling ideas effectively and meeting future organizational and adaptation goals. Hierarchical message orientations, on the other hand, align with the monitor and coordinator roles, which focus on integrating individuals and groups through work processes and systems of control.

Transformational-based messages are aimed at sustaining the ability of the organization to adapt to change. There is a focus on adapting products/markets, branding and reputation management to address interests of external stakeholders (Gotsi & Wilson, 2001). Success is determined by the extent to which framing of communication is insightful, mind-stretching, and visionary.

Promotional messages relate to the mission of the organization to meet external expectations for products, to perform productively to maximize owners' returns on equity, and to enhance performance credibility and organizational accountabiliy (Rose & Thomsen, 2004). Success is determined by the extent to which the communication is framed in a conclusive, decisive, and action-oriented manner.

Hierarchical messages reflect rules of behavior and codified decisions aimed at regularizing interactions between managers and employees. Hierarchical messages characterize the flow and dissemination of formal communications across organizational lines. Success is determined by whether the communication frame seems realistic, practical, and informative. There is a focus on organizational identity, coordination, symbolic convergence, compliance, uniformity, and control (Fairhurst & Putnam, 2004).

Relational messages are aimed at personal relationships, informal interactions, peer communications, and maintaining an awareness of the importance of the individual's role in completing the organization's mission. There is a focus on social identity, common understandings, commitment, and concerns for human development. These messages maintain the circle of interactions within the organization and stimulate opportunities for revising and realigning social networks with the mission and goals of the organization (Scott & Lane, 2000). Members constantly seek to improve relationships through constructive cycles of feedback and positive frames are discerning and perceptive of needs of individuals and groups as important organizational stakeholders.

Recognizing the existence of competing frames can be used as a personal roadmap for self-improvement (i.e., diagramming personal profiles) or as a tool to help managers understand how well they need to balance the different orientations across the quadrants and the steps they can take for improving oral and written communication (Rogers & Hildebrandt, 1993). One application of this approach (which emphasizes style over content) is diagramed in Figure 4.2. In this real life example, the manager seems to place more weight on relational and hierarchical message styles than on transformational and promotional, suggesting a preference toward working with individuals within boundaries of trust, structures, and rules. This manager, however, seems to deflect the need for placing importance of equal value on the right side of the framework where messages are aimed at energizing people toward new ideas and commitment to engage in new tasks. When subordinates, peers, and supervisors provide their inputs (i.e., 360 assessments), this framework can become a powerful tool for guiding improvement efforts based on expectations from others (Belasen, 2008).

By observing the roles and type of messages used by managers, we can also obtain a clearer picture of shifts in emphasis in how each level appreciates its roles and expectations in terms of responses to changes in the task environment (Belasen & Frank, 2010). Under normal conditions the four message orientations or approaches are reflections of administrative responsibilities with top executives communicating strategic priorities

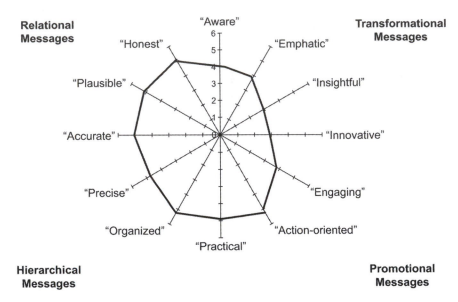

Figure 4.2 Competing Values Framework: Message Orientations and Styles (Belasen, A. T. [2008]. *The Theory and Practice of Corporate Communication: A Competing Values Perspective.* Thousand Oaks, CA: SAGE Publications).

and managers and supervisors translating them into concrete and more practical objectives and tasks that employees accomplish (see Figure 4.3).

Managers reporting to higher levels can gain a number of advantages by using the model of message orientations described in this chapter. Having a strong understanding of the frequency (amount of content), flow (who the message is directed to), and the intensity of the message (power of the message or the source of the message) can help mitigate communication roadblocks as well as clarify organizational directions and expectations. The model is particularly helpful in clarifying expectations during organizational transitions and shifts in importance of organizational goals. Knowing in advance what higher levels communicate and detecting the tone of the messages should also help managers avoid second guessing higher levels and, instead, focus attention on messages that are consistent with the expectations of higher levels.

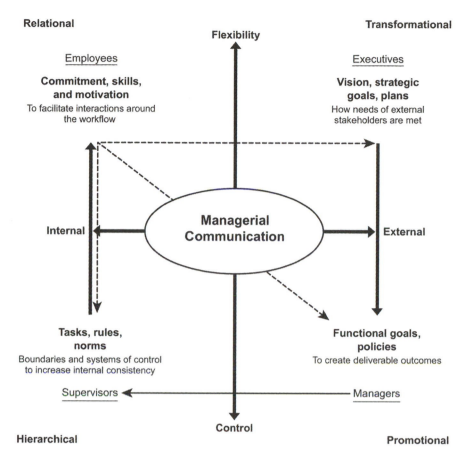

Relational

Transformational

Flexibility

Employees

Executives

**Commitment, skills,
and motivation**
To facilitate interactions around
the workflow

**Vision, strategic
goals, plans**
How needs of external
stakeholders are met

Internal

Managerial
Communication

External

**Tasks, rules,
norms**
Boundaries and systems of control
to increase internal consistency

**Functional goals,
policies**
To create deliverable outcomes

Supervisors

Managers

Control

Hierarchical

Promotional

Figure 4.3   Responsibilities by Level in Downward Communication (Belasen, A. T. & Frank, M. [2010]. A peek through the lens of the competing values framework: What managers communicate and how. *Atlantic Journal of Communication*, 18, 280–96).

When the lines of communication are clear and the messages reach their target audiences with appropriate orientation, the consistency of organizational communication increases. Creating appropriate messages and choosing the right communication channels to deliver messages can help managers align their goals with the expectations of higher and lower levels thus increasing vertical alignment across administrative lines. This should also help reduce the opportunity for miscommunication and the potential for conflict between senders and receivers. Knowing that managers at all levels of the organization demonstrate an awareness of the four orientations also provides an additional tool in developing a common language for sharing expectations across administrative levels. Awareness of these differences could help ameliorate unnecessary frustrations and misunderstandings among the managerial levels especially during organizational transitions (Belasen & Frank, 2010).

Improving Leadership Communication

CVF-based communication audits are often used for highlighting not only deficiencies in organizational communication that cause major breakdowns, but also for improving organizational effectiveness. Managers who use the CVF communication audits reportedly develop a better understanding across managerial and functional lines and work effectively as a management team.

By comparing the results of self-assessment against ratings by others, a manager can take steps to deal with higher expectations (e.g., by increasing personal involvement) or lower expectations (e.g., by decreasing an overemphasis on monitoring behavior) thus reducing tension and the potential for conflict in interpersonal relations. When combined with other techniques (e.g., role analysis transacting technique or responsibility charting method), self-assessment method and the information coming from the composite profile can also be applicable to improve interpersonal communication and enable a more effective work climate. The same communication audit and gap analysis can be used to identify blind spots across managerial levels, the focus of the next section.

For example, while middle-level managers that participated in a communication audit conducted in a service organization believed that their attention was equally distributed across the communication roles, top executives (their bosses) and first-line supervisors (their subordinates) perceived their role behaviors very differently. That is, they felt that the middle managers did not pay enough attention to the producer role. Furthermore, they seemed to signal an overall dissatisfaction with the "scope" of middle managers' role performance (Belasen, 2008). At the same time, first-line supervisors (i.e., direct reports) felt that the middle managers should increase their mentoring and facilitation responsibilities, a need that hinges on the expectation of more communication and feedback between the two levels. Interestingly, these observations were also shared by upper-level managers (the middle managers' bosses) who expected middle managers (their direct reports) to expand their activities.

This kind of comparison gives evaluators, communication analysts, and directors of communication a sense of direction about what needs to be improved (target of audit) and how important the improvement is (outcome of audit). In the situation described above, the middle managers provided their self-perceptions of how well they would like to see themselves performing these communication roles. Of course, these self-perceptions do not always align with the perceptions of others. For example, while middle managers might "agree" that the scope of their attention should include all the roles as also evident in the perceptions of their subordinates (first-line supervisors), upper-level managers (the bosses) might think differently. As described by Belasen (2008) they ended up "pushing" their desired profile further toward the right of the CVF with a clear bias toward external affairs. Is this reasonable? You be the judge!

Successful managers must continually and appropriately respond to environmental changes. Because of the dramatic changes taking place in today's marketplace, such as the rate of technological change associated with the shift to an information age economy, organizations no longer have a choice—they must determine how to change to increase their effectiveness. Managers should create an atmosphere that encourages individuals to monitor, challenge, and discuss each other's ideas to stay open to new ways of doing things. When organizational members are willing to consider multiple perspectives and try innovative ideas, they add complexity to the organization, which allows it to more effectively meet the challenges posed by the complex environment.

Wendy: Becoming a Master Manager

After completing the competing values skills assessment, I learned that as a managerial leader my strengths are in all areas except the innovator and broker roles. These two roles are especially important, because they foster creative thinking, manage change, require negotiation skills, and build power bases. I also noticed that I can improve on my skills in team building and encouraging participative decision making within the facilitator role. Two colleagues and two employees filled out skill assessments on me at the beginning of this course and their results were strikingly similar. The surveys revealed that my strengths lie within the human relations model, the internal process model, and the rational goal model. Therefore, my self-improvement plan focuses on ways that I can improve in the open systems model and build my strengths in developing the competencies within the innovator and broker roles. In addition, I would like to focus on improving team building efforts and encouraging participative decision making.

The innovator and broker roles are currently my weakest roles. Within the innovator role, thinking creatively and managing change are two areas where I need improvement. According to Quinn, "the innovator role involves the use of creativity and the management of organizational changes and transitions, and it provides a unique opportunity for managers to affirm the value of individual employees within the organizational setting" (Cameron et al., 2007, p. 264). I believe that as a managerial leader I am open to change; however, I do not excel at thinking creatively and developing change. I have the tendency to get comfortable within my position, my unit, and if things are operating smoothly, I do not always think about implementing any changes. However, as a managerial leader I should be anticipating possible changes and thinking about ways to improve on current processes to adapt to change. For example, I recently attended a staff meeting and suggested that managers within the organization discuss current processes and inefficiencies. I do feel that I am open to new ideas, but I am not always the creative one to come up with the ideas. Unfortunately, the meeting I mentioned above did not foster any new changes. The organization where I work is very resistant to change, so it is challenging to try and encourage change when the majority of employees wish for things to remain the same.

Within the broker role, networking and building relationships is another weak area for me. Quinn states, "the broker presents and negotiates ideas effectively . . . the broker creates relationships and agreements that result in moving the organization forward" (Cameron 2007, p. 299). I do present ideas within the organization where I work (internally), but I could improve on building and strengthening relationships within the community (externally). Recently, I submitted a self-evaluation to my supervisor, and networking and strengthening community partnerships was one of my goals. Once again, I have the tendency to get comfortable within my position internally; but externally, I could develop relationships with other agencies and staff to strengthen my competencies in the broker role. Specifically, building social capital within the community would be beneficial to this role. As a managerial leader, I would also like to improve on team building and participative decision making. Although I did not score low in these competencies, I could have scored higher and also feel there is true value in mastering these competencies within the facilitator role. Dr. Belasen states, "perhaps, the most important role of the Facilitator is to strengthen group cohesion through team building and development" (2000, p. 288).

In developing a change strategy for myself in the areas of the innovator, broker, and facilitator roles, I have identified some resources and tools to help my self-improvement plan. One strength that will help me to further develop my skills is that I am genuinely a people person and I enjoy meeting new people and learning about new things. Whenever there are opportunities to attend trainings and workshops for my job, I always sign up. In addition, I make an effort to get to know fellow attendees and truly engage myself in workshop activities and discussions. Recently, I received an email for an upcoming training session on grant writing, which is not currently within my job responsibilities, but it is an important skill to have working in the nonprofit sector. I expressed this interest to my boss and she was surprised to learn about my interest, but was very supportive of my idea. I need to involve myself in some creative activities outside of work to develop my creativity at work. Because I enjoy learning new things, I believe I could work on developing my creativity by taking an art or photography class, and possibly implementing more creative project ideas at work. By surrounding myself with creative people it will help me to improve in this area and further build on my networking skills as well. Finally, I could also learn more about team building and participative decision making by getting fellow staff members involved in a task force committee aimed at developing team building within the organization. My plan appears in Table 4.6.

As outlined in the above chart, I have identified action steps that I need to accomplish in the innovator, broker, and facilitator roles to improve in all competency areas. According to Quinn (2007, p. 344) becoming a master manager "requires not only the ability to play all eight roles

TABLE 4.6
Self-Improvement Plan for Wendy over the Next 180 Days

Self-Improvement Plan	30 Days	60 Days	180 Days
Innovator Role • Living with Change • Thinking Creatively • Managing Change	• Reach out to a friend or coworker who is dealing with a difficult situation. Brainstorm for ways to help this individual. • Look into local art classes at the university. • Look at current processes within the agency that could benefit from changes in order to improve greater efficiency.	• Help support this individual as he or she adapts to changing circumstances. • Enroll in an art class and start thinking about creative projects that could be implemented at work. • Provide some factual evidence and bring forth ideas at the next supervisors meeting.	• Serve as a mentor and encourage other individuals to embrace change. Serve as a positive role model to others. • Successfully complete art class and begin fostering that same creativity by introducing ideas at staff and supervisory meetings. • Implement new processes such as technology upgrades that could benefit the agency.
Broker Role • Building & Maintaining a Power Base • Negotiating Agreement & Commitment • Presenting Ideas	• Identify local groups or coalitions that I could join to network. • Memorize Fisher and Ury's four principles for "yes." • Develop an idea to present at the next staff or supervisory meeting.	• Attend community meetings regularly and begin developing referrals, resources and forming partnerships. • Utilize the four principles when faced with a situation that requires negotiation. • Present a new idea to colleagues and fellow staff.	• By the end of 180, I will have increased my social capital and have effectively developed positive networking skills. • I will have mastered the effective techniques to mastering negotiation. • I will have successfully implemented an idea that I introduced.

TABLE 4.6 (*continued*)

Self-Improvement Plan	30 Days	60 Days	180 Days
Facilitator Role • Building Teams • Using Participative Decision Making	• Present an idea to staff advisory on how to utilize team building within the agency. • Utilize participatory decision making within the staff advisory group on team building initiatives.	• Introduce and implement team building initiatives to all units within the agency. • Get all staff involved with the team building initiative including feedback and concerns.	• Evaluate the success of the team building initiative through goal achievement and outcomes. • Survey all employees for feedback on the team building initiatives. Make any necessary changes.

(at least at a competent level), it also requires that the manager have the ability to blend and balance the competing roles in an appropriate way." To achieve this blending, I have outlined action steps that are to be accomplished within 30 and 60 days. Around 180 days, maintenance and follow-up are necessary to evaluate my overall progress, including outcomes. To monitor my self-development plan and track my own progress, I plan to keep a journal; as I complete action steps toward achieving my goals, I will document my progress and accomplishments. In addition, I will document any challenges or barriers that I run into and write down the action steps I have taken to overcome them. If at any time I feel that my self-development plan needs adjustments, I will make them accordingly and document all changes that have been made. I will also entrust a colleague to help evaluate my progress and provide ongoing feedback, guidance, and support along the way.

I feel confident about the self-development plan that I have outlined. The goals I have set for myself are realistic and achievable. As a managerial leader, I feel that my strengths in the human relations model, the internal process model, and the rational goals model will help me to improve on my weaknesses within the open systems model. I feel that I am at the competent stage with my skills in the mentor, monitor, co-ordinator, producer and director roles. What I hope to achieve from my self-development plan is the ability to integrate the competencies from the innovator and broker roles into my current roles. In addition, I want to improve on my team-building skills from the facilitator role as well. I believe that my self-development plan has clearly defined action steps to help me to accomplish my goals. This class has taught me the importance of integrating an open systems model in organizations. For me to be a master manager, I must learn to integrate these competencies into my leadership roles and learn to balance them effectively.

5

Aligning Personality Traits with Leadership Roles

When a manager plays a particular role, the choice of that role is often influenced by personality traits or characteristics. Personality traits and their interrelationships have been documented to affect managerial goals, values, and needs (Herringer, 1998; Sharp & Ramanaiah, 1999) as well as leadership behavior (Hogan et al., 1994). Traits also affect the cognitive, interpersonal, and work styles managers use to reach those goals, values, and needs. Research has also suggested the importance of matching training orientation (Gupta & Govindarajan, 1984), personality (Miller, Kets de Vries & Toulouse, 1982), and leadership cognitive style (Govindarajan, 1989) to situational contingencies.

An important personality theory, FFM or the Five Factor Model (Costa, McCrae & Dembroski, 1989; Digman, 1997) consists of four emotionally stable traits—Agreeableness, Extroversion, Conscientiousness, and Openness (Costa & McCrae, 1992) and a fifth trait, Emotionality (also referred to as Neuroticism). These traits were found to be related to effective transformation and transactional role behaviors (Bono & Judge, 2004; Leung & Bozionelos, 2004), army officers' leadership effectiveness (McCormack & Mellor, 2002), and problem-solving (Spector, Schneider, Vance & Hezlett, 2000). However, the relationship between roles and personality traits takes

Portions of this chapter originally appeared in Alan Belasen & Nancy Frank, Competing values leadership: quadrant roles and personality traits. *Leadership and Organization Development Journal*, 2008, 29(2):127–43.]

on increased relevance when managerial roles are refined into more specific task/skill functions.

Traits, as described by the FFM or similar theories, have been found to affect role related influence tactics (Cable & Judge, 2002), managerial skill assessments (Craik, Ware, Kamp, O'Reilly, Staw & Zedeck, 2002), preferences for four leadership task categories (Nordvik & Brovold, 1998), and the leadership effectiveness of military officers (McCormack & Mellor, 2002). Young and Dulewicz's (2005) study of leadership training outcomes in the British Royal Navy identified four "supra-competency clusters." These clusters were similar to the four CVF role quadrants. Specific traits were found to be related to each of these competencies.

In addition to the relationship between the first four FFM traits, low levels of emotional stability, the fifth trait, would seem to be associated with behavioral extremes indicated by Quinn's (1988) negative zone. Responding appropriately to competing demands requires balanced role strengths along with high levels of emotional stability; whereas, lower levels of emotional stability combined with weaker, unbalanced role behaviors, give rise to reactionary, extreme behaviors that often result in ineffective outcomes.

Less effective managers engaging in restricted, inflexible modes of thinking find themselves confined to the negative zone; whereas more effective managers, able to detect and respond to contradictory signals, emerge within the positive zone. For the current study, an adaptation of the four stable traits—agreeableness, assertiveness, conscientiousness, and openness were used. These traits appear to parallel the CVF quadrants: Agreeableness corresponds to the human relations quadrant; assertiveness to the rational goal; openness to the open systems; and conscientiousness to the internal processes (Belasen & Frank, 2005).

Traits, Mindsets, and Roles: Some Evidence from Recent Research

Do traits also play a role in shaping mindsets? Would it be possible to assume that traits determine the kind of mindsets that push managers to choose certain roles over others? For example, are managers more prone to choosing roles that align with stable organizational conditions keeping untested or weak roles as last resort roles?

To investigate the relationships between personality traits and roles, a representative sample of successful mid-to-upper-level managers was selected from a pool of nearly 300 managers participating in an online MBA. Respondents generally represented higher levels of management within their organizations, with 9% reporting to the CEO, 10% reporting to the president, 20% reporting to the vice president, and 20% reporting to the director. Over half of the respondents represented large organizations, with 16% from organizations with more than 10,000 employees; 9% from organizations with between 5,000 and 9,999 employees; 15% from organizations with between 1,000 and 4,999 employees, and 11% from organizations with between 500 and 999 employees. Finally, respondents represented a wide range of experience within their present position, with at least 25% of the group in their current position for between one and three years, and 25% in their current position for between three and six years.

The primary instrument consisted of 60 items addressing classification and measurement model questions and five additional items measuring each manager's self-perceptions of effectiveness in each of the quadrant classifications. For example, the item related to innovation and openness asked, "To what extent do my skills in adaptation and innovation contribute to my managerial effectiveness?" with possible responses ranging from "Contribute Little" to "Contribute Highly," on a scale of one to seven. The items related to human relations asked: "To what extent do my skills in coaching individuals and facilitating group interactions contribute to my managerial effectiveness?" with the same possible responses ranging from "Contribute Little" to "Contribute Highly." The remaining questions were phrased similarly according to their primary foci. Finally, we asked one final question regarding perceived overall effectiveness: "My overall effectiveness as a manager is . . ." with possible responses ranging from "Lower than I would like" to "High" on a scale of one to seven. The final 65-item research instrument arose from a consolidation of two separate instruments respectively assessing (a) competing values skills; and (b) work-related personality traits as measured by a new instrument.

Using Multidimensional Scaling models (MDS), with input from both ordinal data and latent variables derived from LISREL (Joreskog & Sorbom, 2003) measurement models, we first tested the degree-of-fit between the eight CVF roles and the CVF quadrants to answer the set of questions associated with the first set of research objectives. Like factor analysis, MDS helps reveal hidden structures in multivariate data while also uncovering underlying dimensions in a series of cases. It can also be used as a data-reduction technique. Unlike factor analysis, however, MDS tries to represent these underlying dimensions in a spatial arrangement that allows a visual image of their relationships. We also used LISREL to examine the relationships between traits and roles. The LISREL method estimates the unknown coefficients of the set of linear structural equations.

It is particularly useful in accommodating models that include latent variables, measurement errors in dependent and independent variables, reciprocal causation, simultaneity, and interdependence. The model consists of two parts, the measurement model and the structural equation model: The measurement model specifies how latent variables or hypothetical constructs depend on or are indicated by the observed variables. It describes the measurement properties (reliabilities and validities) of the observed variables. The structural equation model specifies the causal relationships among the latent variables, describes the causal effects, and assigns the explained and unexplained variance.

The MDS analysis included both CVF and personality trait variables in which the alignment between the traits and roles were confirmed. Corresponding traits and roles were distributed into appropriate competing quadrant relationships.

Following confirmation of trait/role quadrant alignments, analysis of causal relationships between traits and roles using LISREL confirmed causal paths from traits to compressed CVF latent variables. Within each quadrant, the hypothesized personality trait predicted its corresponding CVF role. Test results demonstrated causal paths from conscientiousness to analyzer, openness to vision-setter, agreeableness to motivator, and, finally, assertiveness to task master (Belasen & Frank, 2008).

The significance of the competing nature of opposing quadrants applies not only to CVF roles but also extends to traits. Because traits appear to align with the four quadrants, they can also take on a competing or conflicting nature. Competing traits certainly lead to competing values and attitudes. The aggregate outcome of these competing forces, as defined by the incompatible values of the CVF dimensions, is typically reflected in the manner by which individuals react to job responsibilities and their relationships with other people.

Falling Back on Automated Responses

The CVF predicts that balancing the full range of leadership roles should help managers perform their job effectively; yet, limited cognitive and emotional resources constrain employment of the full range of roles. This, too, is consistent with the CVF. Looking back to traits as antecedents to role choices, emotional stability may predict the extent to which managers revert to a restricted array of deeply engrained skills or the basic traits and attitudes that precede more intelligently sophisticated role behaviors. Nevertheless, knowing when to combine conscious deliberation with the ability to quickly size up situations that may depend more on instincts and automated responses is a crucial managerial leadership skill. Perhaps the most important trait influencing the ability to intuitively analyze and assess complex environments is Openness.

Although intelligence—considered by some researchers as equivalent to the "open to new experiences" trait—is only one aspect of a person's overall personality profile, we would venture to state that a person who is open would eventually acquire a broader range of experience. Thus, of the two variables, intelligence and experience, the latter is actually a continuum that grows as an interaction with the fairly stable intelligence variable. Because individuals vary in intelligence and psychological profiles (learning styles, traits, locus of control, self-efficacy), their managerial behaviors and skills, built through years of work experience, will vary accordingly. In other words, any given manager, encountering different work experiences in different environments, could develop a different range of behaviors and skills. Finally, we must ask whether different work and training experiences changes the types of roles managers employ, or whether fundamental personality tendencies influence the types of experience they acquire, thus influencing the roles they choose to play.

The obvious answer to the nature versus nurture question is that both are relatively true. Not everyone shares the same heredity in terms of natural traits and tendencies, nor the same upbringing, community, or life experiences. Heritable tendencies, including different learning styles (Boyatzis, Corver & Kolb, 1995), mixed with life experiences, form an inner core that all future experiences are built on layer by layer. Likewise, not every manager faces the same job demands or organizational environment. Ideally, a seamless fit between a manager's experiences, role styles, attitudes, and traits and specific job requirements and organizational context would be the norm. In reality, however, we recognize that approaching this goal requires an organizational commitment to consider human resource strategies for recruitment, employee retention, and training and development as essential components of long-term organizational strategy (Belasen & Frank, 2004).

Remedying Deficiencies

The new awareness of precursors to CVF role behaviors calls for significantly shifting the focus of training and development efforts away from leadership development strategies designed to simply strengthen weaknesses through training exercises and education. Eventually, management development approaches must target specific weaknesses and their psychological underpinnings, surpassing the typical "shotgun" approach of offering the same leadership training to all managers. Genuine growth and long-term gains in role strength will take place only by concentrating on specific skill growth from an intensely individualized perspective. Management development becomes more relevant when personal tendencies are considered as influencers of role behaviors. Behavioral characteristics, especially deeply engrained tendencies, attitudes, and emotional responses can be quite intransigent and resistant to change. The contingencies of the work environment compound the problem of building and retaining strengths in weaker roles while balancing the remaining stronger roles. A primary advantage of our consolidated model is that it addresses the problem of dealing with competing demands on cognitive resources, demands that are exacerbated by susceptibility to stress, uncertain work environments, and by pressures to shore up additional cognitive resources to deal with uncertainty. With a mastery of transformational and transactional roles, women, by far, have a larger behavioral repertoire to deal with stress than men, often at the cost of becoming hypereffective, examined in the next chapter.

Hermeata: Personal Leadership Development Plan

In consideration of the overall objectives of the four management models and their relationship to the eight different roles of leadership, improving organizational performance is my primary motivation to become a Master Manager. As a managerial leader, it is my responsibility to deliberately make the effort to acknowledge and understand the different and similar roles of the competing values framework and the ongoing process of developing the appropriate competencies. The results of the Competing Values Competency surveys revealed that I am predominantly internally focused. My success or failure in becoming a Master Manager depends on my efforts in the development of externally focused competencies. From my perspective, I have developed performance-based tendencies that have hindered the development of key competencies that are necessary to improve my personal and professional performance.

The results of the first competing values competency survey that was taken at the beginning of the course revealed that my strengths as a managerial leader are within the human relations and internal process models, and my weaknesses are within the open systems and rational goal models. I was not surprised to discover that I am predominantly internally focused. However, I was amazed to discover that the scores of the Competing Values Leadership Roles Profiles from coworkers were strikingly higher than my own evaluation of my performance, which caused me to ask myself questions. Does this mean that I do not realize my competencies in each of the leadership roles? Do I need to develop confidence in my current abilities that my coworkers recognize? Did my coworkers really give their honest opinion regarding my performance? It is significant to note that their results indicated that I was competent in all eight roles of leadership. On retaking the competing values competency questionnaire at the end of the course, I scored myself significantly higher, and the scores were well-rounded. However, I was surprised to note that the control quadrant, one of my strongest leadership roles, was now my weakest.

Careful analysis of the functions that are associated with each of the leadership roles leads me to conclude that my weakest leadership roles are the competencies that are associated with director and broker. I noted weakness in all three competencies in the role as a director, and I believe this is due to years of my commitment to promoting someone else's vision and organizational goals. Even though this behavior induced strengths in the competencies associated with the collaborate quadrant, which is my strongest leadership role, it prevented the development of the externally focused competencies.

My performance was based on aggressively pursuing productivity in the areas of managing, execution, driving for results, and motivating others. I instinctively and aggressively made changes within my own sphere of responsibility, which resulted in the development of my own personal base of power from an internal perspective. My weakness in the role of a broker is due to my strong internal focus on maintaining stability, continuity, cohesion, commitment, and morale. As a leader in this capacity, I had the support of senior management and acquired the necessary resources to maintain organizational goals within my own sphere of responsibility, but I neglected to realize the opportunities to participate in organizational-wide implementation of changes through the presentation of my ideas that could have possibly added value to the organization. My skill in the implementation and control of internal core processes could have been a valuable contribution to the continuous improvement of organizational performance from an external perspective. As noted in the initial survey, the low scoring of myself may indicate that I do not have the confidence within myself to promote change and set goals and objectives on an organizational-wide scale from an external focus. As noted in the second survey, I believe I have gained the needed knowledge to seek ways of developing the competencies that I realize are lacking in my performance as a director and broker.

For the past year, I have been meeting people with thoughts, ideas, skills, or situations that are similar to my own. As shared in my introduction at the beginning of the course, my vision is to establish a non-profit organization that will address the social issues that exist in the Native-American community in Alaska. For the past six months, I have been gathering information and communicating with state officials. I believed this was my first step in building the external networks that are needed to communicate my vision. Needless to say, I have not been able to effectively communicate this need to state officials or the native community. I now realize that from both of their perspectives, I am a threat to the way things have always been done. If my vision becomes a reality, it has the potential of reducing the principal base of income for both the local native community and the local government, and the federally funded social programs that from my perspective restrict the personal and professional development of the native community.

However, I had the opportunity to speak to an individual who has an IT company in Alaska that he has been building for the past ten years, and he has a marketing director who is involved in non-profit leadership. Additionally, we both have the skills, resources, and a small network of individuals who are capable of creating an organization or sustaining an existing organization. Remarkably, I met another individual that has a newly established government contracting company who is in search of business development opportunities involving infrastructure technology. For the next 180 days, I will be reaching out to these individuals in an attempt to communicate the vision of establishing an organization that is capable of producing services that are in demand on both a social and technological level. This is my opportunity to become externally focused in both the director and producer roles by integrating business processes with the dynamics of information technology through the establishment of strong external networks.

Through the insight that I have learned from small business owners and religious leaders regarding their vision and goals, I anticipate having a team of committed and talented individuals that have existing external networks and resources that can be used to obtain community support. My ability to gain the support of the community within 180 days is how I will evaluate my performance as a director and producer. Obtaining community support, which includes establishing long-term relationships at the federal, state, and local levels of government, is an ongoing effort for the entire 180-day period. As a team, I hope to have the resources, statistical data, and real-life examples that will promote the desired results of providing the life-changing social skills to the Native-American community to improve their quality of life. The team's ability to effectively communicate and present our proposal is the determining factor for obtaining federal grants and funds from community-sponsored events. We must present our ideas as a win-win opportunity for the State of Alaska and the native community. If I do not have a well-established team, I will need to make adjustments to reach the desired results of my efforts to obtain community support. Adjustments will include the continuation of building strong networks to reach the goal of establishing long-term relationships within the community.

The results of the Competing Values Competency Survey indicated that my strengths are organizing information flows, encouraging and enabling compliance and the management of execution, and driving for results. According to the gap analysis, there are significant gaps in my ability to implement and sustain change in the create quadrant, developing and communicating a vision in the compete quadrant, and in working and managing across functions in the control quadrant. Because the largest gaps in my performance are developing and communicating a vision in the compete quadrant and working and managing across functions in the control quadrant, I believe I can improve my performance in these areas by making an effort to become more flexible while exercising my strengths as a monitor and coordinator. My strength in those two leadership roles appears to be impacting my ability to implement and sustain change in the create quadrant, which is on the verge of becoming another weakness in my performance.

One of my most challenging performance-based tendencies that will prevent the desired outcome of improving my performance is my low tolerance for ambiguity. I demand the clarity of goals and expectations to measure performance standards. Because my goal is to build my competencies in the leadership roles of broker and producer, I will need to allow more flexibility in the functional area of encouraging and enabling compliance and in my methods of measuring and monitoring performance based on productivity within my own sphere of responsibility. Within a year, I expect to have a team of respected, talented, and committed individuals operating both a non-profit and for-profit organization that are self-sustained and capable of adapting to both internal and external changes in the environment by increasing my personal base of power through the use of external networks.

6

Women's Traits and Leadership Roles: The Danger of Becoming Hypereffective

Although indications of early feminist leadership approaches appeared in the early nineteenth-century social movements, what became known as Feminist Theory actually emerged during the social upheaval of the 1960s and 1970s (Rusaw, 2005). Feminism is comprised of several themes, but one of the most prominent is that gender-based differences in behavior, cognition, and perception are derived from both nature and nurture, from biology and life history. We see these differences demonstrated in personalities, occupational preferences, social role identities, family role expectations, communication preferences, and approaches to interpersonal relationships. Feminism also promotes belief in the caring and compassion for others in the form of social responsibility and issues of social justice (Gilligan, 1981; Helgeson, 1990). Feminist critiques of masculine models of leadership appeared throughout the 1980s and 1990s (Fine & Buzzanell, 2000; Rusaw, 2005).

In addition to beliefs in fundamental differences between the genders, staunch adherence to social justice issues, and condemnation of masculine leadership models, the dominant theme of feminism is arguably its manifest belief that male authoritarianism dominates institutions and that this authoritarianism leads to discrimination and institutional injustice for women (Barton, 2006; Irby, Brown, Duffy & Trautman, 2002; Chin, 2004; Rosener, 1990).

Feminist critiques of management and leadership models argue that management theories and models emphasize power and rational legal approaches while failing to recognize differences between genders in terms of motivation, communication styles, work preferences, cognitive styles, and managerial strengths. Among these differences, for example, is the feminist preference for collegial decision-making approaches and for pluralistic leadership that works toward shared goals and purposes (Barker & Young, 1994). Researchers have found that women tend to adopt a more democratic and participative style than men who prefer a more directive leadership style (Eagly & Johnson, 1990). Feminist theory argues that power is not derived from hierarchy and authority, but rather from shared experience, combined viewpoints, and joint strengths. It should not be surprising that the preponderance of feminist criticism of management theory seems to emanate from academia and the field of education, institutions dominated by male-based hierarchies for centuries (Barton, 2006; Irby et al., 2002). Organizations are viewed as the "products and producers of gender-based power relations, and . . . masculine ways of doing things are inherent in structural, ideological and symbolic aspects of organizations, as well as in everyday interactions and practices" (Hatch & Cunliffe, 2006, p. 274).

Unique Attributes

Literature on women and leadership often seeks to identify unique attributes that distinguish between the styles of male and female leadership, suggesting that gendered leadership styles reflect the power differentials seen in society as a whole and that masculine qualities, such as task focus, assertiveness, authoritativeness, and lack of emotionality are virtually synonymous with leadership within U.S. and European cultures emphasizing power, not influence or empowerment (Izraeli & Adler, 1994; Schein, 2001; Fine & Buzzanell, 2000). Meanwhile, as organizations reinforce these qualities through rewards and incentives (Chin, 2004), images such as "The Glass Ceiling" and "The Glass Cliff" (Weyer, 2007; Ryan, Haslam & Postmes, 2007) continue to reflect reality. When women use assertiveness they are viewed by men as ineffective and less influential and at times as a threat (Carli, 1999). Being dominant, directive, achiever, aggressive, and self-promoting match the stereotypic traits of agentic behaviors while correlating negatively with women's traits.

Mounting evidence that transformational leadership contributes to increased employee motivation and performance has encouraged research into the mechanisms behind its achievements (Alimo-Metcalfe, 1995; Barker & Young, 1994; Eagly, Johannesen-Schmidt & Van Engen, 2003; Rosener, 1990; Kark, Shamir & Chen, 2003; Trinidad & Normore, 2005). There is new support that the success of transformational leadership can be attributed to interpersonal abilities to engender personal identification of the follower with the leader, and to promote social identification with the work unit. The transformational leader affects the feelings of the follower, creating positive identification with both the leader and the work unit. Ironically, this interaction is characterized by both dependence and independence, an interpersonal dependence between the leader and the follower and an empowering independence that encourages work group identification (Kark et al., 2003).

Women's Leadership: Traits, Roles

In spite of the apparent connection between transformational leadership and feminist theories of leadership (Barker &Young, 1994; Alimo-Metcalfe, 1995), however, are we correct in assuming that women in particular are more likely to demonstrate CVF-based transformational behaviors? This question does not hypothesize that transformational leadership is the exclusive domain of women. Rather, it suggests that women can become effective leaders in relational, inclusive, and empowered social settings.

To answer this question, Frank and Belasen (2008) sought additional evidence, through CVF-based studies, that men and women demonstrate different or similar managerial styles. The feminist argument that men and women are biologically, neurologically, and socio-psychologically different would certainly suggest basic dispositional and personality differences between male and female managers. Ruderman and Ohlott (2005), for example, highlighted diverse gender approaches to information processing, motivation, and coping with stress. Other findings highlighted different conceptions of work satisfaction and career goals with women emphasizing intrinsic values (e.g., rewarding roles, personal achievement) and men focusing on extrinsic values such as higher salaries and upward mobility (Sturges, 1999). Research streams support the existence of basic personality differences between male and female (Senykina & Linz, 2007; Judge, Higgins, Thoresen & Barrick, 1999; Xie & Whyte,

1997). Women managers see themselves as being more agreeable; men see themselves as being agreeable at times and assertive at other times. Women often score significantly higher than men on conscientiousness and national cultures often signify this. In Russia, for example, men exhibit internal locus of control, while women were found to have external locus of control (Semykina & Linz, 2007).

Fittingly, in an interview-based study specifically designed to develop leadership training programs that included the feminist perspective, researchers studied perceptions of effective leadership skills (Irby, Brown, Duffy & Trautman, 2002); women were seen as giving more attention to detail, as being more emotional, and as being more likely to seek input from others. Men were seen as more likely to delegate detail work to others.

In terms of D. J. Prediger's (1982) People-Things and Ideas-Data dimensions, both men and women related to the People-Things dimension with women leaning more toward the People side and men leaning more toward the Task side (Lippa, 1998). However, although relation leadership was associated with agreeableness and task leadership was associated with openness and conscientiousness (Won, 2006), there was no support for gender differences in relationship versus task orientation (Toren, Konrad, Yoshioka & Kashlak, 1997; Won, 2006).

Unfortunately, these predictions are unsubstantiated, because research on gender differences within the CVF is scarce, methodologies vary widely, and results are mixed. For example, self-assessments of retail sales managers place women higher than men in mentor and broker roles (Kim & Shim, 2003), female communication and information technology managers preferred the producer role (Parker, 2004), and, finally, 360 assessments of both men and women found no significant differences in perceptions of role performance (Vilkinas, 2000).

Research often focuses on how women lead, while rarely examining the dispositional underpinnings that would explain why their leadership styles might differ (Fine, 2007). Style and skill theories look at "how" managers manage, but only recently have traits (the dispositional "why") been causally connected to managerial styles (Belasen & Frank, 2008). Table 6.1 lists the causal relationships between traits and CVF roles. Because trait research reports both male and female differences, but does not tie traits to CVF managerial role behaviors, this research provides a unique

TABLE 6.1
Relationships between Traits and CVF Roles

	Transformational Roles		
Competing Values Quadrants	CVF Competency Focus	CVF Personality Traits	Feminist Themes
Human Relations	Mentor/Facilitator	Agreeableness	Caring, Empowering
Open Systems	Broker/Innovator	Openness	Collegial, Responsive
	Transactional Roles		
Rational Goal	Director/Producer	Assertiveness	Consultative, Inclusive
Internal Process	Coordinator/ Monitor	Conscientiousness	Fair, Equitable

opportunity to test for male-female differences in traits and their corresponding styles.

Because women are seen as more emotional and people oriented, it would seem that their behaviors would align more closely with their basic dispositions and personality traits, consistent with feminist beliefs that women are biologically and temperamentally different from men. Belasen and Frank (2008) found direct influences of traits on managerial styles, thus indicating that gender differences in traits should correspond to gender differences in managerial styles. Under feminist assumptions, a female manager's behaviors would reflect her innate personality to a greater extent than we would see in men. Women would exhibit different styles, given the extensive support in the literature for different personality trait strengths for men and women.

Women scored higher than men in transactional roles. A path analysis of these items was also conducted, using the relevant CVF roles as latent variables, to indicate a relationship between women and these CVF roles.

All paths were significant between the dummy single indicator gender variable, as indicated by path T-values. A significant path indicates that women scored higher than men for these constructs. There were no areas in which men scored higher than women. These findings were somewhat consistent with the results of the norming sample reported by Eagly and

Johannesen-Schmidt (2001) in which women exceeded men on the trans-formational scales of idealized influence (showing optimism and excitement about the future); inspirational motivation (generating respect and triggering commitment); and individual consideration (developing and mentoring followers). Women also did better than men on the transactional scale of rewarding employees for good performance.

Gender Differences Decrease as Managerial Levels Increase

Why, with so much support for the effectiveness of transformational leadership styles and the tendency of women to display transformational leadership styles, do we not find this in the CVF? One possible answer lies in the findings of previous research. Feminist theory notwithstanding, support for gender differences in transformational leadership styles is not unanimous. For example, no differences were found in task-leadership (Won, 2006; Toren et al., 1997), no support for how significant others perceive effectiveness between genders (Vilkinas, 2000), women were stronger in the producer role (Parker, 2004), women were higher in conscientiousness (Cavallo & Brienza, 2006), women were more analytical (Hays, Allinson & Armstrong, 2004), women were more detailed (Irby et al., 2002), and only small differences in women's tendencies toward transformational leadership styles were found in the Eagly & Johannesen-Schmidt (2001) meta-analysis.

Easing this dilemma of role incongruity requires that female leaders behave extremely competently while reassuring others that they conform to expectations concerning appropriate female behavior. The double-standard requirement, observed or expected, to display extra competence around the CVF roles makes it especially difficult for women to gain recognition for high ability and outstanding achievement. It has been proved that successful managers are tested and honed by experience and education. Viewing the managerial progression as an evolutionary process, upper levels of management are populated with higher proportions of well-balanced, emotionally mature managers. Strong trait and behavioral differences, gender-related or not, are filtered out along the way. Evidence of this leveling process is seen in the differences in role strengths found at the different levels of management discussed earlier in this book, and by Xie and Whyte's (1997) study that gender differences decrease as managerial levels increase.

Women are expected to be friendly, supportive, and skilled in socialization processes, yet agreeableness is a handicap in career advancement (Mueller & Plug, 2006); on the other hand, men who are not friendly (agonistic) are more likely to receive promotions. Women are more conscientious, more analytical, both people and task oriented, and have a transformational leadership style, compared to contractual. Yet while men are granted power automatically, women have to earn it. How do women earn authority unless they act better in areas where they are not competing head-on with traditional male stereotypes? Out of the eight CVF roles, among the four quadrants, is there one particular area, or situational contingency, in which women should excel? Or must they excel in all? Or, as Anna Marie Valerio has pointed out rhetorically: What if men and women leaders "stretch" themselves by learning how to demonstrate some of the opposite gender behaviors? Valerio answered: "Clearly, the outcomes of some managerial situations would be improved if it were more acceptable for female leaders to show more assertiveness and for male leaders to show more caring and empathy" (Valerio, 2009, pp. 30–31).

Leadership Effectiveness

In a study of senior managers' stereotypic perceptions of leadership behaviors, Prime, Carter, and Welbourne (2009) found that with the exception of "networking," female respondents perceived that more women than men leaders were effective at all of the behaviors classified as feminine including "supporting," "rewarding," "mentoring," "networking," "consulting," "team-building," and "inspiring." Male respondents, on the other hand, attributed significantly higher effectiveness to women (i.e., women are better than men) that act out the roles of "supporting others" and "rewarding subordinates." Male respondents perceived male managers as more effective than women in "inspiring others." In terms of "problem solving," "upward influence," and "delegation," male respondents rated male managers as more effective than women on all three variables, while women rated male managers higher on all three except for "problem solving." A follow-up post hoc study conducted by the same researchers revealed mixed results with male respondents designating inspiring, consulting, and rewarding behaviors as gender neutral.

These findings contradict the congruence gender role theory that gender is not a reliable indicator of leadership behavior. Instead, Prime, Carter, and Welbourne's (2009) divergence theory suggests that gender is a reliable indicator of perceived differences in women's and men's leadership performance. In other words, men and women are expected to behave differently from one another rendering gender, a dichotomous variable. Certain mutually exclusive roles are appropriate and socially "acceptable" for men and women and are reflected through organizational norms and expectations. Other than demonstrating the complexity of gender effects on perceptions of leadership effectiveness, these findings have implications for women moving through the corporate ladder and who are evaluated strictly on performance-based criteria such as critical thinking and identifying innovative solutions to problems. This is important because even senior managers may be prone to biases when evaluating women's suitability for leadership positions. "Believing that women lack the expertise to navigate through business problems, the followers of women leaders—especially men—may be more likely to question their recommendations and doubt whether it is worth following their directions. By casting doubt on the problem-solving competence of women leaders, men's stereotypes can potentially make it more difficult for women leaders to gain buy-in from their followers and peers on their problem-solving proposals" (Prime, Carter & Welbourne, 2009, p. 46).

Other studies (e.g., Xie & Whyte, 1997) confirmed that gender differences in personality and needs were stronger than differences in managerial attributes, indicating that although men and women might start from different dispositions and tendencies, only those individuals who adapt to (and allow themselves to be molded by) the requirements of the next level in the hierarchy will increase their chances to climb the corporate ladder. Already playing the CVF roles effectively, the women in the sample studied by Frank and Belasen (2008), for example, seemed to shift their energy from personal, non–value-maximizing behaviors to performance-enhancing activities in areas we could best describe as diligence, thus becoming hypereffective.

The Hypereffective Woman

An earlier study by Belasen et al. (1996), which examined the reactions of middle managers to downsizing, found that managers have become hypereffective in performing their roles. The significant increase in the CVF roles, including the critical transactional roles, suggested that the sample of managers studied may have become not only more effective but what the researchers labeled hypereffective as well. Movement toward the efficiency frontier was not singularly conclusive, but the pattern of change in the tasks and responsibilities underlying the roles suggested a severe loss of discretionary time and an increase in the sense of powerlessness among the managers surveyed. Further, the in-depth interviews supported these preliminary findings.

The reason transactional roles increased was that the managers had been working much longer and harder. Increased organizational efficiencies have come about only in part due to changes in work processes (reflected in part by shifting roles within the Competing Values Framework). The larger source of productivity gain was most likely the result of the vastly increased allocation of managerial activity from personal (non–value-maximizing) activities to activities enhancing organizational effectiveness. It would not take much time for a manager to "burn out" stretching too thin, trying not only to take on each CVF role, but attempting to excel at each of them. Managers have to be able to let go and realize they cannot accomplish each role by themselves.

A later study of the impact of hypereffectivity led the researchers to conclude that this process is unsustainable, requiring top executives and HR directors to pay close attention to the work context that breeds conditions of hypereffectivity and to develop possible remedies (Belasen & Frank, 2004). Reminiscent of the Hawthorne Effects and the dynamics leading female employees to exceed expectations, it is not too uncommon to conclude that women wanting to demonstrate superior skills over their male counterparts tend to resort to overemphasizing the CVF internal process quadrant and its accompanying roles, in particular the monitor (Frank & Belasen, 2008a).

Along with increased responsibilities while learning new competencies in each of the roles of leadership, certain aspects of traditional managerial roles become redundant or less important. In view of the tasks and responsibilities that are depicted in Tables 4.1 to 4.4 in chapter 4, it appears that most of the activities that become less important are those associated with direct supervision or transactional management. To avoid the undesirable state of hypereffectiveness, human resource professionals must establish managerial training and support programs that address the changes and new expectations of managers as well as the shift in the organization's core processes (Belasen & Frank, 2004). Assuming that to be true, we should consider just which CVF areas would be the most advantageous for women to exhibit without running the risk of being perceived as going over into the negative zone. Of the four quadrants, the Internal Processes (lower left) quadrant might be considered the safest area for women. High Human Relations (upper left) competencies would be playing right into gender stereotypes, as would high scores in the vision quadrant. For Rational Goal competencies, very high strengths could be seen as going head-to-head with men, as behaving in a nontraditional way, which might also be perceived as tipping toward the negative zone (Quinn, 1988) for women. Internal Processes roles, however, as long as they are well balanced, are the only ones left where strong skills are highly valued and are not inconsistent with traditional gender role perceptions.

The following anecdote by a woman manager who was perceived as hypereffective and later worked for a hypereffective woman supervisor magnifies the fine line between obsessive monitoring and micromanagement (the excess behaviors in the negative zone of the Internal Processes quadrant) and the perception of hypereffectivity.

I will be the first to admit, when I first became a supervisor, I always felt the need to be in control of everything. If I did not have my eye or hand in every task that was expected to be accomplished by my section then I would actually feel physically anxious. I would go back and re-examine work that had already been completed, even if I trusted the person I assigned the task to, for fear it would not be done correctly. There were even times when I would get home from work, wonder if something was accomplished the way it should be, and when I could not stop my mind thinking about it, I would drive all the way back to the office to check it.

It did not take long for me to realize that I was physically making myself sick by taking on roles, tasks that I had assigned to others because of some great fear it would not be done correctly. Further, my subordinates began to wonder if I actually trusted them to follow through and complete tasks I had assigned to them. Finally, my subordinates finally stopped putting much effort into their jobs because they thought, what's the point, "She is just going to go behind us and check it and re-do it anyway", they used to say. It made for a very uncomfortable work environment for a while. I am not sure what the turning point was for me, maybe it was the ever growing uncomfortable atmosphere that made me sit down with my subordinates to figure out why motivation seemed to be lacking.

Once I addressed the "elephant" in the room, I then had to take a look at myself and what I needed to change. It was not that I didn't trust my subordinates and it was not that I was in fear of losing my job or being replaced, it was about the need for control. It was an internal personal issue more than anything, one for which I actually sought not just assistance from my supervisors, but the advice of a psychiatrist. Learning to let go and allow others to truly take on more roles, made my life and my work section that much better.

Years later, I was then in a position to be the subordinate working for a supervisor who was hyper-effective to the extreme. This particular supervisor was, temporarily, in charge of all the staff specialists and supervisors. She would come up with plans to change processes without even discussing it with section supervisors, she would give us tasks that needed to be completed, but rather than us accomplishing those tasks, she would just say she didn't want to wait, so she completed them herself. Her motto was actually, "if you want it done right, you have to do it yourself." She was grump to be around and you could almost cut the air with a knife. She would run around like a chicken with her head cut off, trying to do her job and everyone else's job, until she was physically and mentally drained. Then she wondered why no one wanted to talk to her, even in causal passerby conversation.

I had always loved my job as a paralegal, but this was one particular short time where I actually dreaded being at work. To make matters worse, it became even more difficult for my subordinates because I would give them tasks, and she would come in and be all over them about how they were not doing it her way, or not quick enough. Often times I would stay late to finish a particular task, but while she was in charge, I could not wait for the end of the day.

(continued)

I am thankful that sooner rather than later, I learned a valuable lesson about the need to "do it all" and learned to let go. Not only was moral high, but productivity was high, and I finally became able to relax and not feel so physically anxious about my job and the quality of the work we, as a team were producing. It even alleviated recurring headaches!

Creating Realistic Boundaries

Hypereffective women constitute essential human capital. Studies of possible negative effects of long-term hypereffective behaviors on the health and careers of women could increase awareness of the perils associated with these behavioral tendencies. Because organizations tend to preserve their resources, any indication that long-term hypereffective performance might place women at risk, thus affecting their continued performance, should lead to the development of intervention programs offered through the human resources training function.

The desire to become a master manager may have both advantages and drawbacks if not carefully monitored. Managers that devote inordinate amounts of time in their pursuits of mastery have a tendency to become hypereffective. On the surface hypereffective managers appear more efficient and have a greater desire to develop success for their organizations. On the negative side, a great deal of personal time is traded to maintain or achieve the goals of the organization. Downsizing, reorganization, and organizational transitions exacerbate these conditions. While managers may be making greater strides in achieving organizational goals—areas of management that were once deemed important are often neglected. There is a tradeoff in that hypereffective managers clearly find few opportunities to diminish the performance of some to increase their attention to others. Ways in which to combat the negative effects of hypereffective management can come in the form of identifying key time management principles, clearly defined goals, empowerment, and appropriate delegation.

A female employee, who I coached in one of my leadership development programs, describes her "hypereffective" female manager: "At first glance, the characteristics of a hypereffective manager appeared to be effective leadership. In fact, I cannot equate my experience with hypereffective management as being unproductive. From my perspective, the hypereffective manager that I worked with inspired me."

"The hypereffective characteristics that she exhibited motivated me to take the necessary steps to be able to perform at that same level. I personally recognize this person as my mentor in the civilian sector. Even with the sudden changes in responsibilities due to the high turnover of senior management, this manager was able to successfully adapt to all eight roles of leadership and develop the competencies to sustain high performance and maintain a cheerful disposition. Even though she is serving in a position as a HR manager, she has taken on the responsibilities of senior management in the critical roles of director, producer and broker for the organization. She is still able to proficiently carry out her responsibilities in the role of a mentor, facilitator and coordinator when managing issues involving employee relations. There is no aspect of her professional life that has been neglected due to the increased responsibilities; however, she has no time to spare for the personal enjoyment of living life free of work. She has cancelled travel and family plans due to unexpected and sudden operational requirements that senior management delegated to her. In my opinion, she is carrying more than her share of the load for a problem that has been created by senior management, and I believe that eventually the added responsibilities will begin to affect her work performance and disposition."

Overall hypereffective managers need to recognize and respect their own limits, both professional and personal. From a professional perspective, placing realistic boundaries on their own capabilities while continuing to strive for success should result in an effective balance. A manager's personal life needs to have equal balance as well. Companies that actively pursue a quality work/life balance often see better results from all levels of an organization. By effectively leveraging the knowledge developed from learning about the CVF, managers are able to continue down the path of becoming master managers while still achieving a high level of work/life balance.

Amanda: Improving Managerial Performance

"You cannot hope to build a better world without improving the individuals. To that end each of us must work for his own improvement, and at the same time share a general responsibility for all humanity, our particular duty being to aid those to whom we think we can be most useful." As we consider the metamorphosis of corporate America, the words penned by Marie Curie, suggest that improvement on the corporate entity is achieved only by improvement in the individuals within the corporation; however, the words of Curie have become more difficult to embrace. Fueled by rapid changes in technology, increased patterns of globalization, and the constant tooling of outsourcing, corporate America has changed in ways that present several challenges to the traditional managerial mindset of old.

Although relics of the loyal lifelong "company man" still exist, the erosion of longtime employment and security calls for a shift in the basic paradigm when considering the value creation expected from aspiring executives. To qualify for promotion, one must effectively execute one's present position's responsibilities. Faced with the paradox of continually creating value in their current position, while exhibiting competencies worthy of executive considerations, managers must learn to tip the scale in their favor with finesse and acumen.

To explain further, top executives are expected and required to demonstrate higher levels of mental, analytical, and conceptual ability. These abilities allow executives to make multifaceted decisions that consider the whole of the organization's mission, vision, goals, and objectives rather than the compartmentalized decisions commonly made by middle managers (Belasen, 2000). Elite executives, with the assistance of an astute management team, move organizations forward by creating value for both internal and external stakeholders. Thus, aspiring executives must demonstrate their capacity to "drive forward" while considering the conditions and climates in which the organization must be driven. Consequently, demonstrating the ability to navigate the paradoxical terrain of an ever-changing corporate landscape, though filled with intricate operations, is achievable through the articulation of scope or the exhibition of a "range of operations."

Range of operations or scope implies an assortment of abilities or skills available for use in varying scenarios and environments. Depending on the size of the organization, scope may be exhibited at varying levels of sophistication. However, the improvement of one's scope must have some measurable genesis for the purpose of tracking growth, development, improvement, or simply put—the expanding range. The Competing Values Framework provides a mechanism for measuring growth and development or systematic change. Whether utilized as a simple or complex tool, the Competing Values Frame may be used to diagnose and implement individual change necessary for forward momentum within organizational culture (Cameron, Quinn, Degraff & Thakor, 2006).

As I consider my own journey toward executive consideration, the Competing Values Framework has been instrumental in identifying competencies and areas in need of development necessary for broadening my range or scope. During the early part of the year, the Competing Values Leadership Roles Assessment yielded a profile in line with my expectations in several areas. Over two months later the assessment yielded nearly identical results. In analyzing these results, both profiles indicated that my strongest competency is found in the upper-right quadrant, in the role of an innovator (6.2), characterized by creativity and creating change (Belasen, 1998). It is also in this quadrant, the create quadrant, that one of my lowest scoring roles lie, that of broker (4.0 initial, 5.4 post), characterized by building and maintaining a power base, negotiating agreements and commitment, presenting ideas effectively, generally coinciding with networking functions (Belasen, 1998).

Evaluation of these results indicates that while I tend to excel in finding creative and innovative methods of creating value within an organization, communicating and winning support for these methods or ideals may be hindered due to a lack of networking activities in a persuasive manner. In others words, the creative ideals are not getting to persons of influence effectively and coherently within the organization. Correspondingly, another area of development was that of mentor (4.0 initial, 5.4 post). The mentor role is characterized by communicating effectively, understanding self and others, and developing subordinates. Both the broker and mentor role, require a high level of emotional intelligence. Individuals with high levels of emotional intelligence possess strong self-awareness, are able to manage their own emotions and their reactions to others, demonstrate empathy, and truly understand and help.

To illustrate these as areas of development, very recently while working with a female subordinate (referred to as D), I expressed my desire to spend more developmental time together for the purpose of promotional preparation. I recognized D's hard work and desired to see her placed in a greater leadership role. Therefore, I changed my schedule for the entire year to include biweekly mentoring with D. At our first meeting, I noticed she was aggravated; however, after making several inquiries of concern regarding her demeanor, I swiftly moved on to the mentoring session.

For the sake of brevity, the mentoring session ended without accomplishing the goals set forth. Ultimately, D expressed that my efforts to support her were insincere and that I had, during the course of our working relationship, been demeaning to her. The manner in which she expressed this to me was in a belligerent fashion. I was able to steer the conversation to a less toxic tone. However, initially, I began to mirror her tone and behavior out of anger and personal indignation. While I cannot justify D's behavior, after consideration, it is my belief that I had not adequately expressed my support in a manner that was significant to her as an individual. By nature, tendencies toward task orientation bear out in the leadership assessment as very focused, which is the lower half of the competing values framework model.

In another illustrative point involving a male subordinate (referred to as T), I had given very clear instruction regarding a matter of importance. The matter in question was instituted to foster departmental cohesion. However, T disregarded the instruction and resorted to formerly acceptable behavior, now deemed unacceptable. My response to T's behavior was to simply question the behavior, with the intentions of redirecting him to proper actions. T responded in an adversarial manner. Again, I mirrored his response. However, I had not taken into account that T was a very influential team member. In hindsight, it would have been more appropriate to have made T an ally by including him as a collaborator in the new directive. Retrospectively, my reaction could have damaged the progress of departmental cohesion.

As previously mentioned, executive leaders exhibit a high level of emotional intelligence. They are able to pilot difficult confrontations with elegance while focusing on the good of the organization. Additionally, they are able to value dissenting opinions in a manner that promotes continued collaboration. These leaders ascribe to a higher standard than the common utterances of "job well done." Rather, they transcend notions of mediocrity through the effectual balancing of human behavior and organizational goals. It is this level of excellence I aspire to. As a result of the Competing Values Framework Assessment, I have been able to discover several areas in need of development, in particular, the brokering and mentoring leadership roles.

Yet discovery, while a key ingredient, is not enough to guarantee transformational change capable of expanding range or scope. It is the identification and implementation of personal improvement strategies that instill lasting change. To that end, it is clear that I, as well as other aspiring leaders, must adhere to a personal development strategy that brings about incremental change over a measurable period of time. Through a pattern of discipline and awareness, growth will occur exponentially, as the mastering current competencies complement the acquisition of new abilities and concepts. With a well-executed personal strategy, good leaders develop into exceptional executives who have demonstrated success in piloting the paradoxical plane of increasing depth and breadth while diligently tending to current responsibilities, and faithfully embracing the ideology of individual responsibility represented in the words of Marie Curie with poise and grace.

7

Women's Self-Development

Recently I had the wonderful opportunity to work with a group of diverse managers in an eight-week leadership development program spanning the eight CVF roles. The program was geared toward helping managers assess their current competencies, draft developmental plans, and consider personal and growth goals. Below are personal accounts with self-assessment and self-development plans from women managers in three different organizations.

Melissa

Being a good leader requires the ability to enter a situation, to see it from contrasting perspectives, and to call on contrasting competencies or roles. The importance of self-development begins with first understanding your strengths and weaknesses. When looking at my pre- and post-competing values leadership roles profiles, my strengths center on the mentor, producer, coordinator, and facilitator roles. The variances between the two tests are very slight with the post-test flattening out even more among all roles. When I asked others to evaluate my leadership style, the strengths they noted were in the director, monitor, and producer roles. As I took the competing values skills profile, the highest skills were in communicating effectively, using participative decision making, working productively, building and maintaining a power base, and understanding self and others. In looking back at our first discussion board, we were asked what we thought after taking the surveys. I made a note in the discussion that all of my results in this survey were relatively even across the board, but the mentor role had a slightly higher score. I think this does describe me well in that I have been described by others as caring, empathetic, helpful, and open and give compliments and credit. I enjoy teaching and training others and want to help people synergize to make the entire team more effective.

In looking at my weaknesses, my lowest two CVF roles are in the broker and monitor roles. I thought I would be higher in the broker role as my role at my job is one of maintaining a good image in the community and helping to raise funds for our organization on an external basis. The competencies associated with the broker role are building and maintaining a power base, negotiating agreement and commitment, and presenting ideas. A broker works to create relationships and agreements that result in moving organizations forward. In an organizational setting power can be divided into four sources: position, which is attached to a formal position; personal power, which comes from personal appearance; expert power, which is based on expertise; network power, which is known as "social capital" (Quinn et al., 2007, pp. 302–303). The other piece of a good broker comes from negotiation skills, which I know I am weak in as I take things as they are and mostly do not argue. A good leader must establish a dialogue of purpose and mutual respect along with insisting on generating ideas beyond what was presented. I can see this as a weaker role of mine because of my relatively junior experience in the workplace. I have yet to build expert or network power, nor do I have the credibility with many to negotiate as they do not know me as a fund developer. They are not familiar with my organization.

The second role I was weakest in was the monitor role. I know this is not my strength because I am far from an analytical person who manages information overload, analyzes core processes, or manages performance or quality. The monitor function focuses the manager's attention on internal control issues in which I have had little experience other than for my own job duties. Looking at the aspect of information overload, I think I excel quite well at this part of the role. I am very organized and have learned that you cannot let things get piled up on your desk. A leader must implement a system such as the "toss, refer, act or file," method. The next competency in the monitor role is analysis of core processes. I quite honestly shut down if too many numbers or theories are put in front of me. It has always taken me longer to understand mathematics or logic, and

I know that is because I am not an analytical person. A good monitor also works to ensure that measures of evaluation and quality are in place.

Plan for Improvement

According to Quinn et al. (2007) a manager must not only have the ability to play all eight roles within the competing values framework, but also have the ability to blend and balance the competing roles in an appropriate way. In looking at a detailed plan for improving my competency in my weakest roles, I plan to implement the following goals over the next 180 days presented in Table 7.1.

High-performance leaders share six principles including: controlling their own destiny, facing reality as it is, being candid with everyone, leading not managing, changing before one has to and knowing if one doesn't have a competitive edge, don't compete (Belasen, 2000, p. 406). Following these principles along with my strengths in the mentor, facilitator, and coordinator roles will help me address my weaknesses in the broker and monitor roles. I hope within the next 180 days to one year, as I am relatively new in my current job, I can evaluate numerous competencies and processes along the way. I will ask for feedback regularly from the board of directors and leadership team as I report to both as well as my peers in the development field. I plan to do this through quarterly meetings with the board and leadership team and conduct a short follow-up survey in what they would like to see me improving. All in all, I think this program was a great way to prepare us for future leadership positions. Being able to balance all roles and have strengths in all roles will make us better leaders. I know my first love is to help people, and I know I have found a career in which I can do that. I know I have strengths that are assets to our organization; yet because of this program, I was able to identify my weaknesses and work on improving them to further my career.

April

When comparing the results of my survey that was taken by me and my peers, across the different management roles, I see that my strongest roles were Mentor and Monitor. My weakest roles were Broker and Facilitator. As I learned about these different roles in the program, the related competencies, and how the roles work together, I began to understand the results

TABLE 7.1

Developmental Goals and Implementation Plans for the Next Six Months

30 days:

Broker role:	Action Step:
Competency: Building a Power Base	Join a civic organization such as the Chamber's Young Executive Network; introduce myself to two trust officers to improve on network power. Increase expert power by seeking out peer learning opportunities with other Community Action Agencies, attend one Nonprofit; Connect professional development seminar on fundraising and compile a two-age fact sheet on poverty stats for grants.
Competency: Negotiation Skills	Negotiate for one corporate sponsorship for upcoming "rock 'n' bowl" event
Competency: Presenting Ideas	Make one community presentation and ask for support with a proposal and prepare for common objections through practice with leadership team
Monitor role:	Action Step:
Competency: Managing Information Overload	Continue to clean on a daily basis all mail and papers from inbox and desk. Put all e-mails in appropriate folders if they are to be saved on a daily basis. Put files to be read into "to read" basket.
Competency: Analyzing Core Processes	Establish in writing the proper process for processing a donor receipt and entering in donations to eTapestry.
Competency: Measuring Performance and Quality	Establish annual development goals along with performance measures for each quarter.

60 days:

Broker role:	Action Step:
Competency: Building a Power Base	Ask for LinkedIn recommendation from three former colleagues/ supervisors. Take criticism from six-month review and create working plan for improvement. Establish rapport with 10 CEOs of companies within the regional community.
Competency: Negotiation Skills	Negotiate for all media given at no cost for entire year with television and radio stations in St. Joseph and ask for semi-monthly editorials to be placed in newspapers.
Competency: Presenting Ideas	Conduct two proposal presentations with bank trust officers for local trusts/foundations.

TABLE 7.1 (*continued*)

60 days:

Monitor role:	Action Step:
Competency: Managing Information Overload	Every two months work on cleaning out e-mail folders and paper folders with information that hasn't been used in that time frame. Establish a method for proposal writing.
Competency: Analyzing Core Processes	Look at process for determining grant criteria and what grants are worth writing and avoiding by analyzing key programs' needs.
Competency: Measuring Performance and Quality	Establish new development committee criteria and seek out new members of fund development committee.

180 days:

Broker role:	Action Step:
Competency: Building a Power Base	Have attended one professional development conference in fund development; seek out information for applying for CCAP certification and CFRE certification. Have met with top 25 CEOs for Breakfast Club.
Competency: Negotiation Skills	Negotiate for new budget for the agency's fiscal year.
Competency: Presenting Ideas	Seek out opportunity to assist satellite officers with community presentations and establish speaker's bureau for agency.
Monitor role:	**Action Step:**
Competency: Managing Information Overload	Recreate eye-appealing yet informational marketing campaign for agency with new website, brochures, annual report, etc.
Competency: Analyzing Core Processes	Evaluate major donor campaign and seek out help from consultant if needed on soliciting more donors and create streamlined approach for handling donor communications.
Competency: Measuring Performance and Quality	Prepare for personal review and upcoming grant cycle with position and establish criteria for my position to be funded continuously.

of my survey. The individuals I worked with the longest in a personal leadership role rated me the highest; the people that I had worked with the least in a non personal, analytical role rated me the lowest; the results of my own survey differed from my peers' results. In some roles I rated myself higher, in some lower, and in some around the same as my fellow coworkers. The results appear in Table 7.2.

As a managerial leader my strengths lie in my people skills and my analytical way of thinking. I have an extroverted personality, or as the Myers-Briggs Type Inventory describes; I am an E-I-T-J. I enjoy working with people, listening to their ideas and motivating them to push themselves. I am always willing to help others or my manager to accomplish a task. I volunteer often for assignments and know when I need to delegate tasks. I take a great sense of pride in my work and in my team's work overall. I like to ensure that we are staying on task and going above and beyond to achieve necessary goals and tasks. In my current role, I am a Business Analyst and manage the performance goals of the team to ensure they are being met at or above our service level agreements.

My weaknesses lie in my ability to take a stand against others when needed. When there is an issue between me and a coworker I tend to either ignore it, or get very frustrated and angry. This issue goes along with my strength, because my human relation skills are so sensitive I can become passive in my abilities to take a stand in a professional and healthy way. I also have a weakness when it comes to change. I am terrified of change and it has affected my professional and personal life. I have been afraid to go after things that I want because of fear of failure. When it comes to my professional life I think the change scares me more because I do not know the impact that it will have on the daily operations. One of my weakest roles listed in my survey results was Broker.

The competencies of the Broker role are: building and maintaining a power base, negotiating agreement and commitment, and presenting ideas. My power base was stronger when I was a trainer for my organization. Since I have moved into a new role I have let myself become a sideline employee. I now take direction more and implement it instead of give direction; this has greatly decreased my influence on others. I think my issue with change comes into play on my negotiating skills. I am good about talking with others and being sensitive to their ideas but at the same time if I don't fully understand it and think it could be a bad solution,

TABLE 7.2
Results

	Director	Broker	Mentor	Monitor	Producer	Innovator	Facilitator	Coordinator
B	4.2	4	4.2	5	4.4	4	4.4	4.6
A	5.4	5	6.2	6.7	5.4	5.2	5	5.6
J	4.6	4.5	4.2	6.5	4.6	6.2	3.8	5.2
M	3.8	3.7	4.5	4.7	4	4.5	4.2	4.2
April 1	4.4	4.5	6.7	5.7	4.6	4.2	4.2	4.2
April 2	5.2	4.5	7	6.5	5.6	4.2	4.8	3.8
Average	4.6	4.4	5.5	5.9	4.8	4.7	4.4	4.6

I tend to stand my ground. Sometimes I can be right but sometimes I can be wrong and my lack of understanding gets in my way. I wouldn't say that presenting ideas is a weak point for me because I am very verbal about what I think we can or should be doing. I am so weak in other areas that they have a negative effect on my ability to present ideas properly.

My second weakest role listed in my survey results was Facilitator. The competencies of the Facilitator role are: building teams, using participative decision making, managing conflict. I have had more of an informal approach style to team building. I have a willingness to help others and I communicate with other members of the team. I have not had the opportunity to build a team and if I was given the chance, I would not yet have the knowledge necessary to put it together. When it comes to using participative decision making and managing conflict, this goes back to my struggles with change. I have to find a way to effectively embrace change and understand the vision of others, without my own ideals clouding the discussion.

I have many available options to help facilitate my journey to become a master manager. My current career has many different classes and workshops that are available to me on leadership. I have many books related to management and leadership that I can learn from. I am able to work on various projects with different groups. I have a good professional support system among my managers and peers. I also have a good personal support system with my family and with the knowledge I am acquiring while getting my Master's Degree. More importantly than any tangible object, I have my drive and motivation to be better.

I understand that this will be a long hard journey, and there will be times that I feel it would be easier to fall back into what I see as comfortable. In order to be successful in life I know I need to push through those tough times to get to what will be better for me personally and professionally. The following is an action plan that I have created for myself on how to better improve the roles of Broker and Mentor.

Broker

30 Days:

1. Become more active in my group by taking on new responsibilities
2. Network with other groups

3. Take a class on managing change

4. Schedule a feedback session with my manager

60 Days:

1. Look for areas of improvement and hold a brainstorming session with people affected

2. Be open to others' suggestions for areas of improvement and learn from new ideas

3. Prepare presentations by offering a list of available solutions

4. Schedule a feedback session with my manager

180 Days:

1. Take on a project where I am able to develop an end to end plan

2. Volunteer to work on a political campaign

3. Reflect on the past 180-day plan and revise plan as needed

4. Schedule a feedback session with my supervisor

Facilitator

30 Days:

1. Get to know the people in my workgroup

2. Attend a teambuilding activity

3. Engage teammates one on one and offer support and help if needed

4. Schedule a feedback session with my manager

60 Days:

1. Read a book on how to deal with conflict

2. Learn how to control my emotions and focus on the issue at hand not the personal feelings

3. Ask my supervisor for opportunities to participate in the decision making process

4. Schedule a feedback session with my manager

180 Days:

1. Work with project managers on how to effectively create meeting agendas
2. Learn how to create a team through education or experience
3. Reflect on the past 180-day plan and revise plan as needed
4. Schedule a feedback session with my supervisor

My main goal through this whole process is to learn and grow through experiences and mistakes. At each step I will schedule a feedback session with my manager to track my improvements. This will help me to see things that I might not be able to see because I am directly involved. This will also give me the opportunity to take advice and revise my action plan accordingly. There may be areas in which my growth is stronger than in other areas. I will need to change my action plans as I begin to change myself.

My hope is that through the new knowledge I have gained while participating in this program, and the future knowledge I hope to gain, I will be able to fulfill my dreams of becoming an activist. Activists also have to be master managers. They have to be well rounded in all of these areas to be effective. They also have to understand that they will need to change roles as needs change and embrace their new roles. I have strong people skills and a sensitive side for helping others. I am also very performance driven; I love to ensure that all tasks are being met. I like to analyze the organizational goals and put logic to what is going on behind the measurements. These skills, while necessary, are only two parts to the puzzle. I have to be willing to branch outside of my comfort zone and learn to encompass and interchange all roles to be more then just successful. I am expecting that this action plan will be a big step in the right direction.

Kim

I conducted a gap analysis of the Competing Values Framework roles using the self survey and those performed by others on me at the beginning and again during the last week of the program. The analysis demonstrates that my four strongest roles are the monitor, mentor, coordinator, and producer roles. After conducting and reviewing the analysis, I enlisted a teammate to join me in performing an evaluation of my strengths and weaknesses to determine which competencies needed further development. We found that my strengths were evidenced through placing value on my job performance, communicating effectively, organizational skills, and utilizing critical thinking in conducting problem-solving. Additional competency strengths are that I manage projects, meet deadlines, and exhibit teamwork in working with my teammates and peers.

The remaining roles of innovator, director, facilitator and broker are my weaker roles. We found that my strengths within these roles are setting goals, designing and organizing systems, living with and managing change, thinking creatively, providing input in decision making as requested, and presenting ideas.

My two weakest roles are facilitator and broker. Within these roles, the competencies of building and maintaining a power base, negotiating agreement and commitment, and managing conflict are my weakest. These weaknesses are primarily associated with the fact that these roles are not key roles within my current position. Because I do not currently have any direct reports, I am not in a position to utilize the managing conflict competency for resolving conflicts between others; however, I do have the ability to manage my own behaviors in dealing with conflict situations. This is a competency that I perform fairly well although it could be developed further through self-awareness and monitoring.

Development Goals

My teammate and I brainstormed potential opportunities to develop and utilize the facilitator and broker roles and competencies further. In relation to the facilitator role, we determined that I could periodically facilitate "Admin and Go Team Meetings" and look for possible training sessions where I could function as facilitator. We also identified a current opportunity to utilize both the facilitator and innovator roles, as a member of a focus group to define the purpose and develop the new charter of the Workforce Leadership Council.

In reference to the broker role, we discussed opportunities for me to utilize this role with my manager and others who I support. The result was to use this role to present ideas for expanding my responsibilities to include oversight of all the administrative issues related to advertising, quality checking others work before it is released, and drafting correspondence on their behalf. Usually, any ideas or concerns that we have in regard to our cross-team relations with Facilities Services are presented to the Executive Assistant Lead, who coordinates with the Facilities Services Lead to resolve such issues. We determined that I could present my ideas via a meeting with the two of them or a special team meeting of both teams.

The following are my action items and goals to achieve within the next six months, which will align with my next annual assessment. I have also included development action items from my last assessment.

30 Days:

- Take on more managerial responsibilities such as drafting correspondence, approving expense reports, and monitoring and managing e-mail
- Meet and talk to senior managers about future career opportunities
- Meet with my mentor to review last assessment and progress of assessment development actions. Also discuss the responsibilities she performs for her managers and identify how I may expand my responsibilities with my managers. Discuss the possibility of trip to corporate to job shadow with her for 1–2 days and meet analytics teams as well as branding teams.
- Complete Take 5 Career Planning course online and complete career plan.
- Complete career plan and set meeting to review with manager.
- Review new assessment processes and forms on line and work with HRM to create training course for managers.

60 Days:

- Complete specialty workshop.
- Begin quality checking work of others.
- Facilitate Admin Team Meeting.
- Participate in Leadership Council Focus Group to determine new purpose and draft charter.
- Work with Branding Group to define advertising objectives and venues.

180 Days:

- Facilitate GO Team Meeting.
- Watch for opportunities to facilitate training in areas of expertise (software, processes, etc.).
- Become a mentor to someone.
- Continue looking for ways to expand responsibilities and build competencies.

Evaluating Progress

Progress of these goals will be monitored through weekly meetings with my manager. Additionally, my manager and I are to conduct quarterly pulse checks of performance and progress of development actions per the last annual assessment. This session is also used to identify new development actions as needed. Progress of these goals will also be monitored and discussed with relevant leaders. Finally, my annual assessment will be an evaluation at the end of the 180 days.

Strengths and Expected Outcomes

My years of experience and expertise along with my education offer me the ability to continue to grow and advance in my career. With the further development of goals specified in this plan, I expect to achieve a promotion to the next level within the next six to eighteen months. By meeting these goals and expanding my responsibilities in Advertising and Human Resources, I may be defining and creating a new role for me in the DBA office. Additionally, as the DBA office continues to grow, more career opportunities will become available for me to explore.

8

Qualities Unique to Women

Burns (1978) used the term "transforming leadership" to describe a relationship in which "leaders and followers raise one another to higher levels of motivation and morality" (p. 18). For Burns, leadership is quite different from wielding power because it is inseparable from followers' needs (Northouse, 2001).

Burns (1978) also introduced the distinction between transactional and transformational leaders. Transactional leadership refers to the bulk of leadership models, which focus on the exchange between leaders and followers. For example, managers who use rewards and sanctions to achieve compliance of employees with stated performance objectives are exhibiting transactional leadership. Transformational leadership, on the other hand, offers an emotional bond that raises the level of motivation and morality in both the leader and the follower.

Building on the initial conceptualization, Bass (1985) extended the concept of transformational leadership to describe those who motivate followers to do more than they originally intended to do by presenting followers with a compelling vision and encouraging them to transcend their own interests for the common good. Transformational roles have typically been categorized into four types: idealized influence, inspirational motivation, intellectual stimulation, and individual consideration. The first trait, idealized influence, refers to leaders who have high standards of moral and ethical conduct, who are held in high personal regard, and who engender loyalty from followers. The second, inspirational motivation, refers to leaders with a strong vision for the future based on values and ideas that generate enthusiasm, build confidence, and inspire followers using symbolic actions and persuasive language. The idealized influence and inspirational motivation are highly correlated and sometimes combined to form a measure of charisma. The third trait, intellectual stimulation, refers to leaders who challenge existing organizational norms, encourage divergent thinking, and who push followers to develop innovative strategies. Individual consideration, the fourth transformational leadership trait, refers to leadership behaviors that are aimed at recognizing the unique growth and developmental needs of followers through coaching and problem-solving communications.

Transactional leadership behaviors are aimed at monitoring and controlling employees through rational or economic means. Using contingent rewards, transactional leaders focus their attention on exchange or trade relationships providing tangible or intangible support and resources to followers in exchange for their efforts and performance and sanctioning undesired behaviors or unattained performance levels. To deal with unexpected surprises or nonroutine events, transactional leaders may also rely on management by exception, revising and updating standards and monitoring deviations from these standards. In the passive version of management by exception, leaders take an inactive approach, intervening only when problems become serious. Active management by exception characterizes enhanced monitoring activities by transactional managers who initiate corrective actions and intensely evaluate progress toward achieving desired performance levels (Bono & Judge, 2004). Bass (1985) included laissez-faire under the transactional leadership label, though it can be viewed as nonleadership or the abdication of leadership responsibilities.

Gender Effects on Transformational and Transactional Leadership

Based on the theoretical ground work by Burns (1978), Bass (1985), Bennis and Nanus (1985), feminist researchers have reasoned that transformational leadership might be particularly advantageous to women because of its androgynous qualities and, indeed, the substantial research literature comparing women and men on these styles has yielded interesting outcomes (Eagly & Carli, 2003). Sex differences in transformational and transactional leadership do have implications for female advantage arguments because researchers defined these styles to identify effective leadership performance. Pursuing these ideas, Eagly, Johannesen-Schmidt, and van Engen (2003) carried out a meta-analysis of 45 studies that compared male and female managers on measures of transformational, transactional, and laissez-faire leadership styles. In general, their meta-analysis revealed that compared with male leaders, female leaders were more transformational and engaged in the contingent reward (i.e., positive reinforcement) transactional behavior.

Male leaders were more likely than female leaders to manifest other aspects of transactional leadership: active management by exception and passive management by exception. Management by exception seems more consistent with the masculine stereotype of focusing on immediate results and administration of rewards and punishments in the short term over building long-term relationships. Men were also higher on laissez-faire leadership. In view of these findings, the tendency of women to exceed men on the components of leadership styles that relate positively to effectiveness and the tendency of men to display ineffective styles (e.g., attending to failures, responding to problems reactively, and abdicating responsibilities) attest to women's leadership effectiveness. "Female leaders were rated as having more idealized influence, providing more inspirational motivation, being more individually considerate, and offering more intellectual stimulation" (Daft, 2011, p. 341).

Leadership effectiveness is positively associated with all of the dimensions of transformational leadership and the contingent reward dimension of transactional leadership. Because women were rated much higher than men in behaviors that contribute to effective leadership as compared with men that were rated higher on the dimensions associated with less effectiveness, then female leadership advantage should be considered seriously and responsibly in promotion to senior level decisions.

Dimensions of Transformational Women Leadership

Porter and Daniel's (2007) definition of transformational women leadership includes the following dimensions: values, vision, action, learning, understanding, ethical practices, and social constructivism. These seven dimensions, when combined, form a robust definition of great leadership that is also consistent with Goleman's (2009, p. 44) description of emotional intelligence as the "sine qua non of leadership." According to

Goleman, EI skills are significantly more important than cognitive abilities and technical skills when moving up the corporate ladder. These EI skills include self-awareness (e.g., self-confidence and acceptance of constructive criticisms), self-regulation (trustworthiness, integrity), motivation (a passion for new challenges, optimism in the face of failure), empathy (developing and coaching others, cultural sensitivity), and social skills (expertise in building and leading teams, persuasiveness). Goleman (2009, p. 45), who developed the notion of emotional intelligence, attested to women's qualities: "When I compared star performers with average ones in senior leadership positions, nearly 90% of the difference in their profiles was attributable to emotional intelligence rather than cognitive abilities."

Because women possess these EI skills and abilities and because, according to Goleman, much of the success of the firm can be attributed to the EI level of its leaders, one can argue that women at the senior ranks can bring business and financial success to the organization, as well as influence stakeholder satisfaction. Women's unique skill sets and the new vision of global economy that calls sensitivity people skills, emotional intelligence, connectedness, and inclusiveness should provide a strategic competitive advantage to organizations. Women bring unique insights into consumer behaviors and preferences and can offer differentially beneficial perspectives on customer needs and overall business direction than male managers can offer (Bilimoria, 2000). Not surprisingly, *Business Week's* cover story concluded that "Men could become losers in a global economy that values mental power over might" (Conlin, 2003, p. 78). It has been shown that having female directors in a company leads to increased profitability. In fact, of the 50 most profitable U.S. companies in the Fortune 500 listing, 82% had at least one female director, and all top ten companies had female directors on their boards (Burgess & Tharenou, 2002), leading Margaret Heffernan of *Fast Company* to proclaim, "the future of business depends on women" (2002, p. 9).

Ruth Simmons, the 18th President of Brown University from 2001

The first component is *values*. In *The Leadership Engine*, Tichy (1997) argued that values are a necessity at the core of effective organizations.

Effective leaders not only bring their values into organizations, they articulate them clearly and use them to shape organizational missions (see also, Rutigliano, 1996). Ruth Simmons is a role model who implements values in the daily operations of her work. She has been President of Smith College, and Provost of Spelman College and Princeton University. She is also the first African American appointed president of any Ivy League university. Simmons's remarkable accomplishments were grounded in her values. She was motivated by her conviction that higher education was crucial to improving the lives of people of color and that elite institutions of higher education had to assume greater responsibility for educating the poor. She contended that institutions always communicate values, whether intentionally or not. Universities should "teach values in the way they hire and treat employees; they teach values in the way they admit students; they teach values in the way they set curricula and requirements. Thus, universities teach values even when they do not set out to do so" (Porter & Daniel, 2007, p. 251).

Meg Whitman, CEO, Hewlett-Packard

The second component is *vision*. An effective transformational leader needs not only to have a compelling vision and plan for the organization but also an effective way to communicate this vision. Too often, leaders think of this vision only as the blueprint for where the organization is going. Transformational leaders motivate their constituents to work for the good of the organization by effectively communicating a collective vision (Burns, 1978). For leaders with broader social values, the vision must provide a clear view of what the organization is, or will be, and how it will behave. Meg Whitman, former CEO of eBay, boasts an impressive record of successful innovations throughout her corporate career. To name a few of her accomplishments, she led the reorganization of the Preschool Division and its return to profitability during her tenure as general manager of Hasbro Inc. At eBay, she realized the huge potential of the Internet in changing the traditional business mode and bringing some new blood to the old-fashioned business operation. She combined the idea of auction with the power of the Internet to offer a new value proposition to customers.

On September 22, 2011, Hewlett-Packard Company announced the appointment of Meg Whitman to the position of president and CEO, replacing unpopular leader Leo Apotheker at the helm of the largest U.S. technology company. The move indicates a long standing view that although the company's strategy to transform its business was sound, it needed new leadership to carry out the plan. Speaking on behalf of the board, Ray Lane, who has moved from non-executive chairman to executive chairman of HP's board, said, "We very much appreciate Leo's efforts and his service to HP since his appointment last year. The board believes that the job of the HP CEO now requires *additional attributes* to successfully execute on the company's strategy . . . We are fortunate to have someone of Meg Whitman's caliber and experience step up to lead HP . . . We are at a critical moment and we *need renewed leadership to successfully implement our strategy and take advantage of the market opportunities ahead.* Meg is a technology *visionary* with a proven track record of execution. She is a *strong communicator who is customer focused with deep leadership capabilities.* Furthermore, as a member of HP's board of directors for the past eight months, Meg has a solid understanding of our products and markets . . . *Meg Whitman has the right operational and communication skills and leadership abilities to deliver improved execution and financial performance.*" Talking about why she chose to accept the role, Meg Whitman said, "This is a chance to help turn around an American icon."

Sources

http://www.nytimes.com/2011/09/23/technology/whitman-expected-to -be-named-at-hp.html?pagewanted=all

http://www.huffingtonpost.com/2011/09/22/meg-whitman-hp-ceo_n_97 6597.html

HP Press release: http://www.hp.com/hpinfo/newsroom/press/2011/ 110922xb.html

Susan Whiting, CEO of Nielson Media Research

Susan Whiting, CEO of Nielson Media Research, offers another example of change and growth. Whiting accepted the appointment of CEO during a time of crisis. In 2002, Nielson was involved in a scandal and was placed under investigation. Whiting took bold measures and ultimately turned the detrimental situation around. While she was in office as CEO, the company went through more changes within one year than it had in the previous 20 years, setting an impressive record in the corporate history of Nielson.

Margaret Blackshere, President of the Illinois AFL-CIO

The third component is *action*: collaborative, community-focused, and respectful action. Working in conjunction with others for a socially healthier and inclusive community, whether in an organizational, civic, or social community, are hallmarks of transformational women leaders. Margaret Blackshere, President of the Illinois AFL-CIO, American Federation of Labor and Congress of Industrial Organizations is a good example. Unlike leaders in hierarchically structured organizations, Blackshere does not view her authority as a matter of power because of her formal authority. Rather, she sees leadership as an ongoing process, and Blackshere sees herself as a team leader, inspiring rather than directing. Her interactions with managers and employees are seldom transactional exchanges of rewards or demotions for superior or inferior performance. Instead, her goal is to coordinate and balance her version of the union with those of her members and employees, transforming these into shared union goals. This is usually translated into forms of interactive and participatory leadership that empower members and employees to adopt her version as their own, while at the same time achieving benefits for workers. On top of that, Blackshere has achieved success not by forcing issues but through developing consensus. She never stops talking and describes her job as bringing people together.

Mentoring

The fourth component is *learning* that is empowering, reflexive, and life-long (Porter & Daniel, 2007). A feminist leader, regardless of setting, should empower others by fostering autonomy, personal responsibility, problem-solving and decision-making skills. Eagly and her colleagues (2003) pointed out that mentoring is a transformational behavior that serves women leaders well; it allows women leaders to deal with lesser authority while creating a participative learning environment that increases everyone's effectiveness. Effective mentoring includes sponsorship, exposure, coaching, counseling, overcoming gender hurdles, and social support. The mentor's transformational traits, particularly idealized influence and intellectual stimulation, may be more congruent with women's protégé's styles enhancing their cognitive abilities to undertake calculated risks to advance their careers. Furthermore, mentor transformational leadership might also help women overcome the absurdity of male-dominated workplace practices, challenge existing values and norms and focus on the context rather than the task. Women reaching out to transformational mentors also benefit from self-development and self-clarity, important influencers on efficacy and confidence. The transformational mentor can help facilitate the attainment of women's development and growth goals in alignment with organizational mission and goals.

Consistent with findings correlating mentoring functions with job-related stress, women who perceive low career development opportunities and discrepancies with career goals resulting from little or lack of managerial support might experience high levels of job stress. Mentoring and coaching, when coupled with effective social support and guidance, can help lower job-related stress and build self-efficacy (Sosik & Godshalk, 2000).

Mentoring can also take shape in group settings with reciprocal relationships in which everyone in the group is a mentor and a mentee; networking mentoring in which two or more women act out overlapping roles of mentor and protégé at different times in the relationship; peer mentoring, a nonhierarchical, organic structure of members with mutual recognition and support; strategic collaboration mentoring with open membership and greater exposure to multiple perspectives; and web-based mentoring with greater flexibility with regard to time and place of mentoring (Paludi et al., 2010).

Networking and mentoring can benefit women through confidence building, career counseling, coaching, and understanding organizational dynamics. While women tend to have a more social orientation to networks through expressive benefits and men have a more utilitarian or instrumental approach to networks—women can certainly benefit from looking to male mentors to provide instrumental career assistance (Hopkins, O'Neil, Passarelli & Bilimoria, 2008).

Phyllis Apelbaum, President and CEO of Arrow Messenger Service, Inc.

Women must also attend to their own ongoing development and self-evaluation, engage in personal and professional reflection, as well as foster these actions in others. Phyllis Apelbaum, President and CEO of Arrow Messenger Service, Inc., is a good example. Apelbaum built an employee-centered culture to achieve the customer service mission. She makes it a point to give back to both the community and industry, using her position as a force to organize others to achieve mutual goals. She focuses on employee relationships and the creation of a corporate culture that minimizes interpersonal conflicts. She is dedicated to relational practices, which include decision-making within an empowered team atmosphere. Her management style can be described as participative, as her employees are highly involved and empowered to make day-to-day decisions.

Alison Chung, President, TeamWerks

Another example is Alison Chung, President of TeamWerks. Chung's education at Wellesley College helped her with confidence and public speaking. Spiritual role models taught her to "see beyond self-interest" and to work for the greater good. Chung believes in the power of a positive mentor. Her strong sense of integrity, ethics, and the importance of creating a corporate culture based on values were her driving force. TeamWerks looks for much more than just a skilled candidate when it makes a hiring decision. Prospective employees must go through a rigorous screening process to be sure that they truly process this ethical and value-based core that Chung has worked so hard to establish at TeamWerks, which she describes as a strong sense of integrity. Chung interacts with every employee on a regular basis to be sure they all understand the direction of the firm and their commitment to the greater organizational goals. Her employees have proven their commitment to the greater organization through their loyalty and dedication. Another way for companies to safeguard their reputation is to foster a culture where employees uphold the values of the firm at all costs. And TeamWerks has done many things to support the community and its clients.

Deborah L. DeHaas, Partner, Deloitte & Touche USA

Consistent with Greenleaf's (1977) servant leadership model focusing on putting service before self-interest, listening first to affirm others, inspiring trust and character, and helping others become whole and accept responsibilities, the fifth component of transformational women leadership is *understanding* of power and boundaries (Porter & Daniel, 2007). Deborah L. DeHaas, Midwest Regional Managing Partner of Deloitte & Touche USA LLP is a good example. Her personal values include integrity, quality of client service, quality of people, and a strong commitment to everyone—clients and staff alike—ensuring satisfaction for all. DeHaas is motivated by opportunities to make a difference and help impact people in a positive way. She likes to get the best out of her people. Her golden rules include being a good communicator and treating colleagues and clients with dignity, respect, and in a fair-minded way. DeHaas encourages them in the consultative process and encourages them to come to the conclusion that creates a solution for the shareholders. In leadership terms, it is about being a servant leader, a truly empowering values-based style that enables followers to accomplish organizational goals. Moreover, she describes herself as most effective with a team of people. DeHaas has always worked in an environment where there has been a team. In her view, you recruit the right people and build a great team around you, members recognize and embrace their roles, and goal-setting comes next.

Eva Maddox, Founder and President of EMA

The sixth component is *ethical practices* promoting inclusiveness, integrity, and responsibility. According to Hood (2003), transformational women leaders should hold different styles of ethical values, and organizations should reflect these values in ethical practices. A woman leader should strive to incorporate people from diverse backgrounds at all levels of an organization and craft a mission and vision with inclusion as a central theme. Eva Maddox, founder and president of EMA, Eva Maddox Associates, is a good example. Maddox's success can be attributed to her determination, hard work, assiduous networking, relentless focus on her vision and goals. Maddox has developed her idea of branded environments into a leadership story that integrates her personal values, creativity, and commitment to design and environmental sustainability with the ongoing evolution of a successful brand and business model. Discussing gender differences, Maddox concludes that there is something especially distinctive about women leaders. They are more engaged in personal relations than men and from a design point of view they understand more about the intertwining of design elements. Often, too, women are more than willing to listen and respond directly to client interests and needs; she believes that women have the ability to take a holistic approach to their profession, not an easy thing to achieve.

The last component is *social constructivism*, which informs one's practice of leadership. A transformational woman leader attends to the social construction of race, class, gender, disability, sexual orientation, and so forth, and how language defines social roles and perceptions of performance. The feminist leader should be aware of the literature on women and people of color in leadership roles, which shows how they are subjected to different expectations, evaluations, and rewards, and attempts to address these issues, when feasible, to mitigate their impact.

Shared Visioning

Unlike leaders in hierarchically structured organizations, women leaders do not view their authority as a matter of power, nor do they think of themselves as persons in superior positions of formal authority (Werhane, 2007). All of the career women described above are not transactional leaders who view leadership as a series of transactions between managers and employees, a trade of promotion or salary for good performance. Rather, they see leadership as an inspirational "buy-in" from employees. This leadership style is characterized by shared vision, which enables leaders as well as followers to agree on organizational values and goals. This is typically reflected through interactive communication and participatory leadership that empower employees and energize them to achieve corporate goals. The leadership processes emphasized by the women are participatory and coaching, rather than directing and authoritarian. In other words, we argue for women's preferences for transformational roles.

As Table 8.1 shows, women would prefer the transformational CVF leadership-role quadrants: human relations and open systems that correspond to the leadership roles, which are mentor, facilitator, broker, and innovator. These preferences are also consistent with empirical studies that show that women managers displayed a greater affinity for the mentor and broker roles than did male managers. When social affiliation and development goals were added as predictors of leadership styles, women, once again, scored higher than men managers in these two roles showing

TABLE 8.1
Women Leaders: Values and Styles

Elements/ Career Women	Dominant Characteristics	Personal Values	Management Styles	Roles of leadership
Phyllis Apelbaum	Agreeable, Friendly	Equality, Fairness	Human relations, Participatory, Devotion to community	Mentor Facilitator Innovator
Margaret Blackshere	Adventurous, Big-picture	Honest, Diligence, Trust in herself and others	Flexible, Transforming (interactive, participatory) Consensus building	Broker Innovator Mentor Facilitator
Eva Maddox	Creative, Determined, Hard work, Visionary	Fearlessness, Challenge	Personal relations, Care, Communication	Broker Innovator Director Mentor Facilitator
Deborah L. DeHaas	Fast-paced, Do-best, Commitment	Integrity, Commitment to others	Servant leadership (empowerment) Team work, Mentoring	Mentor Facilitator Producer
Alison Chung	Confident, Entrepreneurial	Integrity, Ethics	Interactive, Hiring the right people, Corporate Culture	Mentor Facilitator Director Producer Innovator

preference for feedback, giving and receiving feedback (Kim & Shim, 2003).

Ethics and Integrity

Ethics and integrity seem to encapsulate the many differences between men and women in organizations. Gender identity and ethics seem to converge with the stereotypical notion that in contrast to men who display a sense of self-assertion or independence and interpersonal competitiveness, women who place greater value on involvement are also more ethical than men. In a study involving gender differences in upward influence,

Lauterbach and Weiner (1996) found that in contrast to male managers who tend to act alone and often bargain or compromise on issues, women managers solicit diverse views on issues and therefore have higher self-confidence that they "are doing the right thing" because of greater inclusion of people and perspectives. Therefore male managers, fixated on self-maximizing values, may not have the same sense of moral virtue and the need to develop joint accountability on issues of value to the organization.

The feminine sense of "self" is embedded in social interaction and interpersonal relationships in a way that masculine sense of identity is not. Women have a stronger basis for empathy and relatedness or a sense of interconnectedness built into their identity and norms of behavior. While McCabe, Ingram, and Conway (2006) confirmed in their study that "for both men and women, as expressive traits increase so does their propensity to perceive unethical business situations as unethical" (p. 107) and that except for bribery "biological sex differences do not predict differences in overall ethical perceptions" (p. 108), it is fair to say that gender differences in ethics are of enormous importance as one moves up the hierarchy where top executives are also responsible for life-altering decisions (Belasen, 2008). As Eagly and Carli (2007) have pointed out: among the whistle-blowers who have exposed recent ethical violations in corporate and nonprofit organizations, women are prevalent. Women, more than men, disapprove of unethical business practices such as deceiving behavior, misrepresentation, tacit negotiations, bribery, and corruption.

Feminists have accused business ethics scholars and thinkers of skewed business ethics that justify rather than challenge prevailing practices or calling for change. The feminists criticized business ethics for ignoring women disadvantage and for failing to address prejudice and discrimination rather than question, let alone apologize for, these practices (Larson & Freeman, 1999). One crucial survival skill that successful female leaders have in common is *adaptability*. Women are also more likely than men to engage in conversations, elicit opinions and seek to better understand how their superiors, peers, and subordinates would feel about their influence attempts.

Lauterbach and Weiner (1996) found support for the hypothesis that "among those who perceived their influence attempts to be risky, female managers were significantly more likely than male managers to report concern about interpersonal (political) risk as opposed to personal (career) risk" (p. 99). Men, more than women, are likely to engage in enterprising or self-enhancing behaviors such as personal image and reputation. While women use communication to establish relationships with others, men use communication to advance their interests or reinforce status differences (Tannen, 1990; 1994).

Hail Women Whistleblowers

By Anat Maytal, Crimson Staff Writer, Published: Tuesday, May 03, 2005 (http://www.thecrimson.com/article/2005/5/3/hail-women-whistleblowers -last-week-the/#)

Last week, the documentary "Enron: The Smartest Guys in the Room" was released in movie theaters. A detailed account of one of the biggest business scandals, the documentary has its share of entertaining villains, including Enron chairman Kenneth Lay, former CEO Jeffrey Skilling and CFO Andrew Fastow. Yet, what caught my attention was its sole hero— whistleblower Sherron Watkins—who wrote the memo heard around the world, warning Lay that the company's accounting practices were looking very shady.

Seeing Watkins's movie character brought to mind the 2002 cover of Time Magazine, where Watkins was one of three whistleblowers featured on the front cover of the magazine's "Persons of the Year." The other two whistleblowers included Cynthia Cooper, an internal auditor at WorldCom and FBI agent Coleen Rowley. While Cooper mounted an investigation that revealed the largest known bookkeeping scam in corporate history, misstating earnings by at least $3.8 million, Rowley was the one who disclosed incompetence in counterterrorism efforts before the Sept. 11 attacks.

It could not just be a coincidence that these whistle-blowers, in the most significant examples of government incompetence and corporate wrongdoing in our time, were women.

It takes a particular type of courage—the courage to be unpopular—to become a whistle-blower. Initially, Watkins, Cooper, and Rowley were warned to keep quiet but they kept talking, like generations of female truth-tellers before them. Look at Rosa Parks, who refused to move to the back of the bus, galvanizing the country's civil rights movement.

Retired Army Lt. General Claudia J. Kennedy, the highest-ranking female officer, was the one to expose sexual harassment in the armed forces. And it was Erin Brockovich, a minor legal clerk who helped a town triumph over a multimillion-dollar corporate polluter.

The decision for these women to do what's right over what's convenient comes at a very high price. Whistle-blowers get fired, blacklisted, and branded as troublemakers, making it harder to find new employment. The cost can sometimes be even higher—women in the armed forces and police corps often dread filing sexual harassment claims in fear of backlash by their male colleagues for turning against one of their own.

In fact, the three whistle-blowers—Watkins, Cooper, and Rowley—each served as the chief breadwinners in their families, with husbands who were full-time, stay-at-home fathers. For each of them, the decision to blow the whistle meant jeopardizing a paycheck their families depended on. While Rowley was granted whistle-blower protection, she still expressed concern for reprisals in her letters to FBI chief Robert Mueller. There are no guarantees that whistleblowers will not receive some sort of professional punishment, however subtle.

Perhaps it's because women simply act more ethically than men. A 2002 study by two business professors, James Davis at Notre Dame and Jack Ruhe at St. Mary's College in Indiana, found that female business students value honesty and independence far more than do their male colleagues. What's more, the Conference Board of Canada, an independent research group found that 94 percent of corporate boards with three or more women ensured that their companies had conflict-of-interest guidelines, compared with 68 percent of all-male boards. As for verifying audit information, the figures were 91 percent versus 74 percent.

Yet, at the same time, these whistle-blowers had more in common than just being women. Each of these whistle-blowers were outside the boundaries of real power—close enough to see inside, but far enough to have no say in stopping it. It is true that men can be just as angered by illegal behavior, but as an insider in that world performing that immoral activity; it is not as acceptable for a man to reveal ethical breaches. However, the situation is different for women, who are usually not insiders of that world.

(continued)

According to a 2002 study by the U.S. General Accounting Office, American women now represent close to 47 percent of the workforce but only 12 percent of all managerial positions. Moreover, only 5.2 percent of the highest-earning high-level executives at Fortune 500 companies were women. As a result, women in male-dominated industries feel like outsiders and thus are less likely to assume the posture of the three monkeys of evil innocence: Hear no evil, see no evil, speak no evil.

Anita Hill, a different kind of whistleblower who accused then-Supreme Court nominee Clarence Thomas of sexual harassment, believes that women who move up within male-dominated inside circles hold on to their "outside values." In a 2002 op-ed for the *New York Times*, she noted that women often are not accepted by the top rung of the old boys' network and never will be, so they risk less by speaking up.

Perhaps then it is more than a coincidence that the first brand-name whistle-blower was a woman. In Greek mythology, Cassandra had the gift of prophecy. She correctly predicted the outcome of many events, warning the Trojans, for example, in "The Aeneid," against accepting a wooden horse as a "gift" from their Greek opponents. However, when Cassandra spurned the god Apollo as a lover, he retaliated by making anyone who heard her prophecies believe they were lies. It was mostly men who disbelieved her, leading inevitably to disaster and tragedy as it is written, "Cassandra cried, and curs'd th' unhappy hour/Foretold our fate; but by the god's decree,/All heard, and non believed the prophecy."

But is it possible today things have changed? We'll have to stay tuned for the sequel.

Anat Maytal '05, a Crimson editorial editor, is a government and Women, Gender and Sexuality Studies concentrator in Leverett House.

Source: ©2011 The Harvard Crimson, Inc. All rights reserved. Reprinted with permission.

GSK whistleblower details Cidra plant woes

(January 3, 2011—10:36am ET | By Tracy Staton
©2011 FierceMarkets. All rights reserved.

http://www.fiercepharma.com/story/gsk-whistleblower-details-cidra-plant -woes/2011-01-03)

The woman who raised the red flag on GlaxoSmithKline's (GSK) troubled Cidra, Puerto Rico, plant has now spoken to *60 Minutes*. Cheryl Eckard, whose whistleblower suit yielded last year's $750 million settlement and a guilty plea for one of GSK's subsidiaries, gave the news program a behind-the-scenes look at the problems she observed at the plant and the company's reaction to her criticism.

Eckard was a quality control inspector for the company when she found trouble at Cidra in 2002. According to the *CBS News* coverage, Eckard found a host of mess-ups there. "All the systems were broken, the facility was broken, the equipment was broken, the processes were broken. It was the worst thing I had run across in my career," she told *60 Minutes*. Tainted water was used in manufacturing, production lines were turning out too-potent or not-potent-enough drugs, employees were contaminating products and different medications were packed into the same bottles, she now says.

According to Eckard, she informed GSK's North American VP of quality and told him to shut down the plant, stop the shipments leaving the loading dock that day and notify the FDA. But none of that happened, she says. When she alerted higher-ups to a later mix-up, the company denied it ever happened, she says.

The VP Eckard spoke with is no longer with GSK, and the Cidra plant has long been closed and company leadership changed over since then. Indeed, SVP Ian McCubbin told CBS that the company has "worked really really hard to resolve those issues." GSK regrets the plant's problems, he said, "[b]ut we've learned from it."

Megan—Self-Reflection, Self-Analysis

As a grants professional, things like monitoring program performance, encouraging project compliance, and organizing the flow of information are just part of my daily routine. So as I look through the results of my personal CVF assessments, I was not surprised to learn that my greatest strengths are found in the Control quadrant and only improved from pre- to post-assessment. Another one of my highest competencies falls into the Compete quadrant, particularly "managing execution and driving for results." (Please note the quadrants/roles: Create: Innovator/Broker; Collaborate: Mentor/Facilitator; Control: Monitor/Coordinator; Compete: Director/Producer).

When discussing weaknesses identified within the CVF assessment and illustrated in the above charts, I think that it is important to note, as many discussed the first week of class, that low scores do not necessarily imply that a person is poor at something. Because the CVF assessment questions are framed to ask about success frequency, not knowledge, low scores could simply imply that a person does not have experience in certain competencies.

The lowest score on my CVF self-assessment is in the Collaborate quadrant, more specifically in the competency of "mentoring and developing others." The reason it is the lowest score is because I am not in a position currently where that is a regular job function. I do, however, put a lot of value in helping others develop their skills and look forward to "flexing" that competency in the future. The second lowest score is also where my greatest strengths are—in the Control quadrant—specifically, "working and managing across functions." While the rest of my scores in the Control quadrant are exceptionally high (6.2 to 7), I am not surprised that this particular competency is low. I am honest enough with myself that I can see where I don't always do well when having to manage a project across multiple teams or agency functions. This particular competency is part of my 180-day development plan.

The results from the latest CVF assessment are somewhat surprising to me, as eight weeks ago when this class began, I thought of myself as considerably lacking in the Create quadrant. Not only because my initial scores were quite low in this area, but also because I am aware of my own personal feelings of incompetence in this area. I think my coworkers would tend to agree. Though my scores in the Create quadrant came up considerably in the post-assessment, I still feel like there is a lot of improvement to be made in the quadrant as a whole. For the most part, my scores improved because I now have a better understanding of what the statements mean in their context to the everyday functions of the Innovator and the Broker; in the pre-assessment, I gave myself a 1 if I did not know what was being asked. Many of those scores across quadrants changed at post-assessment. Yet still, when it comes to things like fueling and fostering innovation and implementing and sustaining change, I could improve, and these competencies are also part of my 180-day development plan.

Self-Improvement: 180-Day Plan

I have identified three areas related to the CVF competencies that I will actively work toward improving during the next 180 days: (1) working and managing across functions, (2) fueling and fostering innovation, and (3) implementing and sustaining change. These competencies were identified as areas for improvement as a result of both CVF assessment and personal perception of need. Continuing my education and participation in this graduate program will no doubt give me additional opportunities for improving my organizational leadership capabilities. In the meantime, there are practical applications to consider.

To develop my skill at working and managing across functions, in the next 30 to 60 days I will seek out opportunities to be a better Coordinator and bring together people from different departments to improve accomplishment of tasks in developing grants. Many times I bypass pulling in staff because I've experienced issues of staff disinterest and "I don't get paid to do that" attitudes, not to mention that many times I feel like it would be quicker to complete a project myself. I need to work on altering my thinking about the usefulness of project teams in breaking down the work. I also need to work toward being more open to creating processes that include defined interdepartmental tasks instead of leaving them out altogether. Realistically, I just hope that 180 days in, I can get past any pushback from staff and am able to show steps taken to include others in projects.

In regard to fueling and fostering innovation, I will be taking on new duties at my organization in the next 30 days that is going to push me head first into quickly gaining comfort and skill in this area. As a result of declining revenue and a poor economy, my organization laid off a key development position. This has forced some of us to take on the duties of that job. I recently attended Volunteer Management Institute and will be adding volunteer management to my designated job duties. I have experience in volunteer management from my work at other organizations, so it was a fit for me to take on some of this responsibility. However, my organization does not have a history or culture of utilizing volunteers on a day-to-day basis and I will have to put on my Innovator hat to work with staff to think outside the box and creatively develop new volunteer opportunities. In 30 days to 60 days, I will be working to find innovative approaches to not only help a reluctant staff understand the value of volunteers but find ways to include them in their day-to-day work. Within 180 days, I hope to have the program design in place and solid opportunities available for those looking for service work.

Developing competence in the area of implementing and sustaining change is a long process that is best acquired with longevity and experience. I don't anticipate excelling in this area in just 180 days, but there are small things I can do in the short term to initiate the process of being more open to change in general. For example, this past month we have implemented new donor management software at work. Until now, I have not had access to the donor software and this new system will allow for me to change my grant management process some. I've been hesitant to change and start utilizing the new software, but I will take the initiative to be more open to it. In the next 30 days I will work toward learning the software and in the next 60–180 days I will look at ways to use the software to create sustainable improvement of foundation gift and relationship tracking.

Is It Working?

Peter Drucker once said, "Checking the results of a decision against its expectations shows executives what their strengths are, where they need to improve, and where they lack knowledge or information" (www.brainyquote.com, 2011). Evaluating the success of my improvement plan will require me to look at the decisions I made and determine whether my approach for completing outlined goals is working. Identifying what *doesn't* work is a key ingredient in finding out what does. If I'm open to honest self-reflection and external criticism, I will be able to make the changes necessary to ultimately achieve my goals.

In summary, my current strengths tend to lie in those CVF competencies that I utilize on a daily basis. As a grants manager, those mostly fall in the Control quadrant. Weaknesses tend to be in areas where I have little day-to-day experience, such as facilitating innovation and implementing change, which also leads to a discomfort in practical application of those concepts. Not only do I intend to focus on improving areas of weakness, but I will remind myself to take a holistic improvement approach, continually seeking evaluation of my overall core competencies in order to maintain well-balanced and effective leadership. I know that I won't always make the right decisions, but I am committed to being honest and aware enough to learn from the bad ones.

9

Women's Secret Power

There is no question that both leadership and management are demanding, challenging, and vital to the successful operation of organizations. Management and leadership have different centralities: Management is job-centered; whereas, leadership is employee-centered. Management is defined as the attainment of organizational goals in an effective and efficient manner through planning, organizing, staffing, directing, and controlling organizational resources. A key word in that definition is *control*. Managers use centralized authority for *controlling* and *directing* the behavior of employees to ensure that stability is maintained. In management, the executive serves an operational role; he or she centrally possesses *power*, the *control* over resources, and the responsibility for the outcome of the employees' actions. Leadership is defined as a process of influence.

Leadership and management function in dissimilar ways to ensure organizational livelihood, however, because they aim at distinct outcomes it can be very difficult for one to succeed at leading and managing. The differences between management and leadership create two different outcomes. Management maintains stability, predictability, and order through a *culture of efficiency*; while leadership creates change within a *culture of integrity* that helps the organization thrive over the long haul by promoting openness and honesty, positive relationships, and long-term innovation. It is difficult for people to successfully perform management and leadership simultaneously because the two are conflicting in nature. While one strives for productivity, the other strives for change. Management relies heavily on control, whereas leadership relies on shared authority and the empowerment of subordinates.

It can be very difficult for those who are in management positions to manage the burden of vulnerability, especially in hierarchical organizations that share a top-down culture concerned primarily with power structures and results. Fear of losing control, fear of being let down by subordinates, and fear of losing power status can all affect an executive's ability to trust in subordinates and adopt a whole brain approach to leadership. Empowering subordinates or sharing authority with them requires risk on behalf of the manager, and it exposes the manager to vulnerabilities such as employees behaving opportunistically, acting in ways that benefit themselves rather than the organization, taking advantage of the manager's trust, or, most importantly, employees' ignorance or incompetence. Leadership cannot replace management. In fact, for a company or organization to succeed, leadership and management must irrefutably go hand in hand. The challenge for success in both functions lies in balancing management duties with leadership utilities.

Although "manager" and "leader" are typically considered contrasting ideas and because leadership is not bound by position, in theory anyone in an organization can establish leadership, including a manager. The term manager indicates a transactional, authoritative position derived from the organizational hierarchy that is concerned with internal consistency, procedures and policies, setting goals for employees, and emphasizing the task. A leader on the other hand is transformational, informal, and often assumed organically, not assigned. Leadership is based on interacting with others to create a shared reality, influencing and structuring attitudes, helping followers identify their value systems and emphasizing people rather than the task. A transformational leader is described as having behaviors that "communicate the organization's missions, examine new perspectives for solving problems, and develop and mentor followers" (Valerio, 2009, p. 34).

The Paradox of Downplaying Transformational Leadership

Some of the stereotypes about women's leadership have come into existence precisely because of the falsehood that men and women are essentially different. Old arguments that men are naturally tough, strong, and independent while women are weak, emotional, caring, and dependent still have a strong hold on the world of employment. White males have largely been the "authorial voice of leadership in the USA" and the establishment of good leadership practice "has been considered to be the techniques and procedures of white male administrators" (Isaac, Behar-Horenstein & Koro-Ljungberg, 2009). These "implicit biases that stereotypically masculine behaviors are required for effective leadership remain strong" and give males a distinct advantage because their inherent values and demeanor are consistent with this "good leadership practice." This is the first reason that women might downplay transformational roles in traditional fields. Women who have been able to succeed and "break through" have often assumed traditionally male leadership roles, describing themselves as "male-like" and even stating "I don't act like a woman."

In a qualitative study on ten women deans from both male-dominated and female-dominated colleges, several overarching themes were discovered. Women identified male mentors, even in the female-dominated colleges. Indeed, while male managers prefer job experience as a source of learning, women value coaching and mentoring. Experiential vicarious learning seems to fit well for women's success more so than experiential learning alone.

In addressing the contradiction of the necessity of leadership skills when going from lower management to upper management these women felt they were able to learn by doing/adapting and most remarked that they did not set out to be leaders, it just happened. Regardless of the environment, the respondents cited concerns for the "greater good"; however, the language the women used signaled a contradiction that was filled with the masculine discourse of achievement and hierarchy. The language these women used reflected a paradox—on one hand they wanted to generate power by empowering others and creating change via their reproductive roles, and yet at the same time they spoke of leadership in terms of productivity and "winning" difficult situations (Isaac, Behar-Horenstein & Koro-Ljungberg, 2009).

A second reason women might downplay transformational roles is the difficulty of the balancing act between representing masculine qualities without "gender-bending." Gender-bending is violating socially acceptable gender roles, thereby making others feel uncomfortable. In the case of deans in male-dominated colleges, they reported downplaying sensitivity and emotion to succeed. In contrast, a dean from a female-dominated college remarked on how she felt she had "alienated" many of her female coworkers because she was "too different" and often had to be reminded to be more sensitive and caring to relate (Isaac, Behar-Horenstein & Koro-Ljungberg, 2009). Likewise, in a study done on faculty members' views of women chairs in the medical field, one senior female member remarked "She doesn't have all the interpersonal skills to make you feel warm and fuzzy . . . and sometimes isn't schmoozing enough" (Isaac, Carnes & Griffin, 2010).

Third, women are likely to downplay transformational roles and behaviors because of the scrutiny they are undeniably subject to. By assuming an upper-management position, a woman becomes a violation of the norm, and is therefore not defined solely by her job title but also by the fact that she is a woman. This adds to the fear of risk-taking necessary for innovation and change because of a feeling, often warranted, that skeptics are waiting for them to fail and that failure would also let down the women they represent. One woman remarked, "I think it's harder to be a leader in my profession which is a very male profession so I've tried to always compensate by being twice as good . . . I think that women are scrutinized more and critiqued more and if something gets messed up it's easy for the guys to say, 'see I told you so' " (Isaac, Behar-Horenstein & Koro-Ljungberg, 2009).

The result is a communication paradox: people view women leaders differently than they view themselves. Women must be adaptable and often downplay their transformational nature to succeed and blend, but when doing so others view them as lacking transformational roles or presenting socially unacceptable gender roles. Whose picture is more accurate, the leaders or followers? This is a difficult question to answer and being that the contingency approach suggests the effectiveness of a leader is contingent on organizational situations, it is likely a combination of both.

Women and Transactional Leadership

Interestingly, Belasen and Frank (2012) found a different viewpoint—women rated themselves higher in the Competition and Internal Process quadrant. Indeed, women and others perceive women's role strengths differently. If one considers this finding more rationally and critically, women's perception is significantly associated with the barrier they have been facing. Women cannot be good or behave strongly in all quadrants, because of the negative image of women given by society. Clearly, there is no win-win situation for women. If women are strong in the Human Relation quadrant, they will fall right into the gender stereotype of women with regard to being emotional and weak. If they decide to focus strongly on rational goals, they will be seen as aggressive and undesirable. Strength in the Vision quadrant will cause them to be seen as wishy-washy and indecisive. The only quadrant left seems to be the Internal Process quadrant, because they are able to avoid contradicting with common beliefs toward feminism.

As a result, a majority of women are now trying to perform their best on managing skills (Internal Process and Rational Goal quadrants), whereas men can be good at any quadrant in CVF. The empirical study by Ibarra and Obodaru (2008) has also shown that male peers gave female leaders the lowest scores on vision (p. 6). Vision is one of the top requirements of high-level leadership. The fact that others view women as lacking vision is not a good sign, because it shows that they do not have confidence in the leadership role of women as well.

The most difficult barrier for women to overcome with regard to being good at both management and leadership is women themselves. Even though women were found to be stronger in a producer role (Parker, 2004), scored higher in conscientiousness (Cavallo & Brienza, 2006), detailed (Irby, Brown, Duffy & Trautman, 2002), and analytical (Hays, Allinson & Armstrong, 2004), women can still learn and develop their leadership vision and innovativeness. Women can be good at both management and leadership. Problems including cultural stereotypes and self-limiting barriers prevent them from being successful in their careers (Carr-Ruffino, 2005). On the way up the corporate ladder, women often get caught in the stereotype trap that relies too much on what male leadership, behavior, or perspectives are like. This trap prevents women from reaching their full potential in both management and leadership, and also hinders them from pursuing a higher-level goal in their career.

Peer pressure also takes its toll on women's success efforts to climb up the hierarchy. Leadership roles have always been conditioned by a social structure, traditionally dominated by men (Lips, 2009). Women can't go any further if their peers and followers do not support them. As a result, women are departing executive positions. A survey of 103 women voluntarily leaving executive jobs in Fortune 1000 companies found that corporate culture was the number-one reason for leaving. Indeed, the greatest disadvantages for women leaders stem largely from prejudicial attitudes and a heavily male-oriented corporate culture (Daft, 2011, p. 340).

Life Cycle Perspective on Career Development

Similar to the leveling process described by Belasen and Frank (2012) where gender differences decrease as managerial levels increase, Daft (2011) describes how individuals move through five stages of "ethnocentric attitude" cycle. At stage one, differences are seen as a threat against their own comfortable world view and frequently use negative stereotyping or express prejudicial attitudes, while at stage two differences are minimized as much as possible and "leaders don't adequately recognize or respond to the challenges minorities and women face in the organizations" (Daft, 2011, p. 350).

As more organizations transition into the third through fifth stages of "ethnocentric attitude," a change in organizational culture and an increase in the number of women in upper-level positions are expected. In the third stage of "ethnocentric attitude," leaders become proactive and acknowledge that addressing issues of gender, race, disability, and so forth is important not just for the minority employees but also for the health of the organization. Nonetheless, a majority of organizations are still at stage two; where "people attempt to minimize differences and focus on the similarities among all people [and] leaders don't adequately recognize or respond to the challenges minorities or women face in the organization" (Daft, 2011, p. 350).

Organizations really start to become more transformational and more inclusive and empathetic in stage four. However, it is only at stage five that organizations fully integrate diversity and leaders have incentives to create inclusive cultures in organizations that are gender- and color-blind.

O'Neil and Bilimoria's (2005) approach to matching women's career cycle with a differential coaching focus on issues of achievement and confidence as well as work-life balance and self-development goals is particularly relevant. Women's careers typically begin with an idealistic achievement phase followed by a pragmatic endurance and continues with a reinventive contribution phase. At different stages of their careers, women are faced with challenges and the need to balance family and personal interests with career and growth goals. Placing a priority on family life may lead to a temporary suspension of work life. A focus on career may also hinder or delay stated family goals. Given the unique contingencies faced by women, personal coaching that evolves around the holistic nature of women's career cycle and development would be beneficial (Hopkins, O'Neil, Passarelli & Bilimoria, 2008)

Facing the Reality of "Small Numbers"

Evidently women are now holding three times as many managerial positions than they did a decade ago (Parkhouse, 2001), and more women are rising into leadership roles at all levels, including elite executive roles (Eagly & Carli, 2003). Even though women have a barrier that prevents them from being successful at both management and leadership, it is reasonable to believe that women have demonstrative competencies in the two sets of roles. Unfortunately, despite the fact that companies have shown a greater commitment to diversity and inclusion and advancement of women in the workplace, the representation of women in leadership positions remains stagnant (David, 2006). Overall, as more corporate cultures adjust (in part by recognizing diversity and accepting cultural differences), more and more women climb the corporate ranks to the top.

Success in management, whether male or female, is less challenging to achieve than success in leadership. Leadership demands personal mastery, innovation, transparency, and among other things concern for personal relationships that are absent in the execution of management. Fear, lack of determination, and lack of skills are all possible reasons for why an individual may fail at leadership, but the fact that management provides comfort through control and positioning power may better explain why so few people succeed at simultaneously accomplishing the contradictory components of both management and leadership; it is easier to maintain than it is to change from the inside out. Likewise, success in management does not necessarily translate as evidence that managers can succeed at higher levels. If you continue to concentrate on doing what you do best, you may not create the impression that you have the skills needed for upper-level positions. On the other hand, if you do not focus on the competencies to support your current job, you create the impression that you do not have the capacity to handle higher-level jobs, let alone senior-level positions. To be upwardly mobile in today's corporate world, one must show not only competency in their current role, but also exhibit qualities that are required at higher levels.

Nevertheless one can assume that women managers in the future will have a clear advantage and will be more likely to succeed in positions of transformational leadership. The reason: Western men are being oppressed by gender roles as well. They are pressured from a young age not to show emotion, not to compete and be tough, and while this benefited them in the traditional "machine" organization, as organizations change they are being set-up for failure at transformational roles. Women, on the other hand, have proved that they not only possess skills required for managerial roles, they often have the debatably innate traditional female roles that are consistent with transformational values. It is clear, however, that old habits die hard and those remnants of the patriarchal organization will not simply go away, making attaining upper-level positions difficult. Women would do well to learn from the example of the women who have risen to the top because, unlike those women who had only male role models and counterparts to identify with, they have the benefit of strong female figures to aspire to be like. In the near future, hopefully, women who possess a well-rounded CVF and strong adaptability skills will begin to break through to the upper echelons of management in greater numbers.

Striving for the Higher Levels: Two Accounts

The following self-analyses are from two individuals, female and male managers, both targeting upper leadership position in his organization as well as describe their aspirations and plans to move up the corporate ladder. Notice how the starting points for the two managers were somewhat different; however, their conclusions are almost identical including the need to promote and sustain the skills associated with the broker and innovator.

Ana

Being promoted is a recognition obtained for meeting institutional objectives and functions that have changed in complexity and responsibility.

Everyone has dreams of one day being promoted to the position that he/she has worked hard to reach. However, moving up the ladder requires people to be successful in their current position and excel in that position before looking for an upper-level promotion. Finding out what exactly is expected to be promoted is always beneficial.

As there are more highly competitive professionals, it is imperative to prove exceptional performance capabilities and consistently show a positive attitude that demonstrates perseverance to succeed. Ultimately, it is people's responsibility to create and manage their career path. Nevertheless, to have a successful career, individuals have to meet the demands of radical change within an organization's environment. Organizations go through restructuring, process enhancements, mergers, acquisitions, and layoffs in the hopes of achieving revenue growth and profitability. Constant change can be confusing and demoralizing; however, individuals' personal competencies can contribute so that an organization can operate successfully and continue in a clear direction.

Organizations look for qualified, competent individuals; particularly individuals who have managerial potential. The goal is that potential candidates will develop managerial skills to assume future executive responsibilities. Individuals have to assess their development needs and then match those needs to specific developmental experiences. The Competing Values Framework is a useful tool that is used to measure desired results. In fact, leadership development programs look to ensure that candidates excel in competencies and capabilities that exist in different quadrants of the CVF. The particular leadership tools and techniques that receive emphasis with leaderships groups are often determined by the organization's own culture, aspirations for change, competencies of the senior leadership team, or the data feedback that individuals receive from various assessments. This type of program certainly provides candidates with an institutional framework that will help them to perform successfully as an organization's executive.

Furthermore, success in obtaining top management jobs still depends on competences in one's field of expertise. Managers need to have a solid record of success as evidence that he/she is a competent manager. However, for managers to bring greater success to their employees, shareholders, vendors, customers, and overall to society, they need to address diverse problems, threats, and opportunities that affect organizations' progress and profitability. Consequently, to face these challenges, managers must understand their strengths and weaknesses before they can function as effective leaders. The most successful leaders have highly developed skills in the quadrants that are congruent with their organization's dominant culture. It is difficult to align skills with an organization that is constantly changing. Exercising leadership and management skills in a complex environment is a formidable task. The proper knowledge on how to act in problematic situations is only acquired through experience. Very often, companies fail to stay competitive when confronted with disruptive market and technological change. Yet, good leaders are responsible for facing changes to execute organizational strategies.

The company I work for concentrates on military contracts. This organization leads the industry by embracing the creation of new technology. Nonetheless, the organization also aligns Collaborate (Human Relations), Compete (Rational Goal), and Control (Internal Processes) quadrants in an efficient way that allows the company to remain competitive. The CVF self-assessment has helped me to recognize areas of improvement that will allow me to align my objectives with the ones the company strives for. I realize that even though my job as a software engineer requires me to align my competencies with the Creative quadrant (i.e., open systems), I also have to align my competencies with Collaborate, Compete, and Control quadrants if I want to meet with the organization's objectives. Although it is difficult to balance these quadrants, it is important for the success of my organization.

Most certainly, the key to being successful in this company is having the ability to embrace an environment that is constantly adapting to change. To help my company to remain ahead of the competition, I need to act proactively to develop and implement new ways of achieving project success. The post-assessment Creative quadrant has shown an improvement in the innovator and broker role from a 5.0 to 5.5 and 4.2 to 4.7 respectively. In the Create quadrant, the innovator role behaviors consist of fostering a creative environment and creating change. The Broker role behaviors consist of building and maintaining a power base, presenting ideas and negotiating agreement and commitment. Working for this company has helped me to recognize that innovation is crucial for organizations that want to have an opportunity at competing in challenging markets. Yet, an uncertain future may hold opportunities as well as threats. I definitely feel responsible for creating ideas and I am committed to performing to my full potential to execute organizational strategies.

Moreover, since technology is always changing, it is expected that the industry in which my company competes will change. The company needs to move forward and keep a leading edge in designing tools so that competitors don't undercut and acquire competitive advantage. The business is frequently changing, but the company has been able to reinvent itself to remain competitive and innovative. I believe that it is important for me to be aware of what is currently happening in the industry. In this way, I can provide measurable value to our clients. My assessment indicates no improvement in the roles of Producer and Director—from 5.0 to 5.0 and 5.0 to 5.0 respectively. In the Compete quadrant, the Producer role behaviors consist of working productively, managing time and stress, and fostering a productive work environment. The Director role behaviors consist of designing and organizing work including delegation and envisioning the future, and setting goals. I recognize that it is crucial for me not to get too comfortable doing the same things that have gotten me where I am. I am a decision maker that bases my decisions on experience; but growing a business entails doing things that are not necessarily based in what the company has done in the past. It is true that markets change but change also means opportunity. For this reason, I have to concentrate on taking initiative and helping our clients make good decisions that will help our company stay up-to-date by expanding presence on online Web sites.

Through process improvements our company has been able to stay competitive and adaptable to change. Our company was affected by a program cancellation that led to restructuring and layoffs. As a result, site specific processes and procedures had to be eliminated. The goal was to adapt a unified process and a common system that will allow the company to be more cost effective. Process innovation definitely helped the company to sustain competitive advantage. CVF assessment shows improvement in the Monitor and Coordinator roles—from 5.0 to 5.2 and 4.4 to 4.8 correspondingly. The Control quadrant indicates that the Monitor role behaviors consist of monitoring collective and organizational performance while monitoring individual performance. The Coordinator role behaviors consist of managing projects and design work processes across functional areas. As a software engineer, I worked to monitor the performance and availability of the new system; however, I knew that for the system to be successful I needed to work with our clients to reach a common process. As a team we knew that we needed to deliver dramatic results in process improvement. The roadmap to success needed to eliminate the barriers of various cultures, systems, and processes to create an environment of continuous improvement.

Our company had to respond to complex challenges; success would not have been possible without the contribution of various talents, insights, and efforts of employees. Innovative solutions came from individuals that were able to work with an open mind to quickly validate and pursue a solution. The implementation of new initiatives could be executed with strong technical skills, but results would not be attained without individuals with strong communication skills. The assessment shows that there is an improvement in the Mentor and Facilitator roles—from 4.7 to 5.5 and 4.6 to 5.0 correspondingly. The Collaborate quadrant illustrates that the Mentor role behaviors consist of understanding others, communicating effectively, and developing followers. The Facilitator role behaviors consist of building effective teams, facilitating participative decision-making, and managing conflict. This assessment has helped me understand that to be successful in my company, I need the ability to gain cooperation from stakeholders to accomplish project goals. The challenge, I think, is becoming influential enough to bring the project's vision into a workable plan. I understand that it will be very hard to persuade others without strong communication skills.

That being said, I possess the basic knowledge and had limited experience applying influence. I know how to apply the general knowledge but I have limited practical experience in building effective teams. I have important technical skills; yet, only experience will help me gain a broader management perspective. It is important to have personal integrity and develop leadership skills. Team members respect leaders who know how to exercise authority; they need to believe in their leaders, both in terms of the leaders' competence and ethical character. I recognize that I have to prove that I can be trusted before I can start influencing people. By applying competency repeatedly and successfully, I will be able to advance my career. Most of all, I will be able to influence the project team culture and develop more productive relationships with stakeholders.

Significant change requires continuous adaptation to remain ahead of competition. Employees' ability to rapidly adapt to restructuring and leadership will demonstrate my company's agility and innovation. Everyone in the organization is invested in its success; we are all responsible for implementing new ideas that can lead our company to achieve its objectives. Dr. Belasen states that successful managers know how to navigate across the roles to balance the demands from different environments on the organization (Belasen, 2000). Trying alternative paths, and testing ideas to the point of failure, requires people who are encouraged to balance all the CVF quadrants. Like the organization, we must be agile, continually changing, and ready to learn.

Now that I am aware of my strengths and weaknesses, I will try to improve leadership behaviors especially in the area of teachable confidence. In the program with Dr. Belasen, I realized that I base decisions on my skills. There is so much more I can learn from my peers. I definitely admire them for being open to listen to someone else's input. I am hoping to one day become a manager who learned from others as well as her mistakes. Good business training and understanding of the CVF have taught me how to approach problems in my career. Also, beyond focusing on business development studies, I would like to expand my technical skills. Overall, I have to think about how I can make changes that will eventually take me where I want to be.

Dave's Managerial Profile: Similar Assessment and Development Plans

I am being considered for a recently vacated leadership position at an academic institution. In my application letter, I was asked to identify what made me uniquely qualified for this leadership role. In addition to my years of experience as an educator coupled with positive evaluations from my supervisor and faculty evaluations from students, I was able to point out several non-teaching competencies and qualities including instructional design, team leadership, committee leadership, and financial management. It was my contention that these extracurricular competencies made me an ideal candidate for upward mobility and entrance into the college's management levels. As part of the development program with Dr. Belasen I have taken two CVF Assessments with the following results (Table 9.1).

In analyzing the results of my assessments, it appears that while my strongest skills are in the Mentor, Innovator, and Facilitator roles, the

TABLE 9.1
Results of CVF Assessment

Role	Desired	Current	Gap	% change
Mentor	6.7	5.7	1	15
Innovator	5.7	5.5	0.2	4
Broker	5	4	1	20
Producer	5.2	4.6	0.6	12
Director	5	4.2	0.8	16
Coordinator	5.8	4.8	1	17
Monitor	5.2	4.7	0.5	10
Facilitator	5.8	5.2	0.6	10

greatest opportunities for improvement are in Broker, Coordinator, Director, and Mentor roles, showing that I do have a broad cross-section of qualities in all areas of the CVF. These results are consistent with my earlier analysis of chief academic officers in general being in the upper portions of the CVF.

Scope, not gender or perceptions, is key. The ability to look forward, identify possible opportunities, and further identify what competencies and skills are associated with those opportunities is the first steps to reaching the higher levels. The next step is to get into a position to acquire, practice and exhibit those competencies while at the same time maintaining a good balance with existing roles and responsibilities. These steps can be accomplished with the help of a mentor, through the discussion of goals with supervisors and managers, and with good intuition and research about the roles, opportunities, and careers being sought.

Making Boardrooms Smarter

The elements of behavioral complexity of women's leadership help mold more resilient and flexible leadership competencies in boardrooms and executive suites. As the findings of new research on collective intelligence and social sensitivity has recently proved, the more women in the group, the more intelligent the group (*Times Union*, Albany, NY, Oct. 11, 2010, A11). As potential and able as female leaders and managers are, women should exercise flexibility and view obstacles in an innovative context that allows them to acknowledge their struggle on the path to top-level executive leadership positions as a bump in the road to success. Stories of successful women executives who navigated their organizations strategically through sustained growth while overcoming negative stereotyping are described in the next chapter.

10

When It Comes to Leadership, Women Rule

The following are examples of successful women leaders in the media and technology industries who have demonstrated extraordinary talents in initiating and leading change and transformation in their organizations.

Meg Whitman: Change Architect

Meg Whitman, CEO of Hewlett Packard and former President and CEO of eBay Inc., is a perfect example of a change architect. Her leadership style contains many overlapping characteristics of both the Broker and the Innovator CVF roles. Prior to her success at eBay, Whitman served as General Manager of Hasbro Inc., was President and CEO of FTD (Florist Transworld Delivery), and President of Stride Rite Corp.'s Stride Rite Division. Her accolades include being named one of the world's *One Hundred Most Influential People* in 2004 and 2005 by *Time* magazine, one of 25 most powerful people in business and the second most powerful woman in American business in 2004 by *Fortune Magazine*, and ranked number one on *Worth* magazine's 2002 list of *Best CEOs*.

Whitman's major characteristics and qualities as an effective leader include: remaining a steady presence and constantly upbeat, remaining calm but ambitious, moving quickly to defend her company's turf as well as always looking to broaden it, remaining firmly in control of the fast-growing market for online auctions, charming customers by informing them of site changes and welcoming their feedback, possessing tremendous brand and consumer instincts, being mindful of the competition, collaborative yet decisive, serious but loose, and drawing strength from her family. Whitman's style of leadership was instrumental in setting the tone for eBay to expand exponentially within a relatively short period of time from its "flea market" roots to becoming the world's online marketplace and the number one consumer e-commerce site.

With strong vision in place, Whitman reinvigorated eBay's corporate culture by avoiding top-down command tactics that assume she knows everything, and instead remained open to new ideas. She also understood from the beginning what was to be the heart of eBay's success—eBay provides the marketplace, but it is the users who build the company, who bring the product to the site, merchandise it, and then distribute it once it has been sold. Whitman's keen insight recognizes that it is eBay's army of users who figure out what is hot before the top executives even know. Whitman, showing the qualities of a broker, worked with others creating strategic alliances when she and her team deepened the company's relationship with AOL, eventually making eBay AOL's exclusive auction provider. This was a great way to connect to AOL users, and it also prevented AOL from becoming a rival. She also purchased Billpoint, an on-line system that allows payment by e-mail, developed eBay's advertising strategy; recruited executives; and pushed for stores and companies to use eBay as their outlets; as well as installing trust and safety programs that offers insurance to buyers.

Oprah Winfrey: Most Admired Entrepreneur

Oprah Winfrey, founder and CEO of Harpo Productions Inc., and the richest self-made woman in America, is another example. Winfrey started from scratch and built an entire multimedia production empire. As a black woman, her attempt at success was even more precarious. However, the remarkable leadership traits she exhibited in her business development resulted in her incredible success. Oprah's achievements largely depend on her vision setting and groundbreaking moves. She represents a brand of business leadership focusing on long-term value creation, rather than on merely meeting the short-term profit projections. Over the past 15 years, she developed an entire set of partnerships and spin-offs. In the midst of these accomplishments, her team could barely imagine what the next greatness would be. In an interview with the magazine *Black Enterprise*, she remarked that divine inspiration, not strategic planning, was the catalyst for her company's success. Her success formula took Harpo Inc., from a five-person production team to a 430-employee multimedia conglomerate that grossed $345 million in 2007 (Black Enterprise, 2008).

Winfrey's most unique leadership style is her ability to transform and empower her followers. Her capacity to bridge human connections distinguishes her as a transforming leader. When speaking in front of millions of individuals in her TV audience, she has the ability and charisma to elevate their needs and promote dramatic change in them. She communicates values via her media productions that have far-reaching ideological consequences and thus transform and effect change (Klenke, 2001).

Oprah Winfrey exemplifies the value of servant leadership that transcends self-interest to serve the needs of others, help others grow, and provide opportunities for others to gain materially and emotionally. "The only reason to do anything at this point is to be of some service to other people. I'm already in millions of homes each day. I certainly have enough attention, enough money, and enough fame. The only reason (to be so open) is that you can use your life experience to enlighten someone else's" (Koehn and Helms, 2005, p. 17).

Yang Lan: "The Oprah of China"

Oprah Winfrey's remarkable success makes her a role model for women entrepreneurs all over the world. Her Chinese counterpart in the industry, Yang Lan, crowned as "China's Oprah," has also achieved equally glamorous success in her own media business that ranked her the richest female entrepreneur in China by *Forbes Magazine*. Yang Lan and her husband co-founded *Sun Media Investment Holdings Ltd.*, one of China's most prominent private media groups. The business spans television production, newspaper and magazines, as well as on-line publishing. Like Winfrey, Yang is also featured as a strong vision setter who stressed growth, change, and adaptability in her business practices. Her signature talk show, *Her Village*, broke new ground in Chinese television industry— it was the first real women's programming of its kind in China. Over the past decade, Yang has bought and sold, opened and closed properties ranging from print newspapers to new Web sites under the umbrella of Sun Media (Rabkin, 2010).

Although Yang does not experience the same racial discrimination as Winfrey from the Chinese cultural background, the depressing political landscape in China has made her road to success a very rocky one. Yang's innovation and adaptability as a transforming leader also fits with the new market economy that characterizes China's booming growth today. The development of the Chinese media, which appears to be driven by the market force, is essentially the result of the Party's reconfiguration of its regime control in the media industry. Strict censorship still persists, and any media disclosure that challenges the ruling regime is sanctioned in some way. By results, Yang possesses the charisma and personal attributes to influence people. As a Chinese TV host, Yang has gained access to high-profile people across cultures, many of whom are movers and shakers in Western countries, to appear on her celebrity show. In fact, she has astonishingly secured interviews that even China's state-run TV stations cannot land (Rabkin, 2010).

Amy Trask: Most Powerful Woman in NFL

The sports arena is undoubtedly dominated by men. Male athletes, owners, managers, and even fans are often more popular and well known in this field than their female counterparts (if any at all). There are, however, women in the background who shaped the sporting world. One of them is Amy Trask, the CEO of the Oakland Raiders. Her standout performance in board meeting presentations landed her the opportunity to continue as counsel for the football team, and she later assumed the CEO position. Many consider Trask to be a powerful figure in the NFL due to the leadership style she displays and the values she conveys to the rest of the NFL franchise (SI, 10.14.2002). Her educational background includes a political science degree from the University of California at Berkley and a law degree from the University of Southern California. Trask has been described as possessing a stubbornness that is often mistaken as being rude or an unwillingness to listen to others—a double-bind paradox in action?

Ellen Kullman's Quest to Make DuPont Great Again

(Fortune)—The announcement that Ellen Kullman would rise from DuPont's executive ranks to CEO within weeks couldn't have happened at a worse moment. It was made in the historically terrible month of

September 2008, when, as Kullman says, "the world fell apart." For her, the year that followed was somber, matching the gray-to-black national pattern. She oversaw two restructurings, regretfully dismissed thousands of employees, and asked the rest to take a two- to three-week holiday without pay. Kullman, 54, never lost her ready sense of humor nor her laugh, which is big and ringing. But for sure, little about her first year was a laughing matter.

If we assume this target is hit, success needs to be kept in perspective. In 2009, DuPont earned $1.92 per share (compared with a recent stock price of $39). If the $1.92 is to be compounded by an average 20% per year, earnings in 2012 must at least hit $3.32. That would still leave DuPont a bit short of the $3.38 it made four years ago, in 2006, when recession was only a shadowy threat.

At the same time, it's hard to regard Kullman's goal as in the bag, because streaks of good earnings have long been rare at this enterprise. In the past 50 years only four of the nine CEOs who preceded her managed to pull off the three-year, 20% gains she's talking about. And not a single one of those men managed in the fourth year to post a gain—of any size.

Kullman's earnings quest is also an apt metaphor for her broader challenge as CEO: to restore the prestige of one of the most illustrious and innovative companies in American history. In truth, DuPont's legacy is so glorious that no CEO seems likely to restore it. But if Kullman can jolt profits, she can give DuPont a momentum it hasn't had for decades.

Dupont's decline is visible in the decreasing ranking on the Fortune 500. The company ranked 10th in the first list, in 1955. Today it's 86th. Not that there's anything wrong with that, to quote the old Seinfeld line. With $27 billion in revenues and $1.8 billion in profits, DuPont remains both a major multinational and the corporate home of celebrated brands such as today's hits: Kevlar, Nomex, and Tyvek.

A half-century ago, it would have been almost impossible to overstate DuPont's importance. It had, and still has, the richest history in corporate America. Founded on the banks of Delaware's Brandywine River in 1802—if you're counting, that's 208 years ago—DuPont grew up with this country. Its founder, Eleuthère Irénée du Pont, and Thomas Jefferson

(*continued*)

were friends and correspondents, and E.I. and his descendants (who call themselves "du Pont," while the company now renders the name "DuPont") became corporate royalty and a dominant force in Delaware. DuPonts and their inlaws ran the operation for 165 years before ceding the reins to non–family members.

The company grew rich from gunpowder in its first century, and in the second transformed itself into a chemical manufacturer and investor. For years, DuPont controlled General Motors and when trouble hit, put Alfred Sloan in to run it. DuPont gave us nylon before World War II and helped bring that conflict to an end by building uranium and plutonium plants for the Manhattan Project.

Even its slogan—"Better things for better living . . . through chemistry"—was famous. Similarly, the DuPont Way of Doing Business connoted efficiency and sensational profit margins that exceeded 20% in the early days of the Fortune 500 (and that were beaten by very few companies). Businessmen came to Wilmington for daylong tutorials on DuPont financial concepts. Warren Buffett remembers sitting through one in 1967, in company with a Berkshire Hathaway (BRKA, Fortune 500) textile executive who was a rayon customer of DuPont's.

But by that time, in a point not stressed in the tutorials, competition and diminished payoffs from its research dollars had chiseled away at DuPont's imperial margins. As if they were on some long, gentle ski run, the margins slowly dropped, even dipping below 4% in the mid-1970s. The norm today is respectably higher: between 6% and 11% over the past five years. Still, the past few decades have largely taken DuPont out of the public conversation and exposed it for what it is: a cyclical-in-spots, inordinately complex, research-oriented conglomerate fighting for every dollar of profit it can get.

Nothing puts DuPont's position in starker relief than a comparison of its total return (stock appreciation plus dividends) against those of the 19 corporations identified in its proxy statement as its "peer group." The 19 include companies with a reputation in technology and science research, among them 3M (MMM, Fortune 500), Procter & Gamble (PG, Fortune 500), Abbott Laboratories (ABT, Fortune 500), and Monsanto (MON, Fortune 500). (Don't look for Dow (DOW, Fortune 500) on the list: DuPont sees it as too chemical and too commodity.)

Over the past 25 years—as well as the past five, 10, 15, and 20— DuPont ends up third from the bottom of the list. The company (buoyed, as is the whole group, by the bull market that sustained most of this period) had an annualized return of 9.45% for the 25 years. That sounds decent; bull markets do help. But the return puts DuPont miles below the list's leader, Johnson & Johnson (JNJ, Fortune 500), at 16.5%. More telling, only Motorola (MOT, Fortune 500) and Eastman Kodak (EK, Fortune 500) had worse records than DuPont, and who wants to be grouped with them?

Some might blame part of this underperformance on more than a decade of reinvention. These days, DuPont regards itself as a "science company," one that is ardently "green" in thinking. Most of this reinvention was driven by Kullman's predecessor, Charles "Chad" Holliday Jr., a personable Tennessean who was CEO from 1998 through 2008. He talked merger with Monsanto for a bit, then swerved into buying and selling businesses as if he had a compass in his hand that pointed every direction except where DuPont had been. Sold:Conoco, pharmaceuticals, and— most traumatically—the hallowed core of the company, nylon and textiles. Bought: seed producer Pioneer, an enterprise that put DuPont into an entirely new business, one dominated by the same company, Monsanto, with which DuPont had discussed a merger. The logic of the 1999 Pioneer purchase was that there is only so much arable land in the world; yields on it need to be maximized, and DuPont has the scientific talent for the work.

For shuffling the deck so vigorously, Holliday is sometimes viewed within DuPont as a "visionary." But if his concept of creating a sustainable company is to pay off, it will be Kullman or someone else who makes that happen . . . DuPont's stock fell from $57 to $25. Solid dividends undid some of that damage (DuPont has not missed a payout in more than a century) but not enough to cure the pain.

The person charged with consigning this sorry record to the ashcan is Kullman, a savvy operator who appears to be proving that you can go home again. Born Ellen Jamison, she grew up in Wilmington, where she captained her basketball team at prep school Tower Hill and was a math whiz as a student. But as an 18-year-old, she hated Wilmington, she says, because she found it claustrophobic. Her parents always knew what she

(continued)

was doing. And with 26 first cousins on her mother's side alone, she seemed to have family everywhere. So she fled north to college, earning a mechanical engineering degree from Tufts.

After graduation, working as a Westinghouse sales representative near Chicago and covering such establishments as U.S. Steel's famous Gary, Ind., plant, she got her first taste of big business and dealing with customers. She loved it but soon recognized that she had large gaps in her knowledge—how to price, for example. So she signed up for night classes at Northwestern's Kellogg business school, working days to finance her tuition. There she met Michael Kullman, a University of Missouri civil engineering graduate who was a full-time day student at Kellogg—"running up debt," she laughs, "that I eventually helped him repay."

Ellen and Mike married and became a dual-career couple, both joining General Electric (GE, Fortune 500) in 1983 as marketing trainees. Ellen was soon made an assistant to Charles Sheehan, a vice president of corporate strategy who was a troubleshooter for a doughty pair, CEO Jack Welch and vice chairman Ed Hood. Kullman, then 28, occasionally sat in on meetings with the two and says she soaked up knowledge about how GE made things work. (Both men say they have no real memory of her.)

Her retired boss, Sheehan, sounding a bit bowled over by how far this kid has gone, recalls her as "very young" when she worked for him but also energetic, gifted, and sure of herself. He remembers one night when a GE group was meeting customers for dinner in Tokyo and was running late. Kullman sped upstairs to her hotel room and raced back with freshly washed hair that Sheehan remembers as just short of dripping. He thought to himself that she must have "enormous self-confidence" to go out looking like that. And that evening, he says, she was just "dynamite" with the customers.

DuPont came into the Kullmans' picture after both became marketing managers in 1986 for GE's medical systems business in Milwaukee. Ellen's marketing responsibility was CT scanners, and the product brought her in touch with people in DuPont's medical imaging business, who offered her a marketing manager post. She was intrigued, partly because she and Mike, then jointly anchored in one division, were starting to bump into each other and to realize that one of them was probably going to end up working for the other someday. They figured she could join DuPont, and he could land at another Wilmington company or in a nearby city, like Philadelphia. But DuPont pointed out that it had 15 different businesses based in Wilmington. Why couldn't Mike work for one that had nothing to do with Ellen's? And so he did, taking a marketing post in another DuPont division. You might judge it a totally rational plan, as long as one Kullman or the other didn't rise to the corporate executive suite.

That's how, in 1988, Ellen and Mike, both settled in for the long term at DuPont. Mike is a director of corporate marketing today, a job requiring him to, among other things, cogitate about DuPont, the brand. He also has uncontested seniority in judging his wife's ability to set goals and meet them. Recalling their Kellogg days, he says, "From the start, she had a huge capacity for work. She was full of energy and very directed. Her strongest ability, I'd say, is just getting things done." That talent, he adds, extends today to balancing a family with three kids—they have a daughter at Tufts and twin boys studying (and playing basketball) at Tower Hill—and also happens to make her the polar opposite of a procrastinator: "I've become more familiar with to-do lists for both of us than I ever thought I would be," he laughs.

Chad Holliday says he first met Ellen Kullman around 1990 when she came with a team from the medical imaging group to visit the DuPont Japanese operations he was running. Seeing she'd come into the company with rank, he marked her as a comer. Later, when Holliday assumed responsibility for a big global product, titanium dioxide, and she became a candidate to run the business, he successfully backed her even though she lacked some obvious qualifications, like experience in heavy chemicals. Still later, he chuckles, he watched her bid her kids good night while she was doing nighttime videoconferences from home.

After becoming CEO in 1998, Holliday asked Kullman to leave the titanium dioxide business, where she'd done very well, and start up a group that would advise customers on safety and protection. The risk for Kullman was clear. "Absolutely everybody, including my husband, told me I'd be better off staying in my current job," she told *Fortune* in 2008. But she thought the safety and protection field could prosper at DuPont and made the move. A good call, that. The new consulting business blossomed under Kullman and picked up speed after 9/11.

(continued)

The safety and protection unit, with her at its head, became one of five "growth platforms" that Holliday established in 2002. (The others were agriculture and nutrition, home of Pioneer; coatings and color technologies, which included automobile finishes; electronic and communication technologies, among them components for solar panels; and performance materials, such as resins and laminated glass.) Kullman oversaw three franchise brands: Kevlar and Nomex, fibers used in protective gear like body armor or firefighting uniforms, and Tyvek, a nonwoven insulating material for houses that became visually ubiquitous during the homebuilding boom (and that led a widow friend of this writer to sigh, "If only I could meet Mr. Tyvek").

The heads of Holliday's five "growth platforms" gave a presentation in 2002 on the occasion of the company's 200th anniversary, and today one DuPont staff member describes Kullman as the standout. "She has a way of speaking that is compelling, and she painted a picture that people believed of how her business was going to grow," this staff member says. "That's when I knew it, that she was going to be CEO one day." Kullman did in fact keep starring as head of the division for four years, increasing revenues and pretax profit steadily.

In the early years of the decade, Kullman also built a reputation for herself by joining with a colleague to lead a companywide drive to improve DuPont's pricing skills, which were virtually nonexistent and were eroding margins. The very word "pricing" instantly carries Kullman back to the marketing training she got in Kellogg's night school and its add-on value for Ellen the engineer. Applying both disciplines to an analysis of DuPont, she concluded it had a "fundamental skills gap" in pricing and wasn't getting full value for the innovation it was providing customers.

But, as she points out, telling someone you want to raise his price doesn't elicit the response, "Gee, that's nice." So her team set up worldwide training programs for everyone who touches pricing at DuPont. "We taught what a marketing manager needed to do," she says, "what a sales manager needed to do, what the salesman's job was." And, of course, she adds, pricing is a different problem when the market is doing well from when it's not. In an up market, where the customer recognizes that you have raw material costs to pass along, raising prices can be relatively easy. But when the "raws" come down, she says, the customer wants prices to fall also.

Kullman's campaign has paid off, and DuPont has vastly improved its pricing skills—even when the economy has been struggling. In 2008 the company was able to increase its prices faster than then-surging raw materials, and last year it managed to keep ahead on prices even as its costs fell.

Kullman doesn't resemble an imperial CEO in style, partly because she remembers that she had to lay off 4,500 employees during her first year. Free to use DuPont's planes on personal trips if she wants to, she has instead booked her family on commercial flights for most vacations (and was not long ago spotted in a crowded airport waiting to board). Moreover, earlier this year she asked DuPont's board to lower her 2009 incentive pay from $1.7 million to $1.5 million. Asked to explain, she referred to the recession's hard licks: "I think that whenever changes are that horrific, I should participate in some way." The action, she says, took note of not only the sacrifices made by DuPont's employees but those of the company's shareholders as well.

At the least, the restructurings have left DuPont lean and therefore geared up to make those 20% earnings gains. Kullman argues that the company is stronger now for having so painfully tightened its operations. "That's my story," she says, "and I'm sticking with it."

But since many companies have renounced earnings guidance, it is worth asking why Kullman decided to advertise her expectations. She gives the questioner her complete attention, a Kullman trademark. She perhaps listens more closely than anyone the interviewer has ever run into. And then the answer: The reason for articulating the goals, she says, is that DuPont's royalty and licensing income from two hypertension drugs called Cozaar and Hyzaar is running out. That income was $1 billion pretax in 2009, and it is dropping fast. Were Wall Street's analysts left to their own ruminations, Kullman says, they would think that DuPont's earnings could not possibly rise, and might actually drop. So it is important, she argues, to make the case that DuPont not only can earn enough to offset the loss of that income but also has every intention of delivering its 20% gains.

The increases, the DuPont playbook says, are mainly to be drawn from four "megatrends." The first is the world's need for food, a case on which Pioneer will focus. The second is its need to migrate away from fossil fuels;

(continued)

DuPont has photovoltaics for solar panels and two biofuels to throw at this problem. The third is the protection of people, assets, and the environment, which ropes in not only the safety and protection division but also DuPont chemicals of various kinds.

The fourth is growth in emerging markets, where DuPont is already strong. The company gets about $8 billion in revenues, 30% of its total, from these regions, and it is aiming for 35% by 2012. DuPont's revenues in both China and Latin America have been growing by more than 15% a year. In a macabre point, murder makes for a growth opportunity in Brazil, where there are around 40,000 killings a year: DuPont's Sentry-Glas and Kevlar combine to make a product called Armura, which shields cars, at a cost of about $10,000 a vehicle.

Pioneer is another business that Kullman is counting on for profits. This subsidiary, once an uncertain earner, is still way behind Monsanto in genetically modified seeds, and is in fact in constant legal battle with Monsanto over this product. But Pioneer has meanwhile been a lifesaver for DuPont in the recession because it is not cyclical, whereas almost every other part of the company is. Between 2007 and 2009, Pioneer's revenues jumped by 22% to $8.3 billion, while its pretax operating profits rose by 37% to $1.2 billion. DuPont's plan calls for Pioneer to generate revenues of about $11 billion by 2012 and pretax operating profits close to $2 billion.

DuPont's recent 10-K filing with the SEC predicts all of its businesses will enjoy improved results in 2010, helped by their cost cutting—still going on—and a better economic climate. No doubt "pricing" will stay on the agenda.

In Kullman's snappy three-year scenario, there is no telling what new products might take off and make a difference. On this front, she has the full-out help of Thomas Connelly, Chief Innovation Officer (and a onetime contender for the job Kullman won). He has been working for years to speed the passage of DuPont's product innovations from lab to market. "My rallying cry," Connelly says, "is 'launch fast and ramp hard,' " a strategy intended to get the company to peak revenue as quickly as possible. By his calculations, nearly 40% of DuPont's revenues last year came from products introduced within the past five years. That proportion is double the rate of a few years ago.

Most of those products did not come from the "pure science" loved in many labs, including some of DuPont's over the years. Instead, what Kullman and Connelly have embraced is "market-driven science," which means delivering the products customers need. It is indeed intriguing to think of Kullman meeting with a customer to determine exactly what DuPont can do for his business and listening, as she does, with total intensity. A buyer sitting across the table from Kullman and asking for the moon might not know whether he was going to get it, but for certain he would know he had been heard.

One longtime DuPont board member, William Reilly, a former administrator of the Environmental Protection Agency, is totally convinced that Kullman can achieve her goals: "I think," he says, "that she is exactly the right person at this time. She has a reputation—even among people I talk to outside DuPont—as someone who executes."

Kullman herself has a view of her job that's not remotely as short term as her three-year ambitions. "I hope to be here a long time," she says. That would appear to be more of the confidence that's been on display for decades and that has a chance of edging this company back toward its better days.

Source: Carol J. Loomis, senior editor-at-large. April 15, 2010: 7:11 AM ET. http://www.cnnmoneycontrol.com/2010/04/14/news/companies/kullman_dupont.fortune/index.htm. Reprinted with permission, PARS International Corp, Inc. FORTUNE is a registered trademark of Time Inc. and is used under license.

The following transcript is from National Public Radio. NPR's Liane Hansen interviewed Sen. Barbara Mikulski for NPR's Weekend Edition Sunday® on January 20, 2011.

http://www.npr.org/2011/01/30/133348416/Longest-Serving-Woman-Senator-Looks-After-The-Rest

Host Liane Hansen talks with Sen. Barbara Mikulski, who is the longest serving female senator in U.S. history. When Mikulski arrived in the Senate in 1986, there wasn't even a woman's bathroom. Since then, she has become the unofficial dean of the increasing number of women serving in the Senate.

In 1986, Senator Barbara Mikulski became the first Democratic woman to be elected to a Senate seat not held by her husband. With her

(continued)

re-election in the 2010 midterms, the Senator from Maryland has now served in that august body longer than any woman in U.S. history.

Over the years, she's become the dean of Senate women. And in that unofficial role, she holds regular dinner parties with a bipartisan group of women senators and acts as a mentor, sharing the benefit of her decades-long experience on the Hill.

Senator Mikulski is in her office in Washington, D.C., and so are we.

Senator Mikulski, thank you for inviting us to talk to you today in your office.

Senator Barbara Mikulski (Democrat, Maryland): Hi, Liane. As time has gone on, the office has gotten a little bit bigger, but the responsibilities have gotten very significant.

> **Hansen:** No doubt. What it was like, as a woman, to into walk into the Senate 25 years ago?
>
> **Sen. Mikulski:** Well, first, it was an enormous thrill. And it was also very scary, because I felt it was not only Barb Mikulski that was coming into the Senate, but I was bringing half of the population with me. And I felt that if I didn't succeed that people would look down their nose at women succeeding, in truly a pretty big man's world.
>
> **Hansen:** Do you think being a woman at that time helped you politically, or hurt you in terms of getting things done? Because you were only one of a handful, so is the spotlight hotter on you?
>
> **Sen. Mikulski:** Well, first of all, in all of American history, when I arrived only 16 women had served. Now, there—in all of American history, 39 have served. There're now 17 of us serving at one time. So there are more women serving in the United States Senate now than had ever served at all, under any condition, when I arrived. So I went to work trying to work twice as hard to be twice good at being a legislator, in order to prove that we were up to the job and that I could really do the job.
>
> **Hansen:** Do you think with women running for public office today - as you said, there are 17 women senators—does it even bear mentioning now?
>
> **Sen. Mikulski:** It absolutely does. Particularly now, people are so frustrated. They're frustrated with their government. They're frustrated

with the way they perceive we don't get value for the dollar. And I believe what they look to the women are—you know, we work on the big macro issues, that so many of my colleagues chair really important committee: Mary Landrieu on small business, Diane Feinstein on intelligence, Barb Boxer on the environment. But while we work on the macro issues, we also bring the macaroni and cheese issues.

Hansen: Every issue is a women's issue.

Sen. Mikulski: Well, that's what I said and that's all of, really, what the women say on both sides of the aisle. National security is a woman's issue. Fighting and dying for your country certainly is a family issue. You just ask those military families on multiple deployments, with the stress that they have to have. Balancing the budget—well, wow—that's a national issue and it's also a family issue. Because the way we balance our budget impacts the way the families will ultimately balance theirs.

Hansen: What part of your personality, your political savvy can be traced right back to your Baltimore roots, do you think?

Sen. Mikulski: Well, I think I am who I am because of the wonderful mother and father I had, and the wonderful kind of schools that I went to. My mother and father owned a small neighborhood grocery store. And they believed that we—everyone who was our neighbor—was part of our extended family. And if they were having tough times, my father and mother tried to help them over that hump.

I also went to Catholic schools and educated by the nuns. And their emphasis on leadership, service and then also the values of our faith contained in "The Beatitudes," Matthew: 5, "The Sermon on the Mount"; hunger and thirst after justice.

Hansen: It is true you almost became a nun, but the discipline might have been too much? (Soundbite of laughter)

Sen. Mikulski: No. Well, you know, everyone at my age that saw these wonderful women who taught us and dedicated their lives, we all wanted to emulate. But, you know, the nuns take vows of poverty, chastity and obedience. The one for me, the obedience—I think I would have had a tough time. (Soundbite of laughter)

(continued)

Sen. Mikulski: But just ask Harry Reid or George Bush, and they would say the same thing.

Hansen: Senator Barbara Mikulski, Democrat from Maryland, thank you for inviting us to your office on Capitol Hill. And thank you very much for your time.

Sen. Mikulski: Good to be with you.

Source: ©2010 National Public Radio, Inc. NPR® news report titled "Longest-Serving Woman Senator Looks After The Rest" by NPR's Liane Hansen was originally broadcast on NPR's *Weekend Edition Sunday*® on January 30, 2011, and is used with the permission of NPR. Any unauthorized duplication is strictly prohibited.

Ann Marie—Remedying Personal Deficiencies

Cameron et al. (2006) describe value creation as a primary motivation that drives both people and businesses. At a personal level, having a positive impact and making a contribution in an area of personal importance is one of the most basic of human needs. Creating value is the way people achieve self-fulfillment, realize their unique potential, and reach self-actualization.

According to Cameron et al. (2006) the most successful organizations and leaders are those that create superior levels of value that tend to be simultaneously paradoxical. These successful leaders and organizations are more differentiated as well as more integrated than their peer systems. They transform themselves by combining stability and flexibility along with internal and external perspectives.

The process of integrating differentiated concepts can be illustrated by examining the idea of cognitive complexity. Individuals who are deeply experienced in a particular activity have greater cognitive complexity about that activity than those who are novices. Cognitive complexity refers to the degree of sophisticated understanding of a phenomenon that resides in a person's mind. Thus, managers with high cognitive complexity can see the uniqueness embedded in a situation as well as the similarities, because of that vision they are able to pursue advanced management strategies. In other words, people with a greater capacity to differentiate and integrate concepts in a specific activity can add greater value to that activity than others not so experienced (p. 64).

Cameron et al. (2006) point out studies on leadership that have found two key dimensions of leadership behavior, person-centered leadership and task-centered leadership. The research revealed the fact that some leaders tend to show concern for people (the soft side of leadership), whereas others tend to focus on getting things done (the hard side of leadership). However, by analyzing decades of research on the effectiveness of these two leadership styles, researchers noted that the average correlation between the two orientations was statistically significant. Leaders could be either task- or person-focused, however, more effective leaders were both. These leaders exhibited a capacity to integrate concern for people with concern for tasks, displaying soft characteristics as well as hard characteristics. Subsequent research has confirmed the superiority of the integration of these two orientations over an emphasis on either one singly.

The review of this research has had a significant impact on my plan to increase my overall competencies in management. I am the type of leader who is both person-oriented and task-oriented (my self-assessment scores coincide with this statement); however, I have been able to identify that my ability to integrate the two skill sets simultaneously needs improvement. I can identify a multitude of occasions where I have demonstrated both person-centered management and a multitude of occasions where I have demonstrated task-centered management. However, I cannot recall nearly as many times where I have demonstrated management style simultaneously.

The Competing Values Framework has brought to light that achieving valued outcomes in each of the quadrants is crucial for my personal and professional growth, as well as the level of value I add to my organization. As a leader one should consider multiple outcomes in each of the quadrants as they pursue value creation strategies. The Competing Values Framework has provided me the awareness and ultimately the ability to move from either/or thinking to a both/and thinking. This framework will help me focus on the integration of competing values.

In conducting my second assessment I saw point gains in all of the roles with the exception of facilitator and mentor. The second assessment has further strengthened my belief and commitment to developing an improvement plan where these areas are the focus. I can also conclude that my conflict and behavior management skills are particular areas of interest. To successfully move from low/middle level management positions to high level management positions I need to master this particular skill set. This skill set is of particular importance as my intention is to focus some of my coursework in the area of Human Resource Management with the intention to one day exit public sector management and perhaps enter the private sector in Human Resource Management. This desire has also prompted me to become intrigued with the concept of motivation and performance. I am looking forward to including Human Resource Management coursework in my MBA program.

In my current position of Job Developer/Grant Coordinator, I supervise a small staff. This role has been an excellent introductory role to what I hope will become more advanced management roles in the future. I am confident that through gap analysis and the development of a well-rounded outcomes portfolio guided by the Competing Values Framework I will have a prescription for ensuring growth and long-term success (see Tables 10.1 and 10.2).

TABLE 10.1
Evaluation

LEADERSHIP ROLES	POST- ASSESS- MENT SCORE	QUADRANT	COMPETENCIES
Mentor	6.2	Collaborate: Human Relations Model (CLAN)	The Mentor is helpful and approachable, engaging in the development of people through a caring, empathetic orientation.
Innovator	5.7	Create: Open Systems Model (ADHOCRACY)	The Innovator displays creativity and facilitates adaptation and change.
Producer	5.4	Compete: Rational Goal Model (MARKET)	The Producer is task-oriented and work-focused, and motivates members

TABLE 10.1 (*continued*)

LEADERSHIP ROLES	POST- ASSESS- MENT SCORE	QUADRANT	COMPETENCIES
			to increase produc- tion and to accom- plish stated goals (A).
Monitor	5.2	Control: Internal Process Model (HIERARCHY)	The Monitor checks on performance and handles paperwork (C).
Coordinator	5.0	Control: Internal Process Model (HIERARCHY)	The Coordinator maintains structure, schedules, organizes, and coordinates staff efforts, and attends to logistical and hou- sekeeping issues (B).
Director	4.8	Compete: Rational Goal Model (MARKET)	The Director engages in planning and goal setting, sets objectives and establishes clear expectations (A).
Broker	4.5	Create: Open Systems Model (ADHOCRACY)	The Broker is politically astute, persuasive, influential, and powerful and is particularly concer- ned with maintaining the organizations external legitimacy (A).
Facilitator	4.4	Collaborate: Human Relations Model (CLAN)	The Facilitator encourages teamwork and cohesiveness and manages interpersonal conflict (A).

Items marked with A indicate priority areas to focus improvement efforts and should be implemented immediately.

Items marked with B indicate areas of relative importance and should be addressed in the next year.

Items marked with C indicate areas important to future growth, but can be addressed in the long term.

TABLE 10.2
Development Plan

Roles	Job Specific Tasks	Competencies that Support Current Job	Competencies to Perform at Higher Levels Areas of Improvement	Expected Outcomes
Mentor	Supervise staff of employment coordinators	Implement programs and procedure that recognize and support growth of human capital	Develop programs and procedures that recognize and support growth of human capital	Improve my knowledge, skill, and ability to demonstrate person-centered management (C)
Innovator	Grant development and implementation	The development of new programs and processes. The development of continuous improvement plans. The ability to adapt to change.	The ability to help others adapt to change, particularly in times of crisis	Improve my ability to guide others through periods of change (C)
Producer	Make certain that program performance standards are met	Set priorities and tasks based on goals and objectives. Motivate others to achieve program goals.	Develop tools and techniques to related to motivation and performance	Increase my knowledge skills and abilities in the areas of motivation and performance to improve my ability to motivate others and assist others in identifying and reaching full potential (B)

TABLE 10.2 (*continued*)

Roles	Job Specific Tasks	Competencies that Support Current Job	Competencies to Perform at Higher Levels Areas of Improvement	Expected Outcomes
Monitor	Track project progress and document results Write Performance Appraisals Maintain records and reports	Monitor and process records and reports	Develop sophisticated tools for monitoring and tracking progress	Improve my ability to provide constructive feedback. Increase my knowledge and understanding of developing performance appraisal methods and systems (C)
Coordinator	Manage state funded employment programs throughout three counties	Attend to logistical and housekeeping issues	Develop and maintain optimal organizational structure	Demonstrate not only the ability to organize my own effort, but coordinate and organize staff efforts
Director	Grant Writing, Project and Strategic Planning, Grant Implementation	Set objectives and goals, and plan accordingly	Establish clear expectations	Demonstrate the ability to clearly outline expectations both programmatically and personally. This will reduce the amount of time spent on corrective action (A)

(*continued*)

TABLE 10.2 (continued)

Roles	Job Specific Tasks	Competencies that Support Current Job	Competencies to Perform at Higher Levels Areas of Improvement	Expected Outcomes
Broker	Market new projects to consumers, community organizations, state and local governments seeking support for community projects	Maintain the organizations external legitimacy	Being politically astute, persuasive, and powerful	An increased level of confidence in my ability influences others (A)An increased awareness of external factors and influences (A)
Facilitator	Hire, train, and supervise staff	Encourage teamwork and cohesiveness	Ability to efficiently manage differences between coworkers	Demonstrate mastery of conflict resolution/ mediation skills (A)

Items marked with A indicate priority areas to focus improvement efforts and should be implemented immediately.
Items marked with B indicate areas of relative importance and should be addressed in the next year.
Items marked with C indicate areas important to future growth, but can be addressed in the long term.

11

Women as Global Leaders

Case Study: Elizabeth Visits GPC's French Subsidiary

Elizabeth Moreno is looking out the window from her business class seat somewhere over the Indian Ocean on Thai Air en route to Paris-Orly International Airport from the Philippines, where she has just spent a week of meetings and problem solving in a pharmaceutical subsidiary of the Global Pharmaceutical Company (GPC).

GPC has the lion's share of the worldwide market in the ethical pharmaceutical products. Ethical drugs are those that can be purchased only through a physician's prescription. In the United States, GPC has research and manufacturing in New York, New Jersey, Pennsylvania, and Michigan. The company also has subsidiaries in Canada, Puerto Rico, Australia, Philippines, Brazil, England and France. GPC has its administrative headquarters in Pennsylvania.

Because of the diverse geographic locations of its subsidiaries, GPC's top scientists and key managers log thousands of jet miles a year visiting various offices and plants. Its top specialists regularly engage in multi-site real-time video and telephone conferences as well as using electronic mail along with faxes, modems and traditional mail to keep in touch with key personnel.

Despite these technological advances, face-to-face meetings and on-site consultations are used widely. In the case of the French subsidiary, nothing can take the place of face-to-face consultations. The French manager is

(continued)

suspicious of figures in the balance sheet, of the telephone, of his subordinates, of what he reads in the newspaper, and of what Americans tell him in confidence. In contrast the Americans trust all of these (Hill, 1994, p. 60). This is the reason GPC regularly sends its scientists and executives to France.

Elizabeth Moreno is one of the key specialists within GPC. Her expertise in chemical processing is widely known not only within her company but also in the pharmaceutical industry worldwide. She has been working at GPC for more than 12 years since finishing her advanced degree in chemistry from a university in the Midwest. While working with GPC, she has been given more and more responsibilities leading to her current position as vice president of chemical development and processing.

From a hectic visit in the Philippines, her next assignment is to visit the French subsidiary for one week to study a problem with shelf life testing of one its newest anti-allergy capsules. It seems that the product's active ingredient is degrading sooner than the expiration date. During her stay, she will conduct training for chemists in state-of the-art techniques for testing as well as training managers in product statistical quality control. These techniques are now currently used in other GPC locations.

To prepare for her foreign assignments, Elizabeth attended a standard three-hour course given by her company's human resource management department on dealing with cross-cultural issues. Moreover, she recalls reading from a book on French management about the impersonal nature of French business relations. This was so much in contrast with what she just had experienced in her visit in the Philippine subsidiary. The French tend to regard authority as residing in the role and not the person. It is by the power of the position that a French manager gets things done (Hill, 1994, p. 58). With this knowledge, she knows that her expertise and position as vice president will see her through the technical aspects of the meetings that are lined up for the few days she will be in Paris.

French managers view their work as an intellectual challenge that requires application of individual brainpower. What matters to them is the opportunity to show one's ability to grasp complex issues, analyze problems, manipulate ideas, and evaluate solutions (Hill 1994, p. 214).

There are a few challenges for Elizabeth on this assignment. She is not fluent in French. Her only exposure to France and the language was a two-week vacation in Paris she spent with her husband a couple of years ago. But in her highly technical field, the universal language is English. So, she believes that she will not have much difficulty in communicating with the French management to get her assignment successfully completed.

Americans place high value on training and education. In the United States, the field of management has principles that are generally applicable and can be taught and learned. In contrast, the French place more emphasis on the person who can adapt to any situation by virtue of his intellectual quality (Hill, 1994, p. 63). Expertise and intellectual ability are inherent in the individual and simply cannot be acquired through training or education.

It appears that Elizabeth will be encountering very different ways of doing business in France. While she thought about the challenges ahead, her plane landed at Orly-Paris International Airport. She whisked through customs and immigration without delays. There was no limousine waiting for her at the arrivals curbside. Instead she took the train to downtown Paris and checked into an apartment hotel that was reserved for her in advance of her arrival.

After a week in Paris, she is expected back in her home office to prepare reports to GPC management about her foreign assignments.

Case Bibliography

Hill, Richard, Euro-Managers & Martians: The Business Cultures of Europe's Trading Nations (Brussels: Europublications, Division of Europublic SA/NV, 1994).

Source: This case was prepared by Edwin J. Portugal, MBA, Ph.D., who teaches multinational management at State University of New York–Potsdam. It is intended to be used as a basis for discussion on the complexity of multicultural management and not to illustrate effective versus ineffective management styles. Copyright 1995 by Edwin Portugal. Reprinted with permission.

Questions:

1. What can Elizabeth Moreno do to establish a position of power in front of French managers to help her accomplish her assignment in five days? Explain.

2. What should Elizabeth know about high-context versus low-context cultures in Europe? Explain.

3. What should Elizabeth include in her report, and what should be the manner in which it is communicated, so that future executives and scientists avoid communications pitfalls? Explain.

4. How can technical language differ from everyday language in corporate communications? Explain.

5. How does this business trip compare to her previous trip to the Philippines?

Analysis

In reflecting on this scenario and applying concepts from the Schmidt readings, I feel there are several actions that Elizabeth could take to establish a position of power in front of the French managers to help her accomplish her assignment in five days. Because Elizabeth is operating from the position of vice-president of chemical development and processing and has a wealth of experience and expertise in the field, on the surface from a Western perspective she already is operating from a position of power. This perspective, however, is not transferable to the European perspective. Elizabeth must reflect on the potential impact of the following key factors in her role: authority, responsibility, power, time, conflict, risk, communication, organization, and agreements in her role. She must additionally evaluate how those factors might impact the French managers' cultural perspectives of how she operates in her position as a non-French speaking American female executive.

At first glance, the element of time is of the greatest concern as Elizabeth has only five days to complete this assignment. The French are known to exhibit an indifference to time, allowing occurrences to naturally progress, with allowances for the unknown. For this reason, I would suggest that Elizabeth not place an emphasis on the time frame of five days and focus more on relationship building and making connections with the French managers.

In terms of Hofstede's Dimensions of Cultural Variability, Elizabeth must demonstrate a high level of respect and understanding for the French culture's centralized power structures, collectivistic culture, strong uncertainty avoidance, and lower masculinity scores. As stated by Schmidt et al., (2007), "Hofstede's dimensions of cultural patterns and range of social behaviors continue to provide reasonable descriptions of the predominant tendencies in the cultures studied." Utilizing the above-mentioned dimensions of cultural variability as they relate to France, Elizabeth should become very familiar with the characteristics associated with the dimensions to support her effort in establishing a position of power.

In reference to the large power distance culture of France, Elizabeth should understand that the French managers recognize the fact that individuals in positions of power are not to be challenged and are further supported to utilize their power as they choose. In addition, she can expect the French managers to support a paternalistic management style and be accepting of large numbers of supervisory staff. The fact that the French have strong uncertainty avoidance indicates that Elizabeth should utilize the strategy of trying to move the group toward consensus on issues, which is usually done informally prior to official meetings in France. As suggested by Schmidt, "People in high uncertainty avoidance cultures try to ensure certainty and security through an extensive set of rules, regulations and rituals; they resist change and have higher levels of anxiety as well as intolerance for ambiguity" (2007, p. 27). Elizabeth also needs to understand that her authoritative power will be greatly supported by the French collectivist culture if she is able to establish synergy among the group, establish cooperation as a norm, and establish rules to consistently guide stability and order.

In reference to high-context versus low-context cultures in Europe, Elizabeth should have a thorough understanding of the fact that in the work environment the differences in high-context cultures and low-context cultures can result in significant challenges to the exchange of information, as it relates to differences in the quality of communication, quantity of communication, and direction of the communication. As supported by Schmidt, the context of communication relates to the amount of information an individual has to have before communication can effectively occur. Schmidt further states that "Information and rules are explicit in low-context cultures that use linear logic and a direct style of communication. In contrast, information and rules are implicit in high-context cultures that draw upon intuition and utilize an indirect style of communication" (pp. 24–25). I would first suggest that Elizabeth

reacquaint herself with the characteristics associated with individuals utilizing high-context and low-context communication and note the differences found between American and European cultures.

In high-context European cultures like those in France, employees will
adjust the direction of the majority of their communication to people who
represent the inner circle of their communication groups: family, some
coworkers, and close friends. This communication usually expands across
a broad range of issues and is in-depth in nature; as a result, the individuals in the inner circle become very knowledgeable and current regarding
personal and business-related information. All other individuals to which
communication is directed represent the outer circle of communication.
In contrast, low-context cultures, such as those found in the United States
where the direction of communication does not differentiate as frequently
between inner circle and outer circle group communication. Instead, direct
communication based on particular situations and personal characteristics
is exhibited. In addition, individuals only broadly communicate to people
in their outer circle. Individuals in these low-context cultures also communicate minimal information and do not engage in prolonged dialogue with
coworkers.

With the above-mentioned information in mind, in her interactions with
the French Managers, Elizabeth needs to further understand that French
communication has a tendency of being very efficient, where issues are
frequently pre-discussed and agreed on before meetings and then unani-
mously announced during meetings. This contrasts with the American
low-context culture where facts and information are presented in detail
during meetings, with negotiations and bargaining taking place during
meetings to reach a decision. Additionally, Elizabeth should understand
that when communication takes place in high-context cultures such as
France, there is great importance placed on the variables of relationships,
issues of appearance and decorum, method of communication, and status
of the participants involved. Lastly, the high-context culture places interpersonal relationships as the primary source of being able to establish a
foundation of communication at the appropriate context, contrasted with
the American low-culture context where opinions are frequently displayed
before relationships are built.

To provide an effective organizational framework for future executives
and scientists to avoid communications pitfalls, Elizabeth should include

in her report the key issues that relate to effectively dealing with international projects: authority, responsibility, power, communication, time, risk, and organization. In reference to authority/responsibility/power, Elizabeth should outline the importance of establishing lines of communication and control that is acceptable to the culture of the partners that the company is dealing with. The ability of executives and scientists to make these cultural communications of relevance is critical to the avoidance of misunderstandings of messages and the avoidance of conflict.

In reference to risk, Elizabeth needs to emphasize in the report the importance of executives in evaluating the specific societal perspectives on risk-taking in conducting business and the implementation of procedures that minimize risk when needed. In addition, the element of time is a significant factor when dealing with individuals of varying cultural backgrounds, and Elizabeth needs to include in her report the importance for executives to adequately provide time for the communication process when needed. Although the element of risk is a central component of global business, Elizabeth should include in her report the necessity for executives and scientists to manage the risk-based on the cultural perceptions of the individuals involved.

Elizabeth should also highlight in the report the importance for executives to evaluate tasks directly in conjunction with cultural perceptions of business partners. In situations where executives are dealing with relationship-centered cultures, the focus will have to be moving toward relationship building as a priority and this information would be very helpful. Elizabeth should also include in her report references to the country-by-country breakdowns of Hofstede's Dimensions of Cultural Variability (Schmidt, 2007, pp. 25–28) and Hall's Low and High Context Cultures to support executives and scientists in addressing the above-mentioned areas of concern. This report should be communicated in a manner that will support understanding among the various cultural perspectives represented in the GPC and various clients represented worldwide.

Technical language can differ from everyday language in corporate communications in that the vocabulary utilized in communication between parties in technical language can be very specific to a particular field of work, as opposed to everyday language that is communicated in native cultures. As stated by Schmidt, "As individuals communicate in their native language, individual speech behaviors take on distinct variations" (2007, p. 87). These variations were identified as the use of dialect, accents, jargon, and argot. In reference to Elizabeth and her inability to speak fluent French in her interactions, it was mentioned in the scenario that her highly technical field will allow her to utilize technical language in English that is familiar to all. Additionally, French managers are well versed on this occurrence and are not particularly affected.

This business trip has both similarities and differences to her previous trip to the Philippines. The business trips are different for Elizabeth in that the Philippine culture represents a short-term orientation culture; where there is a great appreciation for upholding traditions, obtaining instant results, exchanging of gifts and favors, and personal commitment to self. In addition, the factor of the short amount of time of five days to complete the business trip would be less significant for the Philippine culture because of the desire for quick results associated with the culture. These factors are in direct contrast to France. The similarities in the business trips are that both France and the Philippines have collectivistic cultures. Both cultures are also high context. In addition, both countries utilize the English language as the primary language of use in business interactions.

Women Are Interested in International Assignments

For much of the last 25 years women were largely prevented from reaching global business ventures because it was assumed that locals would not respect or accept them undermining or weakening the business relationship. Another reason that women were not considered was that it was believed (erroneously) that they were not interested in these assignments (Adler, 1994). As a program supervisor and designer of executive education programs, I recall the message from one of our educational partners abroad advising me against assigning women for a particular residency "since the male executives prefer to work with male consultants." Most people believe that women leaders are not welcome abroad, however, that largely depends on the task and level of expertise. In some Asian countries it may not be appropriate for a woman to be an executive; however, when an American woman executive goes there to represent their company, the men don't automatically dismiss her as one would expect.

In fact, they believe so strongly that an American company would not make an error in selecting a less-qualified person for the job. Furthermore, because women may tend to be more nurturing in their management style, they can be more receptive to cultural differences and more sensitive to nuances during conversations or negotiations, gaining respect for their approach.

The 1990s and especially the last decade proved to be a turning point for women in business. As business organizations are becoming more service oriented, relying on global supply chain, distribution channels; competitive intelligence; integrated marketing communication; and a customer relationship exchange system, they are moving away from being simply manufacturing based. This, plus the desire to create a diversified workforce, has triggered a change in hiring—women were now being accepted into lower managerial positions. Although this was a positive shift, the international arena did not see much movement. It seemed women were held to a different standard than men and would be denied positions because they did not have any experience although they could not get the experience without being promoted into the necessary positions. The same vicious cycle described throughout this book appeared to face women aspiring to fit into offshore positions. Male managers seemed to be less of a "risk" in international assignments than women and therefore would be afforded opportunities even without all of the "required" qualifications (Altman & Shortland, 2008).

However, change does occur although the patterns of misrepresentation in top executive positions so pervasive domestically also pervades international assignments. Although women have recently increased their international presence, this is really only due to the fact that men no longer want the positions (Altman & Shortland, 2008). And while more women are being placed on international assignments than ever before, only 22% of senior positions are occupied by women (Thorton, 2011).

Verghese (2008), for example, reported on a survey conducted by Mercer Consulting in 2006 of over 100 multinational companies with almost 17,000 employees working internationally, found a significant increase in the number of women being sent to work in the Asian Pacific region. The companies surveyed indicated that the number of women on international assignments was 16 times greater than in 2001. There has been little research and discussion in regard to women leaders and the cultural implications. In a recent survey over half of the companies (55%) expect the number of female assignees to continue to increase steadily over the next five years, while 35% believe the number will remain the same. Just 4% believe it will decline (http://www.amanet.org/training/articles/New-Study -Shows-More-Women-Being-Sent-on-International-Assignments.aspx).

Women Qualify for Global Jobs!

Will having a woman negotiating an outcome or closing a deal on international agreements increase the company's success with its overseas partners and/or competitors? In this book we advance the argument and provide evidence indicating that women managers and executives do very well once opportunities are opened up for them and once they are provided with important strategic responsibilities. It has also been suggested throughout the book that companies who promote women to senior positions tend to do very well financially.

According to Verghese (2008), extensive research has demonstrated that, in fact, women expatriate leaders are more likely to possess the characteristics that ensure success in an expatriate role, namely cultural empathy, a willingness to take risks, and persuasive motivation and flexibility (Sharpe, 2000). These and other claims that were made in this book about women's education, skills, abilities to deal with stress, and attitudes suggest that more and more women are going to be working and leading across borders and consequently strategies need to be put in place to support this growth.

In February of 2010 *Training Magazine* published an article entitled "How to Develop Your Global Leadership Pipeline" by Sheila Madden. The article points out that, while 86% of top executives think it's "extremely important" to work across boundaries (global and cultural boundaries were part of the study), only 7% think they are doing so effectively. The huge disparity in these numbers illustrates the fact that most global companies need to develop better strategies to improve the effectiveness of cross-cultural endeavors. Madden points to the CCL, Center for Creative Leadership, for suggestions on improving global leadership effectiveness. Some of the approaches Madden writes about, for instance, *increased diversity, cultural intelligence*, and *improved language skills*, mimic the ones laid out throughout this book.

Madden argues that cultural sensitivity is not enough but, rather, cultural intelligence is needed to succeed at international business. This includes not only an understanding of cultural differences, but also knowledge of how to manage these differences. As argued in the following sections, gaining global perspective by learning about cultural factors such as cultural variability and hostility is also important for leadership effectiveness (Schmidt et al., 2007). Additionally, Madden points to the need for a *common language*. She is not speaking so much literally as she is figuratively, however. Broadening our ability to communicate, even in our native language by learning new ways to express our concerns will promote improved communication and encourage synergy.

As globalization infiltrates the world's businesses, executives, men and women, will choose transformational leadership as their means for successfully leading their organization. Transformational leadership, characteristically women's leadership, will become the dominant form of leading in the next wave of conducting business in the global market.

The next sections examine factors (e.g., cross-cultural sensitivity, cosmopolitan leadership, language, conflict resolution) essential for effective global management. As these factors and topics are explored, keep in mind the traits, skills, knowledge, and competencies that women possess and that were discussed throughout the book positioning them well ahead of the learning curve to assume global leadership roles effectively.

Global Leadership

Globalization impacts every area of a company from its customer base, vendors and distributors, marketing strategy to its alliance networks, partnerships, and competitors. Almost no American corporation is immune from the impact of globalization (Javidan, Dorfman, de Luque & House, 2006, p. 67). According to Goldsmith, Greenburg, Robertson, and Hu-Chan (2003) traditional leadership practices are changing as globalism spreads. The new business environment demands that leaders espouse a new range of skills, resources, and market offerings. The consequences of the globalized marketplace command leaders and organizations to adapt to rapid worldwide changes.

Global leadership is not merely a single competency, nor is it a collection of various individual leadership competencies. Global leadership is a process that involves a broad behavioral repertoire, a fascination for learning, an appreciation for diverse cultures, and a profound awareness of international climates. Global leadership is best described by Beechler and Baltzley (2008) as a process of "influencing individuals, groups, and organizations inside and outside the boundaries of the global organization, that represent diverse cultural, political, and institutional systems to contribute toward the achievement of the global organization's goals" (p. 41). Understanding the global market requires that leaders learn to pay attention to changing trends at home and abroad. Leaders must develop an awareness of macro-trends in business, technology, economics, demographics, public policy, government regulation, and politics (Clark, 2008). Because vulnerabilities by and large do not arise in the leader's native market, global literacy has become a crucial tool for organizations' survival. Literacy in global movements will offer leaders foresight into the constant evolutions of the international marketplace and permit them to perceive changes as they unfold, rather than simply reacting to them after they have already begun to impact the business. By proactively seeking out the trends in the global market, leaders can capitalize on opportunities and avoid unnecessary pitfalls.

Today's global marketplace reflects distinct national histories, heritages, and philosophical ideas with global corporations in direct competition over markets and delivery systems. Fluent global leadership is reliant on the ability of the leader to broaden his or her awareness of the various business environments around the world (Ellsworth, 2002). A leader must know the ins-and-outs of how foreign governments operate. Different countries have distinct regulations that impact the ways in which organizations operate. A skilled leader will know how to align company operations with the localized legal courses of action and protect his or her company from consequences of violating international laws (Goldsmith et al., 2003). Additionally, a global leader must also understand the significance of political tensions, ideologies, and characteristics of the people who occupy the regions in which his or her company operates.

Dr. Geert Hofstede, an international research consultant, in an effort to aid leaders in their quests to better understand the mindsets of the people throughout the world, identified what he believed to be important dimensions of national character along four dimensions of national culture:

1. Power Distance or the distribution of legal power across hierarchical lines
2. Uncertainty Absorption or the amount of latitude given to lower levels in decision making situations
3. Individualism versus conforming to group expectations
4. Masculinity or the extent to which the dominant values are assertiveness, money and material things, not caring for others, quality of life, and people.

Understanding the ideologies of other countries is a must for leaders in the global age, not only because they effect mundane political and regulatory stipulations, but also because those ideologies shape the composure of the local workforce. Companies operating across borders must recognize the social ideologies of the people that will be working for them. As Ellsworth (2002, p. 243) put it "the foundation of the free-market ideologies of the other powers range from Germany's social-market economy to the emphasis on the harmony of corporate and national interests in Japan and Korea." To unpack that statement: the social ideologies of the people in different nations determine the purposes of their companies. While one organization may focus on profitability and sustainability, another may focus on the welfare of its people. In each case, executives in the global era must deploy stylistically unique methods of leadership to achieve goals.

Developing Global Competencies

The development of global leaders, in many multinational organizations, transpires though rigorous recruitment and training programs especially because understanding the complexity, interdependence, and multiplicity of international markets is crucial for the success of the business. A growing trend for discovering potential global leaders is the implementation of systematic skill identification programs. Being successful in the global market requires companies to staff their overseas locations with the right combination of people. Selecting employees that will be able to adapt to their new surroundings will help the company retain these employees. According to Leaper (1999) long-term expatriates are vital to the success of the business. Managing culture shock is one way companies can retain its employees. One way to do this is to send the employee into the new culture on a short-term assignment to gain a better understanding of whether or not that person will be able to adapt.

Many organizations require that recruits attend sessions at Intercultural Assessment Centers (IACs). Mendenhall, M. E., Kuhlmann, T. M., & Stahl, G. K. (2001) assert that using assessment centers to identify global leadership competencies is a great way to ensure that the proper candidates for leadership positions are acquired, because IACs confront applicants with intercultural situations in which their responses can be systematically observed using reliable and valid instrument measures. Aspirants often take a number of tests to determine their level of cultural intelligence. Scales such as the Intra-Cultural Development Inventory, The Cultural Intelligence Scale, and The Multi-Cultural Personality Questionnaire are used frequently by cultural assessment centers to detect worthy and well-equipped job applicants (Mendenhall et al., 2001).

Once promising applicants are selected for hire, they must then enhance their leadership competencies including the ability to learn about foreign cultures, craft culturally synergistic environments, interact with foreign colleagues as equals, and use cross-cultural interaction skills (Adler & Bartholomeow, 1992). Preparations for global leadership positions ensure that individuals develop the proficiencies necessary to lead internationally. The skills of developing global leaders are highly dependent on the support and direction of superiors as well as the various training programs designed by human resources departments (Goldsmith et al., 2003). Such programs usually comprise of formal and informal diversity coaching, leadership development programs, cross-cultural as well as language instruction, and team-building procedures. Some companies, such as Avery Dennison, even require their new hire executives to facilitate peer meetings, conduct research, give formal presentations, and participate in one-on-one coaching sessions with superiors (Schuler, 2007).

Beechler and Baltzley (2008) believe that characteristics such as a person's intellect, his or her personal psychology, knowledge, and self-awareness are important characteristics for global leaders to acquire. Other scholars, such as Goldsmith et al. (2003), suggest that, though no particular leadership model will accommodate the needs of all of the unique global leadership roles; successful global leaders will possess at least five universal characteristics. The five characteristics of global leaders are *thinking globally, appreciating cultural diversity, possessing technological savvy, building partnerships and alliances*, and *sharing leadership*. To successfully manage an organization in the global era, the attainment of these skills has become vital for new leaders.

Culture and Gender Factors

Cultures are both geographically based and gender-based. A culture is made up of the assumptions, values, expectations, and attitudes that develop over time among a groups and regions. The widely held belief that as North American we are perceived as successful by other cultures no longer holds true as shown by Wal-Mart's failure to localize its operations in South Korea or position itself in Germany. According to Verghese (2008), an international consultant and author, there are significant gender differences when working in varying regions. For example, Sweden has low gender differentiation, meaning that culturally there are few distinctions between what a man and woman can and cannot do; compared to Japanese society that has a much higher degree of gender differences where the cultural expectations of what is and is not acceptable for men and women is more divided (Brislin, 2008). Gender in the workplace does not just mirror prevailing social norms, but reinforces them and fashions wider social structures and practice.

Leaders can rely on existing research conducted by The Globe Project to assist them in constructing useful leadership strategies that appeal to multiple nations. Project GLOBE was conceived by Robert J. House of the Wharton School of the University of Pennsylvania in 1991, and involved 170 "country co-investigators" based in 62 of the world's cultures (Grove, 2005, http://www.grovewell.com/pub-GLOBE-intro.html). The researchers used qualitative methods to identify nine cultural dimensions. Performance orientation, uncertainty avoidance, humane orientation, institutional collectivism, in-group collectivism, assertiveness, gender egalitarianism, future orientation, and power distance were recognized by GLOBE as the different dimensions of culture. By distinguishing where specific regions lie among the range of cultures, leaders can target elements of motivation and efficiently acclimate their leadership styles.

In addition to the cultural dimension research, GLOBE also created six cultural leadership profiles that label characteristics of different cultures.

These characteristics demonstrate the range leadership responses to cultural differences that prove effective in various national settings. The six leadership dimension profiles are:

1. Charismatic/Value Based: a broadly defined leadership dimension that reflects the ability to inspire, to motivate, and to expect high-performance outcomes from others on the basis of firmly held core beliefs.
2. Team Oriented: a leadership dimension that emphasizes effective team building and implementation of a common purpose or goal among team members.
3. Participative: a leadership dimension that reflects the degree to which managers involve others in making and implementing decisions.
4. Humane-Oriented: a leadership dimension that reflects supportive and considerate leadership but also includes compassion and generosity.
5. Autonomous: a dimension that refers to independent and individualistic leadership.
6. Self-Protective: a dimension of leadership that focuses on ensuring the safety and security of the individual (Petiick, Scheier, Brodzinski, Quinn & Ainina, 1999, p 59).

Like the identification of culture, the goal of the six leadership profiles is to arm leaders with essential information that will help them avoid inaccuracies and miscalculations when attempting to apply leadership techniques. Understanding the six leadership dimension profiles will assist global leaders in their efforts to tailor their leadership designs and assure that they deliver their messages clearly, and in a format that will inspire communal motivation and participation from subordinates across the globe.

Working in collaboration with subordinates and other leaders worldwide requires that leaders share authority and control. Leaders must sacrifice personal control to guarantee the smooth operation of their companies throughout multiple regions of the world. Discrete executive teams diversify international organizational leadership in the global era; as a result, there is an increased demand for both accountability and responsibility (Goldsmith et al., 2003). Traditional hierarchies have no relevance in the global era because global leaders must use multidimensional leadership styles, in correspondence with flexibility, to cohesively consummate their global strategies. Leaders must learn to trust other executives, and to respect the varying styles of leadership that he or she may encounter from such executives as they manage from distant soil.

Because leaders must be able to effectively communicate their vision with executives and teams throughout the world, understanding and forming a deep appreciation for diversity becomes critical. In contrast to previous generations of leadership, in the global era there is no true right or wrong way to lead. This new perspective requires that executives place a significant emphasis on learning about other countries, cultures, and ways of life. Leaders can no longer presume that they share a similar cultural base or outlook with those with whom they work and do business. Leaders must now recognize diverse organizational dynamics and how cultural differences impact the workplace. Leaders have the responsibility to practice what Goldsmith et al. (2003) refer to as *multigenerational leadership*, which is defined as "leading individuals with different frames of reference or ideological differences" (p. 29). Being able to lead from multiple frames of reference demands that leaders know the historical, political, and economic perspectives of people from other regions of the world, and it is impossible to do so without understanding the details of their cultures.

Leaders need to appreciate both the general and the specific contents of cultures; the big and the small things that make various societies unique. Executives must learn to appreciate the different leadership and work styles, as well as the special methods of decision-making, motivating, and rewarding employees that are deemed acceptable by people from other cultural backgrounds. When a leader understands fully the cultural makeup of the people he or she is working with, he or she will be able to effectively manage cultural tension and avoid offenses and embarrassments. Skilled global leaders will employ multiple techniques for learning about other cultures, and he or she will pass on to subordinates all relevant information.

In an effort to learn the detailed structure and composure of foreign cultures, a successful leader will immerse himself in field work, a process that many refer to as "cultural immersion" (Goldsmith et al., 2003). In fieldwork, the global leader travels, for a significant amount of time to a foreign location for the purpose of learning to identify with its people. The leader participates in what Harris et al. (2004, p. 26) refer to as "acculturation," or the process by which an individual effectively adjusts and adapts a particular culture. By doing so, the leader learns the ins-and-outs of the local culture, and gains awareness and appreciation for the traditions, beliefs, and practices of the local culture.

Intercultural Conflicts, Ethics, and Leadership Effectiveness

Communication plays a key role in conflict, both in creating the conflict as well as in resolving the conflict. Communication is fundamental in conceptualizing the dispute and in selecting an appropriate way to handle it. Conflict that involves communication between differing cultures often stems from the involved parties having a perceived incompatibility of goals. According to Schmidt et al. (2007), the conflict gap gets wider based on how divergent the differences in the group membership are. Cultures that have similar beliefs, rules, and communication styles normally should either encounter fewer conflicts, or should have an easier time resolving them. However, because conflict is an integral part of every society, and more and more different cultures are entering the global economy, conflicts occur on a regular basis.

When conflict does arise during intercultural communication, there are several key characteristics to look at that act as cues as to how to negotiate the conflict. Schmidt et al. (2007) identify three categories of conflict-handling strategies. The three most commonly observed strategies are nonconfrontational or yield-lose, solution-oriented or win-win, and control or win-lose. With the nonconfrontational strategy, the communicator will manage the conflict indirectly by trivializing the conflict, avoiding volatile issues, or physically avoiding any incongruity. The solution-oriented strategy leads communicators to manage a conflict by yielding alternative solutions or making compromises. Finally, a communicator that uses the control strategy will deal with the conflict by arguing their position persistently as well as by employing nonverbal messages to express their argument. When employing a conflict-handling strategy it is important to be mindful of how the tactic will be received by the culture with which you are dealing, as choosing the wrong strategy to manage a conflict can damage a relationship.

How you present yourself to the other party can affect the relationship that you build with them. Face-negotiation and face-work are communication strategies that involve, "a socially approved identity we seek when we interact with others . . . it is the verbal and nonverbal efforts we use to strategically construct and maintain our identities during an interaction" (Schmidt et al., 2007, p. 107). Face-work is extremely important in dealing with cultural situations because what may be considered an appropriate face-negotiation strategy in one culture may offend someone in another culture. Lustig and Koester (2003) identified three face needs that can be found among cultures: control, approval, and admiration or respect. These three face needs are believed to be universal among cultures, yet some are more important in certain cultures than others, and some are equal among cultures.

When communicating with a party from a different culture it is important to understand the face needs of their culture so as not to offend them during your interactions. In March and Wu's book *The Chinese Negotiator*, they recount a face-negotiation situation between an Australian brewery designer and a team of Chinese men who were charged with hiring someone to build a large brewery in Guangdong Province, China. In preparing to negotiate with the Chinese the first thing that Benjamin, the Australian brewery designer, did was research the Guangzhou Company that was building the brewery. He found that not only were they tied to the Chinese government because of the tight control on alcohol, but that this particular unit of the government was run by ex-Red guards. The Chinese culture is built on strong loyalty to authority, and their collectivist practices include indirectness and the avoidance of public embarrassment (Schmidt et al., 2007). Based on his research of the Chinese culture, Benjamin realized that the group with which he would be dealing would report back to their government superiors. Therefore, Benjamin understood that he needed to make sure that he made them look good in the eyes of the ex-Red guards (March & Wu, 2007).

Further, Benjamin learned from his research the importance of avoidance in causing the Chinese to lose face. He needed to be sensitive to not pointing out their shortcomings, so he offered to work with them to develop a proposal that would incorporate some of the latest brewing technology that had just been introduced. He felt that by letting them know that the technology was brand new, it would help them avoid feeling that their plans were not adequate. Additionally, he felt that having a proposal that included the latest technology would allow for the lead negotiator for the Chinese to not lose face with his bosses. After weeks of negotiation, Benjamin was awarded the contract to build the brewery.

After working with the Chinese on this project, and eventually on a winery in another province, Benjamin reflected on a few of the valuable lessons he learned in negotiation with the Chinese. His first lesson was not to be distracted by cultural differences. He learned the value of understanding cultural differences and adjusting his communication style. His second lesson was the value of face-negotiation. He learned that the Chinese will do something wrong rather than admit that they made a mistake. Finally, he learned the value of reciprocity as reciprocal favors are common in China, so if you make someone look good, they will return the favor. By working within this framework, Benjamin was able to establish a relationship of mutual respect that allowed for further business dealing with the Chinese (March & Wu, 2007).

Conflicts exist in every culture and can arise in business dealings at anytime. It is vital for managers dealing with intercultural communication to understand the culture with which they are interacting to either avert conflict, or to resolve it in the most productive way possible. Building a solid relationship with the party in which you are involved in a business transaction is important in maintaining the business relationship. Utilizing the correct communication and conflict management styles is essential to the cosmopolitan leaders of today's global corporate industries as a way to foster respectful, cordial working relationships with other cultures.

Contextualizing Communication Relationships

The value a society places on individualism has been cited by Weaver (2001), who noted that American-style ethics reporting places emphasis on lower-level employee's responsibility in assessing and reporting questionable behavior in an organization. However, this contradicts several cultural norms that often require lower-level employees to challenge superiors and colleagues, thereby upsetting cultural harmony. This is not acceptable in high-context cultures. It also disregards such a culture's need for superiors to save face and to allow subordinates the same dignity. The effectiveness of a particular ethics management program will depend on its communication context. Such initiatives will have more success in low-context cultures if they have formal structures, explicit language, written documents, and published codes of conduct.

Conversely, high-context cultures using these same tools are likely to see them as irrelevant (and thus ignored) and therefore ineffective; or if noticed, they are often seen as overbearing or arrogant, and perilous to the organization's harmony and societal legitimacy (two things that are placed at a high premium in high-context cultures).

Weaver (2001) noted that in Eastern and European settings, leaders (who often are placed at a high power distance from subordinates) must encourage acceptance of ethical standards by example. In these high-power distance cultures, it is the leaders, not subordinates, who are to be held responsible for ethical behavior of an organization, because unethical actions (on behalf of lower-level employees) simply reflect their (expected and normative) responsiveness to their leadership. Weaver notes that in a high-power distance society, ethics programs risk "locating blame" at the wrong level in an organization, and "may be perceived as efforts by elites to avoid responsibility for the exercise of their power"; meanwhile underlings may reject such programs, as they may not be willing to reject their superior's requests to enact unethical behavior for the same reason. For these reasons, Weaver (2001) recommends that global businesses focus attention on "organizational elites," and that these elites should take a particularly active role in ethical change and in sharing information across levels of the organization.

Intercultural Competencies

Mendenhall et al. (2001, p. 207) identified a list of "intercultural competencies" that include fostering a "tolerance for ambiguity, goal orientation, sociability and interest in other people, empathy, and non-judgment." Sharon Lobe, author of *Global Leadership Competencies: Managing to a Different Drumbeat*, suggested that personal characteristics, such as tolerance for ambiguity, behavioral flexibility, nonjudgment, interpersonal skills, cultural empathy, low ethnocentrism, motivation, and the willingness to acquire new patterns of behavior and attitudes are predictors of expatriate success (Lobe, 1990, p. 40).

John Pepper, former chairman of the Executive Committee of the Board of Directors of The Procter & Gamble Company, stated in an interview that "of all the career changes that I have had, the international assignment was the most important and developmental . . . It changed me as a person" (Bingham, Felin & Black, 2000, p. 287). Benefits of cultural immersion are numerous. Leaders who participate in international immersion gain a better understanding not only of the business techniques of the local people, but also a personal understanding of how they live their private lives (Goldsmith et al., 2003). In doing so, the expatriates gain the information necessary to successfully market their products and ideas with a well-developed personal touch. Though some researchers may disagree on the necessity for leaders to spend extended periods of time within other countries, most agree that it is wise for leaders to have experience living in different regions, learning other languages, and studying other cultures.

Of course, the ability to appreciate diversity is not a competency that is to be possessed by leaders alone. Awareness of, and respect for, various cultures should be shared by all employees, not only the ones operating at the executive level. Cultures differ in perspectives on religion, race, sex, values, behaviors, and ethics. Most global organizations designated entire units, such as human resources departments, to properly train employees how to interact with individuals and teams from other cultural backgrounds. Adler and Bartholomeow (1992), for example, described the function of human resources departments as one that reflects ideas from multiple cultures in its planning and decision-making processes. Mendenhall et al. (2001), recognized that in a globalized world there is an increased need for specialization in the area of multicultural awareness, and so these researchers developed a model for what they call Strategic International Human Resources Management (SIHRM) and the increased demand for coordination and personal orientation.

Providing employees at all levels of an organization with the skills and information necessary to competently appreciate cultural dissimilarities and efficiently interact with people of diverse backgrounds allow for the creation and use of multicultural teams. Though very little may be shared at orientation stages of multinational team development, employees that are well equipped with the skills to interact with people from all over the world will work through tensions and form cultural synergy. Mendenhall et al. (2001) refer to cultural synergy as collaboration that emphasizes likenesses as well as common concerns, and integrates differences in an effort to enhance relationships. Because almost none of the world's nations are made up of ethnically or racially similar people, stressing diversity within organizations is a must for all global leaders.

Language

A multinational corporation's language design, according to Luo and Shenkar (2006), is driven by strategic rationality, evolutionary path (language and organizational culture is always changing), and bounded rationality constraints. The choice of language used by the parent (home office) affects corporate control, implementation of its strategies, and the performance of its subunits. What the multinational company produces and how it makes its money drives both its global strategy and its functional language decision. It also determines its language intensity, which refers to how heavy handed the parent is in adhering to the functional language throughout its company. For instance, multidomestic companies compete locally and have increased pressure to use the local language. A multidomestic company is more focused on communicating with its customers than with its corporate partners at home. On the other hand, global multinational companies that assume more standardization across national markets and economies of scale, and depend on the transfer of information and innovation across the company, have more pressure to use the language of the parent company.

Schmidt et al. (2007) refer to code-switching as the phenomenon of an individual alternating between languages to accommodate the variables of location of the interaction, the topic of communication, and the background of the other communicators. In reference to the characteristics of language, Schmidt highlights the characteristics in the following ways: language as being symbolic, language as being abstract, language shaping perception, language as a contextual code, language as being rule based, and language as being functional. A multinational corporation with subunits—partners, distributors, wholly owned subsidiaries, sales offices—at some point must decide the primary or "functional" language they will use to communicate with those subunits.

The functional language is the language used in the company's major documents and contracts, major events, and in most of its interactions with subunits. A company's language policy is also a salient policy of company culture as well. Each language has its own rules and codes and carries with it its own cultural markers. As Schmidt et al. (2007) note: "Language is symbolic . . . Language is abstract . . . Language shapes perception. . . . Language is a contextual code" (pp. 88–90).

Luo and Shenkar (2006) also consider the organizational design in the choice of functional language. Subunits and headquarters operate in different environments and face different needs by employees and consumers. This also drives both the choice and the intensity of the language decisions used by the company. Another finding by these same authors is that for multinational contractors, those who use the same language as the parent are in a better bargaining position than a subunit that uses a different language. If a subunit has a better ability to make themselves understood, and vice versa, then they will certainly be in a better bargaining position than a subunit that uses a different language.

Van den Born and Peltokorpi (2010) provide relevant illustrations of how the global communication concepts and concerns we have been studying can interface with the language policy choices that multinational companies make. The first policy is the ethnocentric approach in which a company uses the language of the parent company for all inter- and extra-company communications. Using one official language can unify a company, making communication across different countries easier. When all employees of a company are proficient in the same language, they are able to collaborate more smoothly; and all work units, regardless of location, can feel connected and part of a team. This approach would fit best into a collectivist culture that values harmony and homogeneity, but its rigidity may make communication with those from "outside" the culture difficult.

The polycentric approach to language use emphasizes local languages at individual branches of a multinational corporation (MNC) while still using the parent company language for all extra-company communications. This approach capitalizes on the fact that offices speaking the local language will be better equipped to integrate with the local economy and become a more accepted part of the local business culture. Expatriate managers from the parent company are placed at each branch to interface with and translate directives from corporate management. This stratification between management and local employees can lead to the feeling that branches are cutoff and ignored from the greater organization, and expatriate managers may have trouble assimilating into local culture.

MNCs with geocentric language policies staff international offices with managers from neither the parent nor the local country. The use of a cultural "third party" is intended prevent employees from feeling unduly "ruled over" by a parent company/country. Geocentric companies use a lingua franca or a common language for all official company communications. In many cases, English is chosen as the lingua franca (whether the parent company is located in an English-speaking country or not) and local languages are used for inter-unit communications. While this option may appear to foster the coveted "third culture" for MNCs, it does come with communicative drawbacks. The use of many languages could make it easy for miscommunication to occur between branches; and with a lingua franca that hypothetically is the native language of no one, usage problems can occur.

The Cost of Ignoring Intercultural Differences

Effective communication in the global marketplace is essential for achieving business goals. Technology has changed the way businesses communicate across the world, but the importance of communication has not. Communicating globally is complex; therefore, it is imperative that a business have a communication strategy. Forming an overall strategy and then adapting that strategy to different markets will assist the company in working in different cultures. Knowledge of other cultures will allow businesses to respond quickly to opportunities or crises. The language barrier is a challenge to communicating globally. Language is shaped through symbols, abstractions, and perception. Because of these things one cannot simply rely on the words in a language to communicate. Adjusting a company's communication strategy to correspond with the culture will help the company succeed.

In 1991 Wal-Mart embarked on its first international business venture when it opened a Sam's Club near Mexico City. Over the years, while some of Wal-Mart's international stores have done well, others have not. Wal-Mart's venture in Brazil was an example of a company that did not "understand the local culture" (Blackman & Dann, 2010). Further, a *New York Times* article from August 2, 2006 points out that Wal-Mart encountered problems in Germany because, among other things, it "never established comfortable relations with its German labor unions."

According to the *New York Times*, Wal-Mart began its German chains by placing American executives in charge of operations.

After numerous failures caused by a lack of knowledge of the customs and practices of Germans (i.e., Germans do not like buying prepackaged meat products), Wal-Mart realized it was not in touch with German consumers and began using local management teams. Another venture—this one in Korea—failed because the decision was made to use the same store layout that is used in the United States. But the warehouse atmosphere and packaging that was too large for Korean shoppers, and a store layout that boasted high shelves and a sterile, industrial look were not acceptable to small Korean shoppers who had to use ladders to reach some products. Wal-Mart's international failures were due to a business model that has been successful in the United States but does not translate well to other nations where shoppers have different habits. Companies risk losing large sums of money when they invest billions in foreign markets only to fail when they move forward without adequate cultural sensitivity and awareness.

Wal-Mart's missteps mimic those of other large companies like Euro Disney in France in early 1990 and even McDonald's. McDonald's international ventures went through a period of trial and error during which the company learned to keep most of its menu options in line with its trademarks but to also incorporate local traditions (e.g., Belgian McDonald's restaurants serve beer).

Cosmopolitan Leadership

Putting a local team in charge that has awareness of a culture's traditions is not enough. To maintain the U.S. brand that made a company successful and gain new customers abroad, the people hired to implement and carry out the business plans should be multicultural and multinational. At the very least, the teams should include members from both the company's headquarter-nation and the nation the company wishes to compete within. The problems of these multinational corporations can be described as a lack of *cosmopolitan leadership* and ineffective global team strategies (Schmidt et al., 2007). These teams should be lead by cosmopolitan leaders who understand the points of view of all members of the team and can help a team work toward a unifying goal rather than focusing on the differences between the members of the group.

A true *cosmopolitan leader* is able to navigate between cultures and over language barriers with tact and empathy. By paying attention to the specific intricacies of culture and company structure in all branches of a multinational company, the appropriate language policy can be formulated to minimize conflict and increase synergy within an organization or the local team.

Another important aspect of a company's cross-cultural ventures is the nonverbal behavior of an area's indigenous people contrasted by how the employees of a company express themselves to customers. Wal-Mart executives discovered that German shoppers were uncomfortable with the smiley nature of Wal-Mart employees (Landler & Barbaro, 2006). Problems arose because Wal-Mart's smile policy did not translate well to German communication styles and message orientations. Further, it is not just the nonverbal but also the verbal interactions that international business associates must be aware of. "Have a nice day" is a common American phrase and is used by sales clerks in all of the United States. However, many Germans consider this phrase to be "insincere and superficial" coming from a stranger or acquaintance.

Schmidt and his associates (2007) point out the need to be "precise" when communicating in intercultural situations. These authors also point out that, consequently, the message is most often in the receiver. This means that cross-cultural misunderstandings are often the result of the receiver from one culture misinterpreting the message being sent from a person of another culture. The competitive nature of American businesspeople is not a widely accepted concept in Europe and Asia. Straightforward comments can be taken out of context and affect the overall relationship between people of different cultures and, ultimately, the perception of a company attempting to break ground in a foreign nation.

For companies like Wal-Mart and McDonalds to succeed on an international level, company executives will have to raise their level of cultural awareness and sensitivity and hire more cosmopolitan leaders who will work together as equals with employees from the local cultures. Together these intercultural teams will need to be proactive in the development of strategies for handling cross-cultural issues, and creating an atmosphere where international customers can appreciate the brand of the company while, at the same time, feel that they do not have to forsake their own traditions and customs to do so.

Change and Technology

Another must for global leaders is the ability to adapt to changes. The globalized world moves at a rapid pace, and changes occur constantly. Leadership positions evolve with mergers, partnerships, and alliances; and the traditional roles of customer, competitor, and supplier are nearing their end, giving way to more interdependent functions (Goldsmith et al., 2003). Because customers are increasingly placing demands for simplicity and uniformity among suppliers, many organizations, such as IBM, are beginning to sell competitor products alongside their own. The constant changes in business practices and the blurring of role boundaries within the global marketplace makes it all the more important that leaders are well equipped with communication tools that make it easy for them to deliver messages fast and effectively.

A fundamental aptitude of global leaders is the development of technological savvy. Becoming familiar with technology and being able to use it with ease are inescapable requirements of executives in the age of globalization. Because technology makes it possible for people to communicate quickly, at virtually anytime of day using a multitude of devices such as "smart" cell phones, email servers, networks, video conference equipment and web phones, it is imperative that global leaders master the art of technological developments. People who are not comfortable with technology will not be able to sustain leadership roles in the global era regardless of space and time constraints (Colfax & Santos, 2009).

Because leaders who embrace technology will have the world at their fingertips, being comfortable with learning and using new devices is essential to global leadership. Technological developments have permitted organizations to replace "management by walking around" approaches with "management anytime, any place" (Goldsmith et al., 2003). Technology has dramatically improved the interaction capabilities of multinational organizations and made it easier than ever for leaders to maintain open channels of communication with their worldwide partners and staff. With tools like video conferencing equipment companies no longer have to travel across borders to meet with leadership teams and clients. This allows companies to cut costs and communicate at unprecedented speeds.

Advancements in technology, the development of the knowledge-based workforce, and the globalization of the marketplace have all contributed to the integration of the international boundaries. The disintegration of physical and figurative boundaries gave way to mergers, alliances, and partnerships among the world's organizations, and the concept of leadership has been redefined by a shift in individual competency requirements as well as the reliance on dispersed authority and control. Leadership practices that focused on domestic influence and uniform hierarchical systems have become a thing of the past, and leadership driven by diversity, collaboration, and interdependence have become a norm in the reality of the global era.

Jarvenpaa and Leidner (1999) examines whether trust can be developed and preserved among people working together while geographically and culturally divided and, if so, what characteristics global teams must exhibit. These topics bring attention to an issue that will no doubt be of growing importance to leaders of global companies as they strive to build a workforce in a growing number of countries. Dramatic changes in speed and access via the Internet have significantly influenced international business and contact with other cultures.

To effectively work as a group in a global virtual team, emphasis should be placed on the members of the group being on the same page by actually introducing themselves to one another, positive reinforcement for any and all ideas, allowing each member to work at their best ability without be chastised for their downfalls, and setting timelines and calendars for when work needs to be done while making sure all team members are aware of the deadlines in a respectful and timely manner.

Indra Nooyi, CEO, PepsiCo: A Global Strategist

Ranked #1 of the Most Powerful Women in Business in 2006 by *Fortune Magazine*, Indra Nooyi is not only a woman CEO but is one of the most recognized icons of corporate success to originate from India. Nooyi was named President and Chief Executive Officer of PepsiCo, the fourth-largest food and beverage company in the world. She is the fifth CEO, and the first female CEO, in the company's 44-year history, making PepsiCo the second-largest U.S. firm to be headed by a woman.

Born in Chennai, India in 1955, Nooyi received a bachelor's degree from Madras Christian College in 1974 and an MBA from the Indian

Institute of Management, Calcutta in 1976. After beginning her career in India as a product manager at Johnson & Johnson, Indra traveled to the United States to attend the prestigious Yale School of Management where she earned a Masters of Public and Private Management. After graduating, Nooyi honed her skills directing international corporate strategy projects at the Boston Consulting Group before moving on to work at Motorola where she ascended the ranks to reach the role of Vice President and Director of Corporate Strategy and Planning. After four years, she accepted a similar position as Senior Vice President of Strategy and Strategic Marketing for Asea Brown Boveri (ABB) before joining PepsiCo in 1994 as Senior Vice President of Strategic Planning.

Over the next seven years Indra Nooyi assumed roles of increasing responsibility at PepsiCo before being named as President and CFO and being elected to the Board of directors in May 2001. It was in this role that Nooyi served the company before accepting her current position as CEO five years later. In addition to her seat on the PepsiCo Board of Directors, Indra serves as a member of the Board of the Federal Reserve Bank of New York, Motorola, the International Rescue Committee, and the Lincoln Center for the Performing Arts. She is also a Successor Fellow of Yale Corporation and on the Advisory Board of the Yale School of Management, the Board of Trustees for the Eisenhower Fellowships and Asia Society, and a member of the Executive Committee of the Trilateral Commission.

For the majority of her almost 20-year business career, Nooyi has been leading the course for several major corporations and making powerful decisions around strategic planning and development. At PepsiCo she has been credited with several key decisions that have helped to shape the company's performance today, including the divesture of fast food restaurants (Taco Bell, Pizza Hut, and KFC), the spin-off and public offering of company-owned bottling operations into anchor Pepsi Bottling Group, the acquisition of Tropicana, and the merger with Quaker Oats, bringing in the vital business of Quaker and Gatorade brands. Predecessor Steve Reinemund has been quoted as saying that "Indra's record of transforming PepsiCo speaks for itself . . . She not only co-authored our vision and drafted our strategic blueprint, she has a sharp talent for turning insightful ideas and plans into realities."

It is true, Nooyi seems comfortable in the public eye; she is exceedingly smart with a strong point of view, yet she has spontaneity, a sense of humor, and she is genuine (Ganguly, 2006). She also strongly identifies with her cultural background and puts her family (husband and two teenage daughters) first. In fact, Nooyi views everyone at PepsiCo as part of her extended family, bringing a human appeal to her position of power. For example, she entrusts her receptionist to ask her daughter if she has finished her homework when she calls to ask for permission to play Nintendo (Amardeep, 2006).

Nooyi has a special talent for identifying emerging trends in global markets, an invaluable asset as globalization continues to reshape the way business is done today. She has directed PepsiCo's global strategy; driving critical cross-cultural advisory panels and cross-business initiatives not only to identify the changing needs of consumers and retailers but also to enhance operations and enable PepsiCo to meet these needs. A true global warrior, one might say. Nooyi's insights and rich understanding of emerging markets is uncanny and her leadership is transformative. She believes in constant reinvention; her vision is performance with purpose. Former CEO Roger Enrico says he was immediately struck by her ability to "look over the horizon" and praises Nooyi for her "practicality, vision, and courage—not to mention her unique presence" (Brady, 2006).

Globalization and Women's Leadership

As we move well inside the second decade of this century, it becomes increasingly important to overcome the challenge of unequal opportunity by considering objective factors such as profitability, innovation, and efficiency rather than basing promotional decisions on judgmental biases and irrelevant factors. What an individual competently demonstrates at home provides a solid foundation for what can be accomplished abroad. Hiring managers and top executives should look for women who are self-confident, but not overly so, in their skills and knowledge. They also should consider having a good understanding of the intercultural challenges described above, decision-making styles, communication patterns, and time and space issues as important qualities, which are based on personality, not gender. Providing the means for individuals with families and children to go abroad with their mother/wife expands the talent pool. Having language and cultural classes, social networks, and some type of employment assistance for spouses would also bring about great opportunities for everyone.

It stands to reason that the real challenges for women with regard to overseas assignments may be having access to building and sustaining global management skills as well as joining networks with access to high-visibility positions. Networking provides skill building, peer support, and ways of addressing firsthand how to juggle the demands of personal and professional life especially with international assignments. Women should also pursue key organizational champions proactively to help promote their chances and achieve equal recognition. As will be discussed in the next chapter, schools of business also have an important role advancing women-focused programs or executive education courses and offering flextime options (Ibeh, Carter, Poff & Hamill, 2008).

12

Fundamental Change

On September 28, 2010, President and CEO Ilene H. Lang of Catalyst, a nonprofit, research powerhouse that works globally to advance women and business, addressed the United States Congress to provide the latest findings of women in leadership positions. Overall, her message was that women are more prevalent now than ever in management, professional, and related occupations. However, the numbers are still not indicative of the progress women have made in relation to their male counterparts.

Why Do Many Women Opt Out from Seeking Higher Levels of Corporate Leadership?

Women are criticized for either being too feminine or too aggressive, and many times find themselves in a bind and fighting against a double-edged sword. The overwhelming criticism of executive women in leadership can prove to be a barrier to entry and drive women away from reaching for the two. The executive levels at many organizations are considered "boys clubs," and a glass ceiling to the top blocks women from reaching higher levels within the organization. This also raises serious doubts in women when they think of what it would be like if they entered the executive department.

1. Unequal expectations (double bind)—Women trying to advance in their careers often find themselves in a double bind. They have learned that they need to act and think like men to succeed, but they are criticized when they do so. The band of acceptable behavior is much more

narrow for women leaders that for men . . . When women managers are assertive and competitive like their male colleagues, they are often judged in performance reviews as being too tough, abrasive, or not supportive of their employees.

2. Glass ceiling—an invisible barrier that separates women and minorities from top leadership positions. They can look up through the ceiling, but prevailing attitudes are invisible obstacles to their own advancement.

3. Opportunity gap—the lack of opportunities. In some cases, people fail to advance to higher levels in organizations because they haven't been able to acquire the necessary education and skills.

Women may hold the same position as men but their salaries are significantly different. It is not a secret that women have been outpaced by men in salary throughout their careers. It is clear that for these numbers to continue to shift, there needs to be a fundamental change in how leading companies proactively and diligently break the systemic barriers that prevent women from reaching the top.

Organizations need a fundamental change in the fabric of top leadership positions. They need to reassess their mission statements and remove corporate barriers that limit or inhibit women's access to upper positions. Even a small increase in the percentage of female managers is expected to contribute to the implementation of successful practices, such as participative decision making and interpersonal communication that women tend to promote. Evidence shows that there is positive correlation between employee participation in decision-making and superior organizational performance (Fernie & Metcalf, 1995; Capelli & Neumark, 2001). Hence, many decisions in organizations are made by groups, teams, or committees (Foote, Matson, Weiss & Wenger, 2002). Participative decision making generates more complete information and knowledge, brings more perspectives and heterogeneity into the process, increases diversity of views, and leads to increased acceptance and support. As long as organizations include women in their management teams, they should expect superior performance (Melero, 2011).

Prejudices against female managers are expected to be less intense and their peers and superiors are less likely to perceive them as tokens when women's proportions in decision making authority centers are higher. Tokenism is a phenomenon that leads to the informal isolation of minority members who, in turn, respond by keeping low profiles (Kanter, 1977). If women have preferences for specific leadership styles (i.e., democratic), the likelihood that such styles and practices (i.e., involvement, interpersonal orientation) will become widespread increases. Melero (2011) found that workplaces with a higher percentage of female managers tend to allocate more time to group decision-making processes and to giving and receiving feedback. Managers are also more open to improving the collective performance and discussing career development opportunities with employees.

To push through the invisible wall, women must act in ways that are genuine and honest to their own values. Arguably, if women have to hide their own values and succumb to organizational pressure to mold into current norms and practices their motivation to remain with an organization for a long period of time is lessened (Ruderman & Ohlott, 2004). At the same time, women need to find the right balance of agentic and communal behaviors through feedback, mentoring, and developmental plans. Balanced behaviors will allow women to communicate competence and self-confidence.

Women are encouraged to self-promote and make connections laterally and vertically. This expectation may seem quite rudimentary; however, studies show that men do a better job at networking with other men rather than with women affiliates. Moreover, research has shown that women have limited access to or are excluded from informal networks in the workplace. These networks are vital during socialization processes, decision-making communications, and conflict resolutions. Limited access can also make it more difficult for women to create alliances and be close to point of information leading to limited mobility (Miller, 2006). This is especially true in highly male dominated or masculine settings where women are challenged to act tough and exercise competitive styles to gain acceptance into influential networks (Timberlake, 2005).

Women's networks, mentoring, and coaching provide opportunities for men and women to exchange information about each other's professional experience (Valerio, 2009, p. 83). Often, HR organizations may emphasize the positive skills that women possess, but may not actually follow through on hiring women for top leadership positions. Because of this frustrating situation, women tend to just give up instead of fight the injustice or engage in self-promoting behaviors. As a result, women are also less likely to use self-promoting behavior, are less "networked," and less likely to negotiate their "cards" aggressively.

Women do not tend to promote themselves as well as men do, and they also have less mobility within and between organizations and are more dependent on formal advancement procedures than are men (Lyness & Thompson, 2000). Existing training and development programs tend to focus on current competencies and short-term performance expectations rather than long-term strategic planning goals putting women at obvious disadvantage. Women also often take jobs where there is no opportunity for promotion to the top, such as human resources public relations. Moreover, many of the contributions of women to the companies they work for do not get noticed as much as men's contributions.

Willingness to relocate provides flexibility that can make women both competitive and attractive for employers. According to the survey by *CareerWomen* (2004, p. 1), over 60% of the women sampled stated they would relocate for the right position or promotion. However, when asked how willing they would be to make the move, only 4% responded "very willing." In contrast, 77% of job seekers with MBAs claimed that they would move and of that, 46% replied "very willing." Moreover, 73% of women stated that they have moved for their spouses or partners, while only 9% responded that their spouse or partner moved for them. It appears that while women feel they would relocate for the right opportunity, most women do not actually make the move when the opportunity presents itself.

What Can Be Done?

Two levels of intervention must be considered for lowering or neutralizing the negative effects of evaluative biases: (1) informal or personal initiatives by women and men in organizations; and (2) change in formal organizational mechanisms such as policies, performance evaluation criteria, and codes of behavior. The next section lists ideas and themes that emerged throughout the discussion in this book (see Table 12.1). Many of these ideas and insights were also observed in the profiles and characteristics of successful women leaders discussed in the book.

TABLE 12.1
Response Behaviors and Strategies

Individual Initiative	Organizational Change
1. Go above or around the barrier; initiate a dialogue on gender among peers	1. Use contingent reward leadership
2. Be a strong, skillful, and persistent woman leader	2. The gendered context of organizations must be recognized in any assessment process
3. Compete head-on for those lucrative corporate positions when they become available	3. Create mentoring opportunities that match women with senior managers programs, including women mentors for men
4. Seek out significant impact on how resources are allocated	4. Create a tracking system that monitors the equity by which performance ratings are developed and used
5. Stay connected	5. Clarify the demonstrative outcomes of problem-solving skills in performance evaluation by emphasizing problem-solving competence
6. Pursue executive coaching and role modeling; get an executive mentor	6. Develop transformational-based mentoring programs
7. Get transformational mentor to promote confidence and trust	7. Balance agentic with communal norms and standards
8. Seek out other women that have broken that glass barrier	8. Help women think and act strategically
9. Reframe your work context to make it more meaningful: integrate your roles to achieve wholeness	9. Focus career advancement and management development programs on future, strategic planning goals rather than present, short term
10. Break down institutional gender stereotypes; redefine the power structure, then use it to initiate change	10. Design different approaches to leadership development
11. Actively manage your mentoring relationships	11. Support mentoring systems that sympathize with the need to integrate work and family roles
12. Seek visibility through networking	12. Promote policies that encourage diversity and reward collaboration
13. Be in charge of your destiny; develop agency behaviors (e.g., assertiveness)	13. Increase group diversity by including more women on work groups

(continued)

TABLE 12.1 (*continued*)

Individual Initiative	Organizational Change
14. Follow your deeply held values and beliefs rather than organizational norms and expectations; be authentic —live up to your values	14. Provide employees and managers with leadership training that focuses on upward leadership practices, including self-assertion and involvement strategies
15. Identify alternative routes, including external sources, for self-development and ongoing learning	15. Monitor and encounter disempowering experiences targeted at women managers
16. Develop self-awareness and self-clarity	16. Abolish practices where women constantly need to validate their qualifications before assuming leadership roles
17. Continue to display transformational leadership qualities especially individualized consideration and intellectual stimulation	17. Develop and deliver ethical training programs that focus on commitment and respect for fairness and egalitarianism
18. Continue to develop your CVF leadership competencies; get feedback from others about your strengths and weaknesses; pursue holistic development that considers the balance of family and work life goals in women's careers	18. Initiate radar (360°) assessments
19. Seek out relationship with peers to build rapport and credibility	19. Emphasize different expectations such as challenge, balance, and authenticity in career roles and responsibilities
20. Be proactive in searching creative ideas to resolve the tension between organizational values and your personal values.	20. Use differential coaching methods following the life-cycle approach to development
21. Seek out high risk positions such as international assignments that might lead to greater visibility and leadership opportunities	21. Assign women to high-visibility jobs
22. Demonstrate your success stories; communicate competence and self-confidence	22. Initiate change in organizational and institutional structures, existing performance evaluation criteria and standards

These two levels converge at leadership development and succession plans that integrate management education and development goals with organizational interests and needs. Fulmer and Bleak's (2008) guidelines about successful implementation of leadership development programs in organizations are particularly relevant: Start at the top, connect leadership development goals to the organization itself; establish an integrated leadership strategy; be consistent in the execution of leadership programs; and hold leaders across organizational lines accountable. Because many of these ideas must also include the way executives are trained and acquired essential management and leadership skills, MBA and management education programs have also an important responsibility to incorporate these ideas in their curriculum.

Vision, Change, and Women's Strengths

Visionary leadership must have broad appeal, deal with change, promote faith and hope, reflect high ideals, and identify the path and journey to achieve strategic goals. Vision also gives meaning to work. If a company is struggling, a clear vision can create incentives and motivate employees to do great things and feel like they are a part of something meaningful. The vision helps generate commitment and helps managers garner support; it creates momentum and gets the entire employee base excited and takes ownership to collectively turn things around. When employees understand and embrace the vision, the organization becomes self-adapting. This self-adapting capability could make a significant difference in the company's fate, and it puts emphasis on the entire organization to be empowered and turn things around (that is, as long as the vision is truly what the struggling organization needs to improve).

Strategic leadership is built on four foundations: vision, mission, strategy, and mechanisms for execution. In chapter 3 we discussed reasons and factors that often lead to executive failures and the demise of organizations. This failure is often caused by lack of motivation to implement the vision, proposing a vision that is not in alignment with the core values and culture of the business, failure to take into account the impact on stakeholders when implementing a vision within an organization, and an overall resistance to change. Creating a vision alone is not sufficient or good enough to succeed in today's volatile environments. To sustain the business, a true strategic leader must connect the four foundations mentioned above. It is especially important to have clear vision in a struggling company during harsh economic times or cutthroat competition. Vision links the present with the future; if there are operational problems today, there will likely be operational problems tomorrow if a leader doesn't establish a strategy with a clear vision of where she wants the company to be, what changes need to be made, and how the company will operate in the future. Execution and operations are important to get right for short-term survival, but if leaders take their eyes off of strategy, it is more likely that the struggling company will fail without a clear vision. Creating a vision helps to establish strong communication and direction throughout the organization, which is necessary to find solutions to the company's financial problems.

The vision needs to be supported through the clarity of a mission that is the organization's core broad purpose and reason for existence. The synergistic value of the vision and the mission allows companies to create successful strategy, or general plan of action, to achieve the company's goals. Lastly, with all the foundations in place, an exact plan of execution can be developed to bring the company to realize the goals of the vision that was set by the CEO. The ease of execution depends on the leadership style of the CEO. The most effective leaders will have high strength in both vision and strategy. As discussed earlier in the book, executives with excessive egos frequently have an "it's all about me attitude" to the point that their names become completely synonymous with the company's brand. These executives create a very high-valued vision but without being involved in creating the strategy to achieve that vision. They lack the ability to create the synergistic value that is needed for a company to truly succeed in implementing the right vision.

A truly effective leader with an equally effective vision has the ability to empower employees to look past the bottom line and propose ideas that satisfy the higher needs of their employees. Their inspiration may be effective enough to convince employees to sacrifice in the present for a better future. A successful vision is one that is based on the current reality, but is concerned with a future that is substantially different from the status quo.

Vision is a key element to strategic leadership. A compelling vision will motivate and energize people to want to become a part of it. A vision can also provide a path between where the company is today and where it will be in the future, which provides meaningful work for people as they see job longevity. If people can't align with the vision they will not believe in it and may view it negatively. The vision is not a full strategic plan that has details on definite steps that will be taken but rather a foundation to provide a common objective for all involved with the company. Another reason that stakeholders may question a CEO's vision is that it completely differs from what the company is like now. By using the CVF as a reference, it becomes apparent that analysts are solidly in the lower right hand quadrant—Rational Goal—where all of the focus is on results. Wall Street exemplifies this quadrant with total emphasis on the near term results of a company. It makes sense, then, that analysts would find fault in any CEO who is not in the rational goal quadrant. This is especially true in a struggling company (i.e., results are poor and not to the expectations of the shareholders). Add in a new CEO who is outwardly in the Open Systems quadrant and the analysts will have a field day blasting the poor chap and declaring that the company's stock should be downgraded. Wall Street may forgive a more seasoned CEO who focuses on vision—as long as the company is meeting or beating analysts' expectations.

Creating a vision also provides employees with the view that the company has a future that is necessary to retain employees. Communication becomes increasingly important in crisis situations. If employees are seeing that the company is struggling to survive, they may be more likely to jump ship and find alternative employment. Leaders need to be present in a crisis to show their support. New CEOs will have a harder time stabilizing the company without creating a vision, restructuring the operations of the company, and recruiting and maintaining the talent necessary to follow through with objectives. To use a business proverb: If you fail to plan, then you plan to fail. The credibility issue is especially crucial for a new CEO who has not had the chance yet to garner trust among employees. Setting a strong vision could therefore be misunderstood as lunatic and far from reality. Thus, analysts and shareholders often condemn the efforts of a CEO to formulate new high-reaching visions in troubled times.

Creating a strong vision will help the company's culture embrace any necessary changes, allowing it to successfully "right the ship" without throwing everyone overboard. As shown throughout the book, this is exactly where women executives excel in having vision and anticipation skills and in linking strategic awareness with people skills and implementation of change.

Transactional and Transformational Skills that Add Strategic Value

The most important difference between transactional and transformational leadership is the fact that transformational leaders encourage change and are visionaries of change while transactional leaders are concerned with stability, performance, and control. Transformational leadership is vital for championing change as through the ability to bring about significant change in both followers and the organization. Transformational leaders excel at implementing a new vision in an organization, as they are good at encouraging product and technology innovation. They aid in creating a productive and innovative communication. Through inspiration, the leader motivates and guides people, but places the drive for change in their hands. By inspiring a group, and working with them to manage change, the leader creates a relationship based on confidence and trust. This form of leadership initiates intellectual stimulation by all members of the group, giving everyone the advantage of having a say and placing the individual at the center of motivating and making change. Rather than a leader making change, transformational leadership promotes success in challenging the group to diagnose and resolve problem areas. It instills self-worth and self-satisfaction, promoting teamwork and collaboration.

Transactional leadership is vital for managing transitions as it rewards employees (followers) for their job performance and the leaders benefit as the task is completed. Transactional leadership maintains stability in an organization, focuses on executing according to rules, and is primarily based in the short term. Transactional leadership in itself does not promote change (although it is necessary for leaders to have transactional skills during the change process), rather it focuses on execution. Because of its emphasis on stability, this form of leadership inherently focuses on the present and designing the organization to run smoothly and efficiently. For this reason, transactional leaders have good organizational skills and can interpret and execute a plan very well.

The styles of transformational leadership and transactional leadership differ in a variety of manners. However, the greatest and most important difference between these two leadership styles is how these two distinct styles motivate employees. Transactional leadership motivates employees to perform tasks by recognizing employees' needs and desires and communicating how accomplishing the task at hand will satisfy these needs. In contrast, transformational leadership motivates employees by providing the company with a vision and strategic direction and inspiring employees to get behind this vision and helping them to develop the skills needed to bring about a successful change.

Because these leadership styles are distinct but complementary, each is also suited for different situations. When a company needs to bring about organizational change, transformational leadership is the more effective choice. As transformational leadership focuses on the development of vision and strategic direction, while also motivating employees to become part of the change process, this style is best suited for fostering successful organizational change. When a company needs to effectively manage a transition, transactional leadership may be the better choice. This leadership style focuses on task completion and ensuring that the company continues to run smoothly and efficiently. Transactional leadership ensures that stability is maintained during the transition.

Both transactional and transformational leadership skills are needed to motivate and positively influence followers through the change process by participating throughout the process itself. The skills that transformational leaders have are vital to champion change and for managing transitions. While transactional leadership focuses on the here and now and immediate needs; transformational leadership is geared toward the future and growing and developing employees.

Because women were found to excel in both transformational and transactional elements of initiating and managing change (chapter 8), their advantage in leading organizations and operations adds strategic value to organizations and industries. Leadership effectiveness is positively associated with all of the dimensions of transformational leadership and the contingent reward dimensions of transactional leadership. Because women were rated much higher than men in behaviors that contribute to effective leadership, then female leadership advantage should be considered seriously and responsibly in promoting women from within the ranks of management. Providing women with high-visibility corporate responsibilities and influential positions can only support the strategic objectives of the corporation, add credibility, and create value rooted in ethics and high performance. Furthermore, women are also seen as more effective and in tune with the needs and values of a multicultural environment.

Women naturally bring human relations skills into the workplace, which helps create a productive work environment and build strong relationships. Women leaders also bring unique skills into companies like the ability to foster relationships with employees and use influence rather than authoritative power. Female leaders use cooperation and group decision making, and therefore develop connections with employees and encourage teamwork. Female leaders have also typically been rated higher by followers on task behavior, communication, and ability to motivate others. If the trend of women opting out of business organizations over the next decade continues because of discrimination and lack of incentives, important skills like empathy and human communication will suffer. A shift in culture will encourage more women to seek high-level corporate positions because organizational climates will be more accepting of them. This process of cultural acceptance and an increased desire to pursue high-level management will create a progressive effect that will equalize the gender demographics of corporate leadership.

Overall, the increase in female acceptance into senior executive positions will likely help organizations over the next decade. Studies have shown that female leaders are better able to manage the increasingly diverse workplace, focusing on interpersonal relations, verbal communication, and listening to subordinates. Additionally, today's employees often rate female leaders as providing more idealized influence, inspirational motivation, individual consideration, and intellectual stimulation than male leaders, which are important for developing fast, flexible, and adaptive organizations. In addition, companies with a significant percentage of female senior managers and board members have been found to be better performers. One study of Fortune 500 companies found that those companies with three or more female board members achieve an average of 83% greater ROE than those companies with a smaller number of female representation. In all, based on results from today's companies with strong female leadership presence, the increase of female leaders in the workplace over the next decade will likely be a great asset to those companies who embrace women's interactive leadership styles and their contributions to the organizations they lead.

As companies go global, there are new responsibilities that they need to be accountable for. Alongside corporate responsibility, there is a need to incorporate social responsibility and environmental accountability in corporate strategic plans. Though it is difficult for companies to think beyond corporate walls, as globalization moves forward, there will be an increasing demand for corporations to take social and environmental responsibility for the communities in which they employ their workers and environments from which they extract their resources. In the next decade, it will be increasingly important for companies to have leaders that seek balance in corporate responsibility, social responsibility, and environmental responsibility. As companies infiltrate underdeveloped countries, no one is in a better position to positively impact the people, society, and the economy than the corporations that are penetrating these impoverished areas.

Fitting Business and Management Education

Most critics of business and management curriculum have argued that the practice of management is fundamentally "soft" (Mintzberg, 2004) and that business and management education programs do not do enough to include leadership development, communication, diversity, and interpersonal skills in their core curricula (Belasen & Rufer, 2011). As business enterprises are increasingly forced to compete in global markets, the level of skills and competencies needed to deal with the added complexity must be further elevated. Global managers must manage the often diametrically opposing requirements of complexity and adaptability and align the value system with the goals and strategies of the organization.

Business schools, it was noted, have failed to teach students to grapple with complex, multilayered issues faced by business executives in global markets (Pfeffer & Fong, 2002). Later in their careers, MBA students transfer classroom experience and a strong preference toward a single functional orientation into a multicultural approach to decision making rather than a more fitting hybridized approach in which assimilation and sensitivity to individual, local, and cultural differences occur (Shimoni & Bergmann, 2006). These and other criticisms came close to suggesting that MBA programs breed smart talk, compartmentalization, and trained incapacity and are prone to fail students in global ventures by creating and reinforcing a vicious cycle of underperformance.

Growing interest in transformational leadership has signaled a promising shift in attitudes toward understanding how men and women play
leadership roles. Mounting evidence that transformational leadership contributed to increased employee motivation and performance has encouraged MBA designers to balance quantitative skills with people and
diversity skills (Belasen & Rufer, 2011). In the early 1980s Hofstede
(1983) identified femininity, as compared to masculinity, as one of the
determinant attributes that affect leadership. Most of Hofstede's work supported the idea that these characteristics come from cultural differences
that affect leadership. However, work by Zagoršek, Jaklič, and Stough
(2003) has indicated that gender differences may be more significant than
that of national origins. Yet, school of business and management education programs failed to include women's studies, diversity, and women's
leadership in their curricula.

Ibarra and Obodaru (2008) found that generally women managers display stronger skills than men in all performance areas, including process
and practicality. Unfortunately for women seeking career advancement
to higher levels of the organization, vision and innovation are strong
benchmarks for upward mobility. A primary reason is the perceived causal
path that exists between vision and forward thinking, business performance, financial performance, and overall stakeholder satisfaction
(Cameron, Quinn, DeGraff & Thakor, 2006; Hart & Quinn, 1993).
Strengths in other areas may not always compensate for perceptions of
weakness in innovativeness and vision. Innovativeness is also a stronger
predictor of promotions than relationship skills (Frank & Belasen, 2008a).

The curricular design of new business and management education programs should place heavy emphasis on transformational qualities and strategic vision skills. Taught by both women and male faculty experts,
students gain access to a variety of field experiences, from radar assessment
to effective presentation of final projects with strategic value (Belasen &
Rufer, 2011). Having women faculty, as part of the faculty cadre, may
lessen the effect of gender as seen by Reuvers, Van Engen, Vinkenburg,
and Wilson-Evered (2008). As students become familiar with the cultural
and style differences between the female and male faculty members, they
may also develop responses to transformational women leaders similar to
that of their male counterparts. Thus, diversity in faculty need to mirror
the demographics served as well as students' expectations. Curricular

design that takes into effect leadership diversity is also relevant and accountable.

Closing Thoughts

The challenge associated with becoming a master manager is developing the natural impulse to know when and how to effectively integrate the various roles of leadership to capitalize on the strengths of the organization through the effective use of human resources. Becoming competent in effectively communicating organizational vision and goals that promote the idea of high performance and increased productivity is based on power that has the ability to influence work performance and behavior. Master managers are challenged with developing the ability to create a strong organizational culture that operates on a social construction of organizational-wide influence on internal and external networks that are controlled by a system of beliefs and values that are embedded into the organizational culture (Belasen, 2000, p. 386).

In his book *Where Have All the Leaders Gone?*, Lee Iacocca, former CEO and Chairman of Chrysler Corporation, lists the "Nine C's of Leadership," which help distinguish effective from ineffective leaders: *Curiosity, Creativity, Communication, Character, Courage, Conviction, Charisma, Competence, and Common Sense.* All nine characteristics appear to coincide with women's strengths in interpersonal and social skills and contribute to their expertise as leaders and managers. I am not surprised that a great leader in an industry that was bailed out by the government has come up with this list. My hunch is that if women had led the automobile industry, many companies and their employees would have been saved from the demise of the 2007–09 recession.

References

Adler, N. J. (1994). Competitive frontiers: Women managing across borders. *Journal of Management Development, 13*(2), 24–41.

Adler, N. J., & Bartholomeow, S. (1992). Managing globally competent people. *Academy of Management Executive, 6*(3), 52–65.

Alimo-Metcalfe, B. (1995). An investigation of female and male constructs of leadership and empowerment. *Women in Management Review, 10*(2), 3–8.

Altman, Y., & Shortland, S. (2008). Women and international assignments: Taking stock—A 25-year review. *Human Resource Management, 47*(2), 199–216.

Amardeep (2006, August 16). Two lessons from Indra Nooyi. Retrieved May 31, 2007, from Sepia Mutiny Web site http://www.sepia mutiny.com/sepia/archives/003694.html.

Arfken, D. E., Bellar, S. L., & Helms, M. M. (2004). The Ultimate glass ceiling revisited: The presence of women on corporate boards. *Journal of Business Ethics, 50*(2), 177–86.

Barker, A. M., & Young, C. E. (1994, October). Transformational leaderships: The feminist connection in postmodern organizations. *Holistic Nurse Practitioner, 9*(1), 16–25.

Barton, T. (2006). Feminist leadership: Building nurturing Academic communities. *Advancing Women in Leadership On-Line Journal.* Retrieved from http://www.advancingwomen.com/awl/fall2006/barton.htm.

Bass, B. M. (1985). *Leadership and Performance Beyond Expectation.* New York: Free Press.

Bass, B. M., & Avolio, B. J. (1994). Introduction. In B. M. Bass, & B. J. Avolio (Eds.), *Improving Organizational Effectiveness through Transformational Leadership* (pp. 1–9). Thousand Oaks, CA: Sage.

Beechler, S., & Baltzley, D. (2008). Creating a global mindset. *Learning Officer, 8*(5), 32–44.

Belasen, A. (2000). *Leading the Learning Organization—Communication and Competencies for Managing Change.* Albany, NY: State University of New York Press.

Belasen, A. T. (2008). *The Theory and Practice of Corporate Communication.* Thousand Oaks, CA: Sage.

Belasen, A. T., Benke, M., DiPadova, L. N., & Fortunato, M. V. (1996, Spring). Downsizing and the hyper-effective manager: The shifting importance of managerial roles during organizational transformations. *Human Resource Management Journal, 35*(1), 87–118.

Belasen, A. T., & Frank, N. M. (2004). The perceptions of human resource managers of the shifting importance of managerial roles in downsizing organizations. *International Journal of Human Resources Development and Management, 4*(2), 144–63.

Belasen, A. T., & Frank, N. M. (2005). Roles managers play: A deeper look at the Competing Values Framework. Academy of Management Conference, August, Hawaii.

Belasen, A. T., & Frank, N. M. (2008). Competing values leadership: Quadrant roles and personality traits. *Leadership and Organizational Development Journal, 29*(2), 127–43.

Belasen, A. T., & Frank, N. M. (2010). A peek through the lens of the competing values framework: What managers communicate and how. *The Atlantic Journal of Communication, 18*(3), 5–30.

Belasen, A. T., & Rufer, R. (2011). Meeting the diversity challenge: Using the Competing Values Framework to design responsible business education. In Michele A. Paludi, & Breena E. Coates (Eds.), *Women as Transformational Leaders* (pp. 147–78). Santa Barbara, CA: Praeger.

Belasen, A. T., & Frank, N. M. (2012). Women transactional leadership: Using the competing values framework to evaluate the interactive effects of gender and personality traits on leadership roles. *International Journal of Leadership Studies*, forthcoming.

Bennis, W., & Nanus, B. (1985). *Leaders*. New York: Harper and Row.

Bilimoria, D. (2000). Building the business case for women corporate directors. In R. J. Burke & M. C. Mattis (Eds.), *Women on Corporate Boards of Directors: International Challenges an Opportunities* (pp. 25–40). Dordrecht, The Netherlands: Kluwer Academic.

Bilimoria, D., & Piderit, S. K. (1994). Borrad comité membership: Effects of sex-based bias. *Academy of Management Journal, 37*, 1453–78.

Bingham, C. B., Felin, T., & Black, J. S. (2000). An interview with John Pepper: What it takes to be a global leader. *Human Resources Management, 39*(2), 287–92.

Blackman, S. & Dann, J. (2010, February 23). Why Wal-Mart Failed in Brazil. The CBS Interactive Business Network. Retrieved from http://www.bnet.com/blog/mba/why-wal-mart-failed-in-brazil/1902.

Bluestone, B., & Bluestone, I. (1993). *Negotiating the Future*. New York: Basic Books.

Bolman, Lee G., & Terrence E. Deal. "Reframing Organizations." http://www.tnellen.com/ted/tc/bolman.html (accessed 4/25/11).

Bolman, L. G., & Deal, T. E. (1995). *Leading with Soul: An Uncommon Journey of Spirit*. San Francisco: Jossey-Bass.

Bono, J. E., & Judge, T. A. (2004). Personality and transformational and transactional leadership: A meta-analysis. *Journal of Applied Psychology*, 89(5), 901–10.

Boyatzis, R. E. (1982). *The Competent Manager: A Model for Effective Performance*. John Wiley & Sons.

Boyatzis, R. E., Cowen, S. S., & Kolb, D. A. (1995). *Innovation in Professional Education: Steps on a Journey from Teaching to Learning*. San Francisco: Jossey-Bass.

Bradford, D. L., & Cohen, A. R. (1984). *Managing for Excellence: The Guide to Developing High Performance in Contemporary Organizations*. New York: Wiley.

Brady, D. (2006, August, 14). PepsiCo shakes it up. *BusinessWeek*, Retrieved May 19, 2007, from Buckingham, Marcus (2005). *What Great Managers Do, Computerworld;* 3/28, 39 (13), p. 52.

Brigham, S. E. (1993). TQM lessons we can learn from industry. *Change*, May/June, 42–48.

Brislin, R. (2008). *Working with Cultural Differences: Dealing Effectively with Diversity in the Workplace*. Westport, CT: Praeger Publishers.

Buckingham, M. (2005). *What Great Managers Do, Computerworld*; 3/28, Vol. 39 Issue 13, p. 52.

Burgess, Z., & Tharenou, P. (2002). Women board directors: Characteristics of the few. *Journal of Business*, 27(1), 39–49.

Burke, J., & Mattis, M. C. (Eds.). *Women on Corporate Boards of Directors: International Challenges: An Opportunities* (pp. 25–40). Dordrecht, The Netherlands: Kluwer Academic.

Burns, G. (2006, October 24). Enron's Skilling gets 24-year prison term; Judge rejects his plea for leniency. *Chicago Tribune*. http://articles .chicagotribune.com/2006-10-24/news/0610240207_1_chief-executive -jeffrey-skilling-district-judge-sim-lake-less-restrictive-institution.

Burns, J. M. (1978). *Leadership*. New York: Harper & Row.

Cable, D. M., & Judge, T. A. (2002). Managers' upward influence tactic strategies: The role of manager personality and supervisor leadership style. *Journal of Organizational Behavior*, 24(2), 197–214.

Cameron, K. S., Quinn, R. E., DeGraff, J., & Thakor, A. V. (2006). *Competing Values Leadership: Creating Value in Organizations*. Cheltenham, UK: Edward Elga.

Capelli, P., & Neumark, D. (2001). Do "high performance" work practices improve establishment level outcomes? *Industrial Labor Relations Review, 54*, 737–75.

CareerWomen. (2004). "Relocation presents dilemma for today's career women" careerwomen.com. Available from: http://www.women mobility.org/wmob/modules.php?name=News&file=article&sid=14.

Carli, L. L. (1999). Gender, interpersonal power, and social influence. *Journal of Social Issues, 55*(1), 81–99.

Carroll, J. (2006). Americans prefer male boss to a female boss. http://
www.gallup.com/poll/24346/americans-prefer-male-boss-female
-boss.aspx.

Carr-Ruffino, N. (2005). *The Promotable Women*. Franklin Lakes, NJ:
Book-mart Press.

Case, J. (1993). A company of business people. *INC.*, April, 79–93.

Catalyst (2009). 2008 Catalyst census of women corporate officers and top
earners of the Fortune 500 (written by: Laura Jenner and Rhonda Ferguson)
—published March, 2009—Available from: http://www.catalyst.org/
publication/295/2008-catalyst-census-of-women-corporate-officers-and
-top-earners-of-the-fp500 (accessed 09/07/ 2009).

Cavallo, K., & Brienza, D. (2006). Emotional competence and leadership
excellence at Johnson & Johnson: Emotional intelligence and leadership study. Downloaded September 3, 2007 from www.Corpconsulting
group.com.

Chin, J. L., Lott, B., Rice, J. K., & Sanchez-Hucles, J. (Eds.). (2007).
Women and leadership: Transforming Visions and Diverse Voices.
Malden, MA: Blackwell.

Chin, J. L. (2004). Feminist leadership: Feminist visions and diverse
voices. *Psychology of Women Quarterly, 28*, 1–8.

Clark, H. (2009). Are women happy under the glass ceiling? *Forbes
.com*—Available from http://www.forbes.com/2006/03/07/glass-ceiling
-opportunities—cx_hc_0308glass.html.

Clark, J., & Koonce, R. (1995). Engaging organizational survivors. *Training & Development, 49*, 24–30.

Clark, T. M. (2008). *Epic Change: How to Lead in the Global Age*. San
Francisco, CA: Jossey-Boss.

Colfax, R. S., Santos, A. T., & Diego, J. (2009). Virtual leadership: A
green possibility in critical times but can it really work? *Journal of
International Business Research, 8*(2), 133–39.

Conlin, M. (2003, May 26). The new gender gap: From kindergarten to
grad school, boys are becoming the second sex. *Business Week*. http://
www.businessweek.com/magazine/content/03_21/b3834001_mz001.htm.

Costa, P. Jr., & McCrae, R. (1992). *NEO-PR-R Professional Manual.* Florida: Psychological Assessment Resources, Inc.

Costa, P. T., Jr., Terracciano, A. & McCrae, R. R. (2001). Gender Differences in Personality Traits Across Cultures: Robust and Surprising Findings. *Journal of Personality and Social Psychology, 81*(2), 322–31.

Craik, K. H., Ware, A. P., Kamp, J., O'Reilly, III, C., Staw, B., & Zedeck, S. (2002). Explorations of construct validity in a combined managerial and personality assessment programme. *Journal of Occupational and Organizational Psychology, 75*(2), 171–93.

Crouch, J. M. (1992). *An Ounce of Application is Worth a Ton of Abstraction.* Greensboro: LEADS Corporation and Piedmont Pub. Partners.

Daft, R. (2011). *The Leadership Experience* (5th ed.) Mason, OH: South-Western, Cengage Learning.

Dastmalchian, A., Lee, S., & Ng, I. (2000). The interplay between organizational and national cultures: A comparison of organizational practices in Canada and South Korea using the competing values framework, *The International Journal of Human Resource Management, 11*(2), 388–412.

Denison, D. R., Hooijberg, R., & Quinn, R. E. (1995). Paradox and performance: Toward a theory of behavioral complexity in managerial leadership. *Organizational Science, 6*(5), 524–40.

Digman, J. M. (1997). Higher-order factors of the Big Five. *Journal of Personality and Social Psychology, 73*(6), 1246–56.

DiPadova, L. N., & Faerman, S. R. (1993). Using the competing values framework to facilitate managerial understanding across levels of organizational hierarchy. *Human Resource Management, 32*(1), 143–74.

Drucker, P. F. (1993). *Managing for the Future.* New York: Truman Talley Books.

Drucker, Peter F. http://www.brainyquote.com/quotes/authors/p/peter _drucker.html (accessed 05/04/2011).

Dudley, G. W., & Goodson, S. L. (2008). *The Psychology Of Sales Call Reluctance: Earning What You're Worth In Sales.* Dallas, TX: Behavioral Science Research Press.

Eagly, A. H., & Carli, L. L. (2007). *Through the Labyrinth: The Truth About How Women Become Leaders*. Cambridge, MA: Harvard Press.

Eagly, A., & Johnson, B. (1990). Gender and the emergence of leaders: A meta-analysis. *Psychological Bulletin, 108*, 233–56.

Eagly, A. H., & Carli, L. L. (2003). The female leadership advantage: An evaluation of the evidence. *The Leadership Quarterly, 14*, 807–34.

Eagly, A. H., & Johannesen-Schmidt, M. C. (2001). The leadership styles of women and men. *Journal of Social Issues, 57*, 781–97.

Eagly, A. H., Johannesen-Schmidt, M. C., & Van Engen, M. L. (2003). Transformational, transactional, and laissez-faire leadership styles: A meta-analysis comparing women and men. *Psychological Bulletin, 129*(4), 569–91.

Eagly, A. H., & Karau, S. J. (2002). Role congruity theory of prejudice toward female leaders. *Psychological Review, 109*(3), 573–98.

Eddy, P. L., & Cox, E. M. (2008). Gendered leadership: An organizational perspective, *New Directions for Community Colleges, 142*(summer), 69–79.

Ellsworth, R. R. (2002). *Leading with Purpose: The New Corporate Realities*. Stanford, CA: Stanford University Press.

Fairhurst, G. T., & Putnam, L. L. (2004). Organizations as discursive constructions, *Communication Theory, 14*(1), 5–26.

Fernie, S., & Metcalf, D. (1995). Participation, contingent pay, representation and workplace performance: Evidence from Great Britain. *Britain Journal of Industrial Relations, 33*(3), 379–415.

Fine, M. G. (2007). Women, collaboration, and social change: An ethics-based model of leadership. In J. L. Chin, B. L. Lott, J. K. Rice, & J. Sanchez-Hucles (Eds.), *Women and Leadership: Visions and Diverse Voices* (pp. 177–91). Boston, MA: Blackwell.

Fine, M. G., & Buzzanell, P. M. (2000). Walking the high wire: Leadership theorizing, daily acts, and tensions. In P. M. Buzzanell (Ed.), *Rethinking Organizational and Managerial Communication from Feminist Perspectives* (pp. 128–56). Thousand Oaks, CA: Sage.

Finkelstein, M. (2003). *Why Smart Executives Fail*. New York, NY: Penguin Books.

Fiorina, C. (2006). *Tough Choices: A Memoir.* New York: Penguin.

Foote, N., Matson, E., Weiss, M. L., & Wenger, E. (2002). Leveraging group knowledge for high-performance decision-making. *Organizational Dynamics, 31*(2), 280–95.

Frank, N., & Belasen, A. (2008a). Roles women transform—Roles women play. In M. Paludi (Ed.), *The Psychology of Women at Work: Challenges and Solutions for Our Female Workforce* (pp. 101–18). Santa Barbara, CA: Praeger.

Frank, N., & Belasen, A. (2008b). *Roles Women Transform—Roles Women Play: Extending the Research.* Anaheim: Academy of Management.

Fulmer, R. M., & Bleak, J. (2008). What have we learned about strategic leadership development? In C. Wankel & R. DeFillippi (Eds.), *University and Corporate Innovations in Lifetime Learning* (pp. 161–79). Charlotte, NC: Information Age.

Galbraith, J. R. (1993). The business unit of the future. In J. R. Galbraith, E. F. Lawler III and Associates (Eds.), *Organizing for the Future: The New Logic for Managing Complex Organizations* (pp. 43–64). San Francisco: Jossey-Bass.

Gallos, Joan V. (Ed.). (2008). Making Sense of Organizations: Leadership, Frames, and Everyday Theories of the Situation. In *Business Leadership: A Jossey-Bass Reader.* San Francisco: Jossey-Bass.

Ganguly, D. (2006, September 23). Nooyi was wooed in style, reveals Chris Sinclair. *The Economic Times*, Retrieved May 19, 2007, from http://economictimes.indiatimes.com/articleshow/2019285.cms.

Gilligan, C. (1981). *In a Different Voice: Psychological Theory and Women's Development.* Cambridge, MA: Harvard Press.

Gmür, M. (2006). The gendered stereotype of the "good manager": Sex role expectations towards male and female managers. *Management Review, 17*(2), 104–21.

Goldsmith, M. G., Greenburg, C. L., Robertson, A., & Hu-Chan, M. (2003). *Global Leadership: The Next Generation.* Upper Saddle River, NY: Prentice Hall.

Goleman, D. (2009). What makes a leader? *Harvard Business Review*, Winter, 44–53.

Gotsi, M., & Wilson, A. M. (2001). Corporate reputation management: "Living the brand," *Management Decision, 39*(2), 99–104.

Govindarajan, V. (1989). Implementing competitive strategies at the business unit level: Implications for matching managers and strategies. *Strategic Management Journal, 10*, 251–70.

Greenleaf, R. K. (1977). *Servant Leadership: A Journey into the Nature of Legitimate Power and Greatness*. Mahawash, NJ: Paulist Press.

Gupta, A., & Govindarajan, V. (1984). Business unit strategy, managerial characteristics, and business unit effectiveness at strategy implementation. *Academy of Management Journal, 27*, 25–41.

Harris, P. R., Moran, R. T., & Moran, S. V. (2004). *Managing Cultural differences: Global Leadership Strategies*. Boston, MA: Elsevier.

Hart, S. L., & Quinn, R. E. (1993). Roles executive play: CEOs behavioral complexity and firm performance. *Human Relations, 46*(5), 114–22.

Haslam, S. A., & Ryan, M. K. (2008). The road to the glass cliff: Differences in the perceived suitability of men and women for leadership positions in succeeding and failing organizations. *The Leadership Quarterly, 19*(5), 530–46.

Hatch, M. J., & Cunliffe, A. L. (2006). Organization Theory: Modern, Symbolic, and Postmodern Perspectives. New York: Oxford University Press.

Hays, J., Allinson, C. W., & Armstrong, S. (2004). Intuition, women managers, and gendered stereotypes. *Personnel Psychology, 33*(4), 403–17.

Heffernan, M. (2002, August). The female CEO, *Fast Company*, 61, Retrieved from http://www.fastcompany.com/magazine/61/female_ceo.html.

Heilman, M. E., Wallen, A. S., Fuchs, D., & Tamkins, M. M. (2004). Penalties for Reactions to women who succeed at male gender-typed tasks. *Journal of Applied Psychology, 89*, 416–27.

Helgeson, S. (1990). *Women's Way of Leading*. New York: Doubleday.

Herringer, L. G. (1998). Relating values and personality traits. *Psychological Reports, 3*(1), 953–54.

Hofstede, G. (1983). National Cultures in Four. *International Studies of Management & Organization, 13*(1/2), 46–74.

Hogan, R. T., Curphy, G. J., & Hogan, J. (1994). What we know about leadership: Effectiveness and personality. *American Psychologist, 49*(6), 493–504.

Hood, J. N. (2003). The relationship of leadership style and CEO values to ethical practices in organizations. *Journal of Business Ethics, 43*(4), 263–73.

Hopkins, M. M., O'Neil, D. A., Passarelli, A., & Bilimoria, D. (2008). Women's leadership development: Strategic practices for women and organizations. *Consulting Psychology Journal: Practice and Research, 68*(4), 348–65.

Huffman, M. L., & Cohen, P. N. (2004). Occupational segregation and the gender gap in workplace authority: National versus local labor markets. *Sociological Forum, 19*(1), 121–47.

Iacocca, Lee (2007). *Where Have All the Leaders Gone*. NYC: Scribner.

Ibarra, H., & Obodaru, O. (2008). Women and the vision thing. *Harvard Business Review*, 85(1), 40–47.

Ibeh, K., Carter, S., Poff, D., & Hamill, J. (2008). How focused are the world's top-rated business schools on educating women for global management? *Journal of Business Ethics*, 83(1), 65–83.

Irby, B. J., Brown, G., Duffy, J. A., & Trautman, D. (2002). The synergistic leadership theory. *Journal of Educational Administration, 40*(4/5), 304–22.

Isaac, C., Behar-Horenstein, L., & Koro-Ljungberg, M. (2009). Women deans: Leadership becoming. *International Journal of Leadership in Education, 12*(2), 135–53.

Isaac, C., Griffin, L., & Carnes, M. (2010). A Qualitative Study of Faculty Members' Views of Women Chairs. *Journal of Women's Health, 19*(3), 533–46.

Izraeli, D. N., & Adler, N. (1994). Competitive frontiers: Women managers in a global economy. In N. Adler, & D. N. Izraeli (Eds.), *Competitive Frontiers: Women Managers in a Global Economy* (pp. 3–21). Cambridge, MA: Blackwell.

Jarvenpaa, S. L. & Leidner, D. E. (1999). Communication and trust in global virtual teams. *Organization Science, 10*(6), 791–815.

Javidan, M. G., Dorfman, P. W., de Luque, M. S., & House, R. J. (2006, February). In the eye of the beholder: Cross cultural lessons in leadership from project Globe. *Academy of Management Perspectives*, (20), 67–90.

Jones, D. (2009, January 1). Women CEOs slowly gain on corporate America. *USA Today*, Retrieved from http://www.usatoday.com/money/companies/management/2009-01-01-women-ceos-increase_N.htm.

Joreskog, K., & Sorbom, D. (2003). *LISREL*. Scientific Software International, Inc. *Journal of Business Ethics*, *37*, 39–49.

Joyce, W., Nohria, N., & Robertson, B. (2003). *What Really Works: The 4 Plus 2 Formula for Sustained Business Success*. New York: HarperBusiness.

Judge, T. A., Higgins, C. A., Thoresen, C. J., & Barrick, M. R. (1999). The big five personality traits, general mental ability, and career success across the life span. *Personnel Psychology*, *52*(3), 621–52.

Kanter, R. M. (1977). Some effects of proportions on group life: Skewed sex ratios and responses to token women. *American Journal of Sociology, 82*, 965–90.

Kanter, R. M. (1977). *Work and Family in the United States: A Critical Review and Agenda for Research and Policy*. New York: Russell Sage Foundation.

Kanter, R. M. (1983). *The Change Masters: Innovation and Entrepreneurship in the American Corporation*. New York: Simon & Schuster.

Kark, R., Shamir, B., & Chen, G. (2003). The two faces of transformational leadership: Empowerment and dependency. *Journal of Applied Psychology*, *88*(2), 246–55.

Kell, T., & Carrott, G. T. (2005). *Culture Matters Most, Harvard Business Review*, 83(5), 22–24.

Kelly, J., & Nadler, S. (2007). Leading from Below: CEOs can't change companies on their own; The secret is to foster a leadership mentality throughout the ranks. *The Wall Street Journal* (March 3).

Kharif, O. (2003, May 29). Anne Mulcahy has Xerox by the horns. *BusinessWeek*, Retrieved from http://www.businessweek.com/technology/content/may2003/tc20030529_1642_tc111.htm.

Kim, H., & Shim, S., 2003. Gender-Based Approach to the Understanding of Leadership Roles Among Retail Managers. *Human Resource Development Quarterly, 14*(3): 321–42.

Klenke, K. (2001). Cinderella stories of women leaders: Connecting leadership contexts and competencies. *Journal of Leadership and Organization Studies, 9*(2), 18–28.

Koehn, N., & Helms, E. (2005). *Oprah Winfrey.* Boston, MA: Harvard Business School, Harvard Business School Publishing.

Konrad, A. M., Ritchie Jr., J. E., Lieb, P., & Corrigall, E. (2000). Sex differences and similarities in job attribute preferences: A meta-analysis. *Psychological Bulletin, 126,* 593–641.

Kulich, C., Ryan, M. K., & Haslam, A. S. (2007). Where is the romance for women leaders? The effects of gender on leadership attributions and performance-based pay. *Applied Psychology: An International Review, 56*(4), 582–601.

Landler, M. & Barbaro, M. (2006, August 2). Wal-Mart finds its formula doesn't fit every culture. *New York Times.* Retrieved from http://www.nytimes.com/2006/08/02/business/worldbusiness/02walmart.html?_r=3&pagewanted=1.

Larson, A. L., & Freeman, E. (1999). *Women's Studies and Business Ethics: Toward a New Conversation.* New York: Oxford University Press.

Lauterbach, K. E., & Weiner, B. J. (1996). Dynamics of upward influence: How male and female managers get their way, *Leadership Quarterly, 7*(1), 87–107.

Leaper, Norm. How Communicators Lead at the Best Global Companies.Communication World. 16, April–May, 1999.

Leung, L. L., & Bozionelos, N. (2004). Five-factor model traits and the prototypical image of the effective leader in the Confucian culture, *Employee Relations, 26*(1), 62–71.

Lippa, R. (1998). Gender related individual differences, and the structure of vocational interests: The importance of the People-Things Dimension. *Journal of Personality and Social Psychology, 74*(4), 996–1009.

Lips, H. (2009). *Women and Leadership: Delicate Balancing Act.* Retrieved December 9, 2010 from http://www.womensmedia.com/ lead/88-women-and-leadership-delicate-balancing-act.html.

Lobe, S. A. (1990). Global leadership competencies: managing to a different drumbeat. *Human Resources Management, 29*(1), 39–47.

Luo, Y., & Shenkar, O. (2006). The Multinational Corporation as a Multilingual Community: Language and Organization in a Global Context. *Journal of International Business Studies, 37*(3), 321–39.

Lustig, M. W., & Koester, J. (2003). *Intercultural competence: Interpersonal communication across cultures.* Boston: Allyn and Bacon.

Lyness, K. S., & Thompson, D. E. (2000). Climbing the corporate ladder: Do female and male executives follow the same route? *Journal of Applied Psychology, 85,* 86–101.

Maddock, S. (2002). Modernization requires transformational skills: The need for a gender-balanced workforce. *Women in Management Review, 17,* 12–17.

Maddock, S. (1999). *Challenging Women: Gender, Culture and Organisation.* London: Sage Publications.

Mainiero, L. A., & Sullivan, S. E. (2006). *The Opt-out Revolt: Why People are Leaving Companies to Create Kaleidoscope Careers.* Mountain View, CA: Davies-Black Publishing.

March, R. M. & Wu, S. W. (2007). *The Chinese Negotiator: How to Succeed in the World's Largest Market.* Japan: Kodansha International Ltd.

McCabe, A. C., Ingram, R., & Dato-on, M. C. (2006). The business of ethics and gender, *Journal of Business Ethics, 64,* 101–16.

Mceldowney, R. P., Bobrowski, P., & Gramberg, A. (2009). Factors affecting the next generation of women leaders: Mapping the challenges, antecedents, and consequences of effective leadership. *Journal of Leadership Studies, 5*(2), 24–30.

McCormack, L., & Mellor, D. (2002). The role of personality in leadership: An application of the Five-Factor Model in the Australian Military. *Military Psychology, 14*(3), 179–97.

McDermott, L. C. (1993, September). Jump-starting managers on quality. *Training and Development,* 47(9), 37–40.

McKinsey & Company. (2007). *Women Matter: Gender Diversity, A Corporate Driver.* http://www.mckinsey.com/locations/paris/home/womenmatter/pdfs/women_matter_oct2008_english.pdf.

Melero, E. (2011). Are workplaces with many women in management run differently? *Journal of Business Research, 64*(2011), 385–93.

Mendenhall, M. E., Kuhlmann, T. M., & Stahl, G. K. (2001), *Developing Global Business Leaders: Policies, Processes, and Innovations.* Westport, CT: Quorum Books.

Miller, D., Kets de Vries, M., & Toulouse, J. (1982). Top executive locus of control and its relationship to strategy making, structure, and environment. *Academy of Management Journal, 25,* 237–53.

Miller, K. (2006). *Organizational Communications: Approaches and Practices.* USA: Thomas Wadsworth.

Mintzberg, H. (2004). *Managers not MBAs: A Hard Look at the Soft Practice of Managing and Management Development.* San Francisco: Berrett-Koehler Publishers.

Morgan, G. (1986). *Images of Organizations.* Newbury Park: Sage.

Mueller, G., & Plug, E. (2006). Estimating the effects of personality on male and female earnings. *Industrial & Labor Relations Review, 60*(1), 3–22.

Neff T., Citrin, J., & Brown, P. (1999). *Lessons from the Top: The Search for America's Best Business Leaders.* NY: Random House.

Nordvik, H., & Brovold, H. (1998). Personality traits in leadership tasks, *Scandinavian Journal of Psychology, 39*(2), 61–64.

Northouse, P. (2001). *Leadership: Theory and Practice.* Thousand Oaks, CA: Sage.

Oakley, J. G. (2000). Gender-based barriers to senior management positions: Understanding the scarcity of female ceo's. *Journal of Business Ethics, 27*(4), 321–34.

O'Neil, D. A., & Bilimoria, D. (2005). Women's career development phases: Idealism, endurance, and reinvention. *Career Development International, 10,* 168–89.

Ouchi, W. G. (1981). *Theory Z: How American Business Can Meet the Japanese Challenge.* Reading, MA: Addison-Wesley.

Paludi, M. (in press). Teaching about gender, race, sexual orientation, ethnicity and power in a graduate MBA program: Preparing future employees for the realities of work life. In M. Paludi (Ed.), *Managing Diversity in Today's Workplace. Vol. 1: Gender, Race, Sexual Orientation, Ethnicity and Power.* Santa Barbara, CA: Praeger.

Paludi, M., Martin, J., Stern, T., & DeFour, D. C. (2010). Promises and pitfalls of mentoring women in business and academia. In Rayburn, C. A., Denmark, F. L., Reuder, M. E., & Austria, A. M. A. (Eds.), *Handbook for Women Mentors: Transcending Barriers of Stereotype, Race, and Ethnicity* (pp. 79–108). Santa Barbara, CA: Praeger.

Paludi, M. (Ed.). (2008). *The Psychology of Women at Work: Challenges and Solutions for Our Female Workforce.* Westport, CT: Praeger.

Paludi, M., & Neidermeyer, P. (Eds.). (2007). *Work, Life and Family Imbalance: How to Level the Playing Field.* Westport, CT: Praeger.

Parker, K. L., (2004). Leadership styles of agricultural communications and information technology managers: What does the Competing Values Framework tell us about them? *Journal of Extension, 42*(1). Retrieved September 4, 2007 from http://www.joe.org/joe/2004february/a1.shtml.

Parkhouse, S. (2001). *Powerful Women: Dancing on the Glass Ceiling.* New York: John Wiley & Sons, LTD.

Perry, A. (2009). "Women climbing corporate ranks: Study," *Toronto Star,* Friday, March 06th, 2009 issue—Business Section—page B3.

Peters, T. J. & Waterman, R. J. (1982). *In Search of Excellence.* New York: McGraw-Hill.

Petiick, J. A., Scheier, J. D., Brodzinski, J. D., Quinn, J. F., & Ainina, M. F. (1999). Global leadership skills and reputational capital: Intangible resources for sustainable competitive advantage. *Academy of Management Executive, 13*(1), 48–66.

Pew Research (2008). Men or Women: Who's the Better Leader? A Paradox in Public Attitudes, http://pewsocialtrends.org/2008/08/25/men-or-women-whos-the-better-leader/.

Pfeffer, J., & Fong, C. (2002). The end of business schools? Less success than meets the eye. *Academy of Management Learning and Education, 1*(1), September, 78–95.

Pinker, S. (2009). "Why women earn less, men are fragile and more," Today-MSNBC.com. Available from: http://www.msnbc.msn.com/id/23558979/ (accessed 11/1/2009).

Piore, M. J., & Sabel, C. F. (1984). *The Second Industrial Divide: Possibilities for Prosperity.* New York: Basic Books.

Porter, N., & Daniel, J. H. Developing transformational leaders: Theory to practice. In Chin, J. L., Lott, B., Rice, J. K., & Sanchez-Hucles, J. (Eds.). (2007). *Women and Leadership: Transforming Visions and Diverse Voices.* Malden, MA: Blackwell.

Prediger, D. J. (1982). Dimensions underlying Holland's hexagon: Missing link between interests and occupations? *Journal of Vocational Behavior, 21*, 259–87.

Prime, J. L., Carter, N. M., & Welbourne, T. M. (2009). Women "Take Care," Men "Take Charge": Managers' stereotypic perceptions of women and men leaders. *The Psychologist-Manager Journal, 12*, 25–49.

Quick, Gordon. (2007, April 15). They're Not All Bad, Just Big-Headed: Executives need to harness their egos and rediscover their humility. *St. Louis Post.* Retrieved from http://business.highbeam.com/435553/article-1G1-162083247/theyre-not-all-bad-just-bigheaded-executives-need-harness.

Quinn, R. E. 1988. *Beyond Rational Management.* San Francisco: Jossey-Bass.

Quinn, R. E., Faerman, S. R., Thompson, M. P., & McGrath, M. R. (2007). *Becoming a Master Manager—A Competency Framework.* New York, NY: John Wiley & Sons, Inc.

Quinn, R. E., & Rohrbaugh, J. A. (1983). A spatial model of effectiveness criteria: Toward a competing values approach to organizational analysis. *Management Science, 29*, 363–77.

Rabkin, A. (2010). A star in the East. *Fast Company*, September, *148*, 76–109, 6 p.

Reuvers, M., Van Engen, M. L., Vinkenburg, C. J., & Wilson-Evered, E. (2008, September). Transformational Leadership and Innovative Work Behaviour: Exploring the Relevance of Gender Differences. *Creativity & Innovation Management, 17*(3), 227–44.

Rogers, P. S., & Hildebrandt, H. W. (1993). Competing values instruments for analyzing written and spoken management messages. *Human Resource Management Journal, 32*(1), 121–42.

Rose, C., & Thomsen, S. (2004). The impact of corporate reputation on performance: Some Danish evidence. *European Management Journal, 22*(2), 201–10.

Rosener, J. B. (1990). *Ways women lead. Harvard Business Review, 68*(6), 119–25.

Ruderman, M. N. & Ohlott, P. J. (2004). What women leaders want. *Leader to Leader*, 31(winter), 41–47.

Ruderman, M. N., Ohlott, P. J., Panzer, K., & King, S. (1999). How managers view success: Perspectives of high achieving women, *Leadership Briefing, 18*(6), 6–10.

Rusaw, C. (2005, June). Proposed model feminist public sector leadership. *Administrative Theory & Praxis, 27*(2), 385–94.

Rutigliano, K. H. (1996). Bringing LOVE back into business. In J. Renesch and Bill Defoore (Eds.), *The New Bottom Line: Bringing Heart and Soul to the Business* (pp. 92–100). San Francisco: New Leaders Press.

Ryan, M. K., Haslam, S. A., & Postmes, T. (2007). Reactions to the glass cliff; Gender differences in the explanations for the precariousness of women's leadership positions. *Journal of Organizational Change Management*, 20(2), 182–97.

Schein, V. E. (2001). A global look at psychological barriers to women's progress in management. *Journal of Social Issues, 57*(4), 675–88.

Schmidt, W., Conaway, R., Easton, S., & Wardrope, W. (2007). *Communicating Globally: Intercultural Communication and International Business*. Los Angeles, CA: Sage Publications.

Schmidt, W. H., & Finnigan, J. P. (1992). *The Race without a Finish Line*. San Francisco: Jossey-Bass.

Schmidt, W. H., & Finnigan, J. P. (1994). *TQManager*. San Francisco: Jossey-Bass.

Schuler, T. (2007). Building global leadership at Avery Dennison. *Global Business and Organizational Excellence*, 26(4), 6–17.

Scott, S., & Lane, V. (2000). A stakeholder approach to organizational identity. *The Academy of Management Review, 25*(1), 43–63.

Semykina, A., & Linz, S. J. (2007). Gender differences in personality and earnings: Evidence from Russia. *Journal of Economic Psychology, 28*(3), 387–410.

Sharp, J. P., & Ramanaiah, J. P. (1999). Materials in the five-factor theory of personality. *Psychology Reports, 8*(1), 327–30.

Sharpe, R. As Leaders, Women Rule. *Businessweek Online*, November 20, Shimoni, B., & Bergmann, H. (2006). Managing in a changing world: From multiculturalism to hybridization: The production of management hybrid cultures in Israel, Thailand, and Mexico. *Academy of Management Perspectives*, August, 76–90.

Sosik, J. J., & Godshalk, V. M. (2000). Leadership styles, mentoring functions received, and job-related stress: A conceptual model and preliminary study. *Journal of Organizational Behavior, 21*, 365–90.

Spector, P. E., Schneider, J. R., Vance, C. A., & Hezlett, S. A. (2000). "The relation of cognitive ability and personality traits to assessment center performance." *Journal of Applied Social Psychology, 30*(7), 1474–91.

Sturges, J. (1999). What it means to succeed: Personal conceptions of career success held by male and female managers at different ages. *British Journal of Management, 10*, 239–52.

Tannen, D. (1990). *You Just Don't Understand: Women and Men in Conversation*. New York: Ballantine Books.

Tannen, D. (1994). *Talking from 9 to 5: Women and Men in the Workplace*. New York: Avon Books.

Thorton, G. (2011). http://www.internationalbusinessreport.com/Press-room/2007/women-in-senior-management.asp.

Timberlake, S. (2005). Social capital and gender in the workplace. *Journal of Management Development, 24*, 34–44.

Toren, N., Konrad, A. M., Yoshioka, I., & Kashlak, R. (1997). A cross-national cross-gender study of managerial task preferences and evaluation of work characteristics. *Women in Management Review, 12*(6), 234–43.

Trinidad, C., & Normore, A. H. (2005). Leadership and gender: A dangerous liaison? *Leadership & Organization Development Journal, 26*(7/8), 574–90.

Trist, E., & Murray, H. (1993). *The Social Engagement of Social Science*. Philadelphia: University of Pennsylvania Press.

Tsiantar, D. (2006, April 30). Anne Mulcahy. *TIME*, Retrieved May 19, 2007, from http://www.time.com/time/magazine/article/0,9171,1186972,00.html.

Twenge, J. M. (1997). Changes in masculine and feminine traits over time: A meta-analysis. *Sex Roles, 36*, 305–25.

Twenge, J. M. (2001). Changes in women's assertiveness in response to status and roles: A cross-temporal metaanalysis 1931–1993. *Journal of Personality and Social Psychology, 81*, 133–45.

United States Department of Labor. (2009). Women in the labor force: A data book. *Bureau of Labor Statistics*. Retrieved from http://www.bls.gov/cps/demographics.htm#women.

Valerio, A. M. (2009). *Developing Women Leaders: A Guide for Men and Women in Organizations*. UK: Wiley-Blackwell.

Van den Born, F., & Peltokorpi, V. (2010). Language policies in multinational companies. *Journal of Business Communication, 47*(2), 97–118.

Verghese, T. (2008). Women Leading Across Borders, http://www.culturalsynergies.com/resources/Women_Leading_Across_Borders.pdf.

Vilkinas, T. (2000). The gender factor in management: how significant others perceive effectiveness. *Women in Management Review, 15*(5/6), 261–71.

Vollmer, L. (2004, December). Mulcahy took a no-nonsense approach to turn Xerox around. Retrieved May 19, 2007, from Headlines—Stanford Graduate School of Business Web site: http://www.gsb.stanford.edu/news/headlines/vftt_mulcahy.shtml.

Vroom, V. H. (1973). A new look at managerial decision making. *Organizational Dynamics*, Spring, 66–80.

Vroom, V. H., & Jago, A. G. (1988). *The New Leadership*. Englewood Cliffs, NJ: Prentice-Hall.

Walker, Tom. (2007, March 12). What leads some CEOs into scandal? Theories abound about executives who may believe they're invincible.

Houston Chronicle. Retrieved from http://www.chron.com/CDA/ archives/archive.mpl/2007_4302143/what-leads-some-ceos-into-scandal -theories-abound.html.

Weaver, G. R. (2001). Ethics Programs in Global Businesses: Culture's Role in Managing Ethics. *Journal of Business Ethics*, *30*(1), 3–15.

Werhane, P. (2007). Women Leaders in a Globalized World, *Journal of Business Ethics, 74*(4), 425–35.

Weyer, B. (2007).Twenty years later: Explaining the persistence of the glass ceiling for women leaders. *Women in Management Review, 22*(6), 482–96.

Won, H. (2006). Links between personalities and leadership perceptions in problem-solving groups. *The Social Science Journal, 43*(4), 659–72.

Xie, J., & Whyte, G. (1997). Gender differences among managers and non managers: An analysis of assessment data. *Canadian Journal of Administrative Sciences*, *14*(3), 340–53.

Yoder, J. D. (1991). Rethinking tokenism: Looking beyond numbers. *Gender & Society*, 5, 178–92.

Yoder, J. D. (2001). Making leadership work more effectively for women. *Journal of Social Issues, 57*(4), 815–28.

Young, M., & Dulewicz, V. (2005). A model of command, leadership and management competency in the British Royal Navy. *Leadership & Organization Development Journal, 26*(30), 228–41.

Zagoršek H., Jaklič M., & Stough S. (2003). Cultural Contingency of Leadership Comparing Leadership Practices Between Slovenia, Nigeria, and United States, International Conference Enterprise in Transition, Conference Proceedings, pp. 684–98.

Index

Page numbers followed by f indicate figure.
Page numbers followed by t indicate table.

About the Author

Alan T. Belasen, PhD, is professor of management and chair of the business, management, and leadership programs at State University of New York, Empire State College. He holds degrees from the Hebrew University, Jerusalem, Israel, and State University of New York at Albany. He has taught organizational behavior, leadership communication, human resources, international business, and corporate communication at the University at Albany, and the AACSB Accredited MBA program at Union Graduate College. His published works include *Leading the Learning Organization: Communication and Competencies for Managing Change* and *The Theory and Practice of Corporate Communication: A Competing Values Perspective.* His most recent articles appear in *Leadership & Organization Development Journal; Journal of Human Resource Management; International Journal of Human Resources Development and Management; The Journal of Health Administration Education; The Atlantic Journal of Communication; The International Journal of Leadership Studies;* and the *Proceedings of the Academy of Management.* Belasen also contributed chapters in a number of books on topics such as self-managed work teams, women's leadership, and executive education.